D0571715

23,36

Ballistic Missile Proliferation
The Politics and Technics

Stockholm International Peace Research Institute

SIPRI is an independent international institute for research into problems of peace and conflict, especially those of arms control and disarmament. It was established in 1966 to commemorate Sweden's 150 years of unbroken peace.

The Institute is financed mainly by the Swedish Parliament. The staff and the Governing Board are international. The Institute also has an Advisory Committee as an international consultative body.

The Governing Board is not responsible for the views expressed in the publications of the Institute.

Governing Board

Professor Daniel Tarschys, Chairman (Sweden)
Sir Brian Urquhart, Vice-Chairman (United Kingdom)
Dr Oscar Arias Sánchez (Costa Rica)
Dr Gyula Horn (Hungary)
Dr Ryukichi Imai (Japan)
Professor Catherine Kelleher (United States)
Dr Marjatta Rautio (Finland)
Dr Lothar Rühl (Germany)
The Director

Director

Dr Adam Daniel Rotfeld (Poland)

sipri

Stockholm International Peace Research Institute
Frösunda, S-171 53 Solna, Sweden
Cable: SIPRI
Telephone: 46 8/655 97 00
Telefax: 46 8/655 97 33
E-mail: sipri@sipri.se
Internet URL: http://www.sipri.se

Ballistic Missile Proliferation
The Politics and Technics

Aaron Karp

sipri

OXFORD UNIVERSITY PRESS
1996

Oxford University Press, Walton Street, Oxford OX2 6DP
Oxford New York
Athens Auckland Bangkok Bombay
Calcutta Cape Town Dar es Salaam Delhi
Florence Hong Kong Istanbul Karachi
Kuala Lumpur Madras Madrid Melbourne
Mexico City Nairobi Paris Singapore
Taipei Tokyo Toronto
and associated companies in
Berlin Ibadan

Oxford is a trade mark of Oxford University Press

Published in the United States
by Oxford University Press Inc., New York

© *SIPRI 1996*

All rights reserved. No part of this publication may be reproduced,
stored in a retrieval system, or transmitted, in any form or by any means,
without the prior permission in writing of Oxford University Press.
Within the UK, exceptions are allowed in respect of any fair dealing for the purpose of
research or private study, or criticism or review, as permitted
under the Copyright, Designs and Patents Act, 1988, or in the case of
reprographic reproduction in accordance with the terms of the licences
issued by the Copyright Licensing Agency. Enquiries concerning
reproduction outside these terms should be sent to the Rights Department,
Oxford University Press, at the address above. Enquiries concerning
reproduction in other countries should be sent to SIPRI.

British Library Cataloguing-in-Publication Data
Data available

Library of Congress Cataloging-in-Publication Data

Karp, Aaron.
Ballistic missile proliferation: the politics and technics /
Aaron Karp.
— (SIPRI monographs)
Includes index.
1. Ballistic missiles. 2. Arms race. 3. Arms control.
I. Title. II. Series.
UG1312.B34K37 1996 327.1'74—dc20 95–44961
ISBN 0–19–829173–6

Typeset and originated by Stockholm International Peace Research Institute
Printed in Great Britain on acid-free paper by
Biddles Ltd., Guildford and King's Lynn

WIDENER UNIVERSITY
WOLFGRAM
LIBRARY
CHESTER

DISCARDED
WOLFGRAM UNIVERSITY

Contents

Figures

Preface

The end of the cold war brought about many changes in the international security environment. Weapon proliferation, which for many years had been on the agenda of the arms control debate, took on a new dimension. The new challenges include not only nuclear weapons but also other weapons of mass destruction and their delivery systems. As a result of the collapse of the Soviet Union and the formation of over 20 new states in Europe, on the one hand, and the development of new technologies, on the other, the proliferation of weapons and delivery systems may easily get out of control.

The proliferation problem has evolved in the past 30 years in ways no one could have foreseen. Fewer countries have the weapons we once feared they sought, but far more have the capability to create those weapons. Although proliferation is often associated with one—the nuclear—dimension, we also have to deal with numerous other threats. Six principal non-proliferation regimes have emerged: nuclear, biological, chemical, conventional, weapon-related technology and—last but not least—that for missile technology control. These regimes are reflected in networks of treaties, transparency measures, export control measures and diplomatic activities, such as the talks on Safe and Secure Dismantlement (SSD) of nuclear weapons and the Missile Technology Control Regime (MTCR). Previously a secondary or tertiary issue on the international agenda, proliferation has risen to an undisputed place at the top of our concerns.

The uncertainty that characterizes the proliferation problem is nowhere more serious than in discussions of ballistic missile proliferation. The problem is relatively new, the trends are unclear and the dangers subject to bitter debate. Aaron Karp's contribution helps to reduce some of the uncertainty that plagues our understanding of this demanding issue. Previous books have introduced the general problem and examined possible policy responses. His study paves a new road by examining the basic forces shaping emerging proliferation problems and our ability to deal with them. Newcomers to the issue will appreciate his systematic review of the forces that give missile proliferation its essential significance. Experienced observers will benefit from his examination of the political and technical factors regulating proliferation, channelling proliferators along specific paths and easing the problems of control.

Dozens of countries have some ingredients of rocketry development and many can acquire rudimentary ballistic missiles. This study shows that only a handful of emerging powers have the resources to develop long-range systems and that the most serious danger comes not from the largest missiles that emerging powers can imagine, but from the less ambitious technologies that they can manage. As in other fields of arms control and disarmament, its not always the most exotic and powerful weapons that are most destabilizing; rather, it is often the more common and mundane.

I wish to thank Aaron Karp for this book, written and published under the auspices of SIPRI. Special thanks go to John Stares and Connie Wall for editing and preparing this volume for publication. The index was prepared by Peter Rea.

Adam Daniel Rotfeld
Director of SIPRI
1 July 1995

Acknowledgements

The origin of this book owes much to the support and encouragement of three men: Maurice Eisenstein, who as an official of the US Arms Control and Disarmament Agency in the late 1970s introduced me (and much of the US Government) to the issue of missile proliferation; Walther Stützle, SIPRI Director in 1986–91, who brought me back to the issue and urged me to write this book; and Adam Daniel Rotfeld, SIPRI Director since 1991, who made its completion possible.

Over the years one accumulates innumerable intellectual debts, only a few of which can be acknowledged in a brief monograph. Many debts are owed to journalists and newspaper correspondents whom I never met but whose work was essential to this undertaking. Others are owed to acquaintances—government officials, military officers, engineers in government laboratories and private industry, scholars and professional analysts—most of whom had no reason to suspect that their ideas would have the influence they did here.

This book would be much less satisfactory if not for the work of two leading proliferation specialists: W. Seth Carus, currently with the US Department of Defense, whose ability rapidly to make sense of emerging information is unrivalled; and Kenneth R. Timmerman, a uniquely talented journalist. While I was preparing this study it often seemed as if Ken and his wife Christina have endured unparalleled chaos in their lives so that people like myself can work in calm and concentration.

This study has been influenced heavily by two remarkable books, although neither is cited in the chapters that follow. Lewis Mumford, in *Technics and Civilization* (1934), his unsurpassed study of the challenges of technological change, makes clear the argument that technology develops only through human desire and planning. Technical change, he shows, always remains within our control, if only we are willing to express it. A very different kind of book, Charles Oman's *A History of the Art of War in the Sixteenth Century* (1937), shows that the effects of new weapons are due not so much to their intrinsic capabilities as to the reactions they elicit. In a nutshell, these two ideas are what this book is all about.

On the practical side, the book was edited by John Stares and Connie Wall, an editor of unrivalled skill. Miyoko Suzuki prepared the manuscripts, making a genuine pleasure of the work through her competence and friendship.

Many of the ideas and unacknowledged concepts here emerged only through the constant collaboration of my wife, Gina. Some of the ideas presented here are hers while others are the better for her judgement. Thanks to her talents, competence and good advice, the work on this volume went forward efficiently and pleasurably.

Aaron Karp
1 July 1995

Acronyms and conventions

ALCM	air-launched cruise missile
ASLV	Augmented Space Launch Vehicle
ASM	air-to-surface missile
ASRAAM	Advanced Short-Range Air-to-Air Missile
ATACMS	Army Tactical Missile System
ATBM	anti-tactical ballistic missile
BCCI	Bank of Credit and Commerce International
BNL	Banca Nazionale del Lavoro
CBW	chemical and biological weapons
CEP	circular error probable
CFE	(Treaty on) Conventional Armed Forces in Europe
DFVLR	Deutsche Forschungs- und Versuchsanstalt für Luft- und Raumfahrt (now DLR)
FAE	fuel–air explosive
FATF	Financial Action Task Force
FOBS	fractional orbital bombardment system
FROG	Free Rocket Over Ground
G-7	Group of Seven (industrialized states)
GNP	gross national product
GPALS	Global Protection Against Limited Strikes
GPS	Global Positioning System
GSLV	Global Space Launch Vehicle
HARM	High-Speed Anti-Radiation Missile
ICBM	intercontinental ballistic missile
IMF	International Monetary Fund
INF	intermediate-range nuclear forces
INS	inertial navigation system
IRBM	intermediate-range ballistic missile
LRCM	long-range conventional missile
MIRV	multiple independently targetable re-entry vehicle
MLRS	multiple-launcher rocket system
MTCR	Missile Technology Control Regime
MW	megawatt
NASA	(US) National Aeronautics and Space Administration
NPT	Non-Proliferation Treaty
PGM	precision guided munition
PSLV	Polar Space Launch Vehicle

PTP	trinitrotoluene-proxylin
R&D	research and development
RFNA	red fuming nitric acid
SALT	Strategic Arms Limitation Talks
SAM	surface-to-air missile
SDI	Strategic Defense Initiative
SLV	space launch vehicle
START	Strategic Arms Reduction Treaty
TNT	trinitrotoluene
UDMH	unsymmetrical dimethyl-hydrazine
UNSCOM	UN Special Commission on Iraq
VLS	Veículo Lançador de Satelites

Conventions in tables

..	data not available or not applicable
–	nil or a negligible figure
( )	uncertain data or author's estimate
$	then-year US $, unless otherwise indicated
b.	billion (thousand million)
h	hour
I_{sp}	specific impulse
kg	kilogram
km	kilometre
kt	kiloton
m	metres
m.	million
Mt	megatonne
psi	pounds per square inch
t	tonne
T_c	combustion temperature

1. Introduction

On 1 March 1980 a new rocket flew from a military research facility deep in the Libyan desert. The result of some five years of development by a German team, the long and thin rocket bore little resemblance to missiles developed by the established missile powers. Its makers claimed that it was intended to lead to a low-cost space launcher capable of lifting satellites into orbit, but to outside observers it made sense only as the basis for a new kind of ballistic missile. In reality, it was poorly designed and had little serious potential in either role. Although the project seems unlikely ever to amount to anything, 15 years later it continues to absorb Libyan resources and to arouse national ambitions and regional anxieties.[1]

For all its shortcomings, the Libyan rocket symbolized a new problem in international affairs. For most of the international community, the Libyan launch was a shocking introduction to a world in which long-range rockets had ceased to be a monopoly of the established powers. Perhaps the Libyan effort was doomed from the start, but the idea it represented was of greater moment than was its mediocre technology. Other countries would follow and some of them would be more successful. It foreshadowed a day when almost any country with the money and inclination could launch satellites into space or send warheads across continents.

With the end of the cold war the problem of ballistic missile proliferation has become much more acute. Not only are more countries trying to acquire long-range missiles but the passing of superpower tensions has also elevated the visibility and importance of regional missile forces—those forces emerging outside the established missile powers—making them one of the most destabilizing elements of the new world order. With the spread of long-range rockets, even the best defended countries—countries previously all but immune to foreign attack—are vulnerable to sudden military blows. While the extent and implications of this change are unclear, no one can deny its effect on perceptions of the nature of international conflict. Along with several other proliferation challenges—especially the spread of nuclear, chemical and biological armaments as well as cruise missiles—the spread of long-range rockets will remain a serious problem for many years to come.

---

[1] *Aviation Week & Space Technology*, 3 Mar. 1981) p. 25; and Miller, J., 'U.S. uneasy over military potential of commercially produced rockets', *New York Times*, 12 Sep. 1981, p. 4. The fullest account is given by Barth, K. G., 'Gahdafis geheime Raketen-oase' [Gaddafi's secret rocket oasis], *Der Stern*, no. 22 (1987), pp. 20–26. Evidence that Libyan research on long-range rockets continues came in June 1993, when Ukrainian authorities intercepted a shipment of Russian-manufactured ammonium perchlorate, a high-energy oxidizer for large rockets, that was bound for Libya. Gordon, M. R., 'U.S. tries to stop Russia–Libya deal', *International Herald Tribune,* 24 June 1993, p. 3.

Despite wide recognition of the issue, the understanding of missile proliferation remains nascent. In previous studies there has been a tendency to go directly to the question of how to deal with the problem, overlooking the more fundamental problem of understanding the political and technological forces that make missile proliferation possible to begin with. This study systematically explores the forces and processes governing the global spread of ballistic missiles. It aims to help establish an independent basis for evaluating the implications of missile proliferation in general and the efforts of specific countries to master ballistic missile technology.

What is the significance of missile proliferation, the processes governing the spread of ballistic missiles and the ability of countries to acquire them? All too often the nature of the problem varies depending on the situation. A recurrent theme here is the *contingency* of proliferation. Acquiring large rockets is not as simple as collecting bits and pieces of equipment. Nor does missile control amount simply to erecting fences around a few key technologies. Whether a regional power—be it in Latin America, Africa, the Middle East or Asia—can master any demanding technology ultimately depends not on universal rules or general trends. Any country's ability to develop long-range missiles, whether its efforts can be stymied or whether they matter in the first place, depends on specific circumstances. In order to deal with ballistic missile proliferation, several key questions must be resolved.

Does missile proliferation really matter, or is it something one must simply learn to live with?

Can missile proliferation be controlled or even reversed, or should efforts be made more modestly to reduce the dangers of a phenomenon largely beyond control?

When are regional rocketry programmes most likely to succeed? What must a country do to develop, manufacture and deploy long-range ballistic missiles?

How can outsiders evaluate whether a country's rocketry programme will lead to successful deployment and when it will end in failure?

When are regional rocketry programmes most amenable to outside control?

Which policies are mostly likely to slow or halt the spread of missiles?

Chapters 2 and 3 of this book examine fundamental questions about the nature of missile proliferation. Chapter 2 reviews the arguments that the spread of technology is beyond control. Often heard during the worst moments of the superpower confrontation, these arguments have gained new life in response to rising fears of missile proliferation. The implication is that nothing can be done to halt proliferation: that it can perhaps be slowed but not stopped or reversed. Instead of emphasizing non-proliferation, this outlook leads to the implication that sound policy should stress the extremes of optimism or pessimism. If it is true that control and reduction of weapon proliferation are not possible, the only responses are extreme ones: to create a new and harmonious world order in which advanced weapons are irrelevant and illegal, or to learn to live with weapon proliferation by managing its most destabilizing features.

Contrary to excited newspaper headlines and the alarmed statements of officials just discovering the issue, acquisition of ballistic missiles is neither easy nor uncontrollable. The main conclusion of this volume is that proliferation remains a human problem, subject to human will and judgement. Although the forces responsible for the diffusion of advanced technology are strong, they are neither ineluctable nor beyond the influence of policy. Far from leading to a single result, regional missile projects collapse or continue unproductively just as often as they lead to successful deployments. Experience shows that renegade programmes can be halted and often reversed.

Another general critique of missile proliferation, evaluated in chapter 3, challenges the significance of the problem. While the interest of emerging powers in acquiring long-range rockets is undeniable, this important school of thought urges the international community not to get overexcited about it. Other weapons that are already widely available, especially tactical aircraft, give countries even greater military capability. While most objective studies have concluded that ballistic missiles rarely offer entirely novel military capabilities, some analysts go so far as to maintain that the spread of ballistic missiles has little or no serious effect on international security.

The conclusions here emphasize that the effects of missile proliferation depend on too many factors for facile generalization. Without nuclear armament, ballistic missiles are rarely the most destructive weapons in a country's arsenal, and their effect on the outcome of battles and wars is usually not decisive. Yet there are cases in which they have played a critical role in armed conflict or could have been decisive under slightly different circumstances. Their greatest effect, however, is not as military implements in wartime but as political instruments in times of peace. It is as a symbol of power and a source of psychological pressure that the ballistic missile gains its greatest effect.

The requirements for and processes of developing and manufacturing ballistic missiles are examined in chapters 4–7. While long-range rockets can be purchased when a willing supplier can be found, buying missiles is an exclusively political and financial process. The emphasis here is on domestic development, a far more demanding process with much greater long-term implications for the international system. It is entirely feasible that country-to-country sales of ballistic missiles and space launch vehicles (SLVs) may cease in the near future. By the mid-1990s, only North Korea and possibly China continued to sell whole rockets capable of ranges of over 300 km, and sales of smaller systems were becoming rare. While other suppliers may occasionally drift into the market in the future, the trade in finished rockets increasingly appears to be a relic of the cold war. Domestic development, however, will continue to be a viable option for a long time to come.

The analysis here focuses on domestic development of long-range ballistic missiles and rockets that can be modified for ballistic roles. Because of the similarities between them, it is vital to pay attention to domestic efforts to master all kinds of rocket technology, but four deserve special attention: artillery rockets, sub-orbital sounding rockets, space launch vehicles and ballistic missiles themselves.

Defining a ballistic missile is not easy. For the purposes of this study, a ballistic missile is any unmanned, actively guided, rocket-propelled vehicle that can be fired ground-to-ground along a ballistic (or parabolic) trajectory. In reality, in the more than 50 years since the first flight of the German V-2 rocket, missile technology has grown to include too many exceptions to permit a comprehensive definition. There have been experiments with manned ballistic missiles (the Dynosoar), with missiles fired along flattened (or depressed) trajectories, missiles with long range but no guidance, and missiles with manœuvring warheads (like the Pershing-2 or the US Army's Tactical Missile, ATACMS). Ultimately, there probably cannot be a definition that applies to all missiles. It may be easier to recognize a rocket standing four metres or higher with an explosive warhead as a ballistic missile than to define it scientifically.

The study stresses the domestic development of long-range missiles, which in regional contexts are usually understood to mean those capable of carrying a payload of 500 kg a distance of at least 300 km. While the emphasis here is on ballistic missiles, similarities in the technology make it essential to devote equal attention to efforts to acquire other large rockets, especially space launch vehicles. Some smaller, short-range rockets are also relevant, especially when they use technologies that can be directly applied to larger systems. Other short-range systems, such as sounding and artillery rockets, involve a different and much simpler technology. The latter are important for most countries as their first contact with modern rocketry.

Chapter 4 discusses the soft, or invisible, technology of rocket development. Although not usually associated with weapon development, factors such as personnel, organization and finance are the 'software', the invisible technology of innovation. They are included here as elements of technology in its broadest sense, meaning the techniques or means of creation. From this perspective, the 'technics' of rocket development—the science and art of building large rockets—stretch from equipment to the structure of government and society itself. The challenge of rocket development is to get all of these factors right at the same time and place. Chapter 4 also examines the most important political and economic elements of a rocket programme—those most likely to cause serious problems for a country trying to develop its own ballistic missile or space launcher.

The more orthodox aspects of rockets and missiles, the hard technology, are the subject of chapter 5. The long list of technical problems enumerated in this chapter leads to the conclusion that rocket development is anything but easy. Almost any country can build small artillery rockets. Many can seriously consider building *short-range* ballistic missiles, especially missiles with a range of less than 120–150 km (the exact cut-off point is obscure). The technology of greatest concern today lies on a *technical plateau*, a realm of technology that is more demanding than that of short-range rockets but free of the huge challenges encountered in developing technology for the greatest missile ranges. Within this plateau, where technology allows for ranges of 150 to roughly 1000 km, regional powers can aspire to eventual technological independence. It is over the technologies within this plateau that the most important battles of proliferation control will be fought. At greater ranges the technical requirements become progressively more demanding. The development of extremely *long-range* missiles, those with ranges greater than 1000 km, involves a different class of technology beyond the reach of all but a few countries. At this level, outside control potentially can be much easier and effective.

Ballistic missiles will always be thought of as nuclear-armed missiles. Yet any of the other armament options evaluated in chapter 6 are far more likely to be chosen to fill the nose-cones of regional ballistic missiles. While conventional high explosives are not highly effective as missile warheads, they will continue to be far and away the most common ballistic missile armament. The threat of chemical or biological warheads on ballistic missiles must also be taken seriously, if not for their military capability at least for their frightening appearance. They are not, however, a 'poor man's atomic bomb'. On the contrary, their development requires large investments and considerable technological skill, while in use they have many of the disadvantages of conventional explosives. Several technical problems must still be overcome before any country can deploy them confidently. As the 1993 Chemical Weapons Convention gains adherents and moral authority, moreover, countries clinging to chemical and biological weapon (CBW) options will find themselves compelled to pay ever greater diplomatic penalties for their fascination.

Nuclear weapons, examined in chapter 7, may be the least likely but undoubtedly the most important missile armament. The synergism between nuclear weapons and ballistic missiles is natural since only nuclear weapons can guarantee the military effectiveness of ballistic missiles. The connection between the two may be natural, but it is not automatic. Once a country acquires the ability to build nuclear weapons, several major hurdles must still be overcome before the two technologies can be integrated and nuclear missiles deployed with its armed forces. In addition to the problems of acquiring a basic nuclear weapon capability, a bomb must be designed for missile delivery and its destructiveness must be increased in order to accomplish specific military objectives. Nuclear weapons, in other words, are no panacea for missile ineffectiveness.

General rules and processes are the basic forces behind the proliferation challenge, but no general policy will ever offer a sufficient response. The principal theme of this study is *contingency*, the importance of distinctive national capabilities and choices in shaping the process of proliferation. Chapter 8 stresses that efforts to counter ballistic missile proliferation can never be complete. Proliferation rather is an interactive process—a contest between would-be proliferators with many alternative paths at their disposal and would-be controllers with their own choices to make in response.

Successful rocket development is contingent on the ability simultaneously to focus essential resources where they are needed and manage their application efficiently. This is the real technics of rocketry. The physical technology alone is a permissive force, making proliferation possible but not inevitable. Whether or not an emerging power succeeds in its efforts to create advanced weapons such as ballistic missiles depends—is contingent—more on its ability to organize its resources efficiently. Even rudimentary levels of technology can be sufficient if well organized, while no amount of the finest equipment can compensate for bureaucratic incompetence. The contingent relationship between the politics and technics explains why proliferation is so difficult to predict and to control.

The contingency of proliferation should come as no surprise to students of domestic politics, who are only too aware how hard it can be to translate policy into real accomplishments.[2] In foreign and security policy, however, it is easy to fall victim to the fallacy of assuming that it is simpler for other countries to do things that our own countries find extremely difficult to do. The reality is, of course, that hard tasks like the creation of major weapon systems are no easier anywhere, even in countries possessed of broad resources and immense determination.[3] Proliferation may be likely, but in no sense is it inevitable. It follows that control efforts may not be guaranteed success, nor are they doomed to failure.

There is no simple road-map to successful development of a long-range rocket, but there are rules which most programmes must respect if they are to have much chance of success. While all countries and programmes are unique, all are constrained by the nature of the technology itself. Any development programme must deal with the inherent problems of organization, personnel and finance as well as the physics, chemistry and engineering of rocket flight. The constrained path of missile development has direct consequences for control efforts. Just as there is no single route to successful missile development, there is no single solution to controlling and reversing it.

The greatest shortcoming of this study is perhaps the weakness of the data on which it relies. Compared to superpower strategic assessments of the cold war era, with their enviably exact numbers, regional rockets seem shadowy and ephemeral. Often amazingly little is known about regional programmes— sometimes only general characteristics such as the approximate age of a programme and range of a missile. In some cases not even the names of the mis-

---

[2] This perspective owes much to the work of Theda Skocpol and Charles Tilly. The clearest statement is by Skocpol, in 'Bringing the state back in', eds P. Evans, E. Rueschemeyer and T. Skocpol, *Bringing the State Back In* (Cambridge University Press: Cambridge, Mass., 1985), pp. 3–37; see also Barnett, M. N., *Confronting the Costs of War: Military Power, State, and Society in Egypt and Israel* (Princeton University Press: Princeton, N.J., 1992); Migdal, J. S., *Strong Societies and Weak States: State–Society Relations and State Capabilities in the Third World* (Princeton University Press: Princeton, N:J:, 1988); and Zuern, M., 'Bringing the second image (back) in: about the domestic sources of regime formation', ed. V. Rittberger, *Regime Theory and International Relations* (Clarendon Press: Oxford, 1993), chapter 12.

[3] Jervis, R., *Perception and Misperception in International Politics* (Princeton University Press: Princeton, N.J., 1976), pp. 319–29.

siles are known: the designations of some of the most well-known ballistic missiles—such as the Israeli Jericho or the North Korean NoDong—are Western terms improvised in lieu of their real names. Not surprisingly, the only reliable data available are those for missiles originally transferred from the United States and the former Soviet Union.

To compensate for the poor quality of the information on many regional programmes, particular technical problems are often illustrated with examples drawn from the French, German, Soviet and US experiences in developing their early ballistic missiles. The development of missiles such as the US Atlas intercontinental ballistic missile (ICBM) or the French S-2 intermediate-range ballistic missile (IRBM) was undertaken in very different political environments, but many of the technical problems encountered in these programmes remain important considerations for contemporary missile newcomers. Regional rocket makers are under no obligation to repeat the experiences of their predecessors. Rather, the problems and choices faced by the first countries to develop long-range rockets are used here to illustrate the kinds of problem which all countries entering the field must confront. Repeated references to a few regional rocket programmes, especially those of China and India, may seem unbalanced as well but were necessitated by the availability of data.

2. Can missile proliferation be stopped?

I. Introduction

The swift rise of missile proliferation to the top of the international agenda in the late 1980s often gave the impression that it had a furious, almost inevitable momentum. Previously unknown, this new threat emerged seemingly full-grown and beyond control. The reality is less dramatic. Although missile proliferation is one of the most serious challenges facing the international community today, its rise has not been as sudden or ineluctable as it is often portrayed. Some programmes are clearly bound for success. Other regional programmes, including some that seem to be the most threatening today, have been running for 20, 30 or 40 years and will undoubtedly continue for many more years without results, and a few programmes that were most alarming in the 1980s have since collapsed altogether.

The emergence of the proliferation issue owes much to serendipitous turns of events. As long as regional space launch vehicle and ballistic missile programmes were overshadowed by the superpower competition, missile proliferation did not attract the attention it deserved. For missile proliferation to become a leading issue, older issues had to disappear and spectacular events had to capture public attention. The wider transformations of international politics in the late 1980s facilitated just this shift in priorities. Only a few months after the superpowers completed their first serious disarmament treaty—the Soviet–US Treaty on the Elimination of Intermediate-Range and Shorter-Range Missiles (INF Treaty)—in 1987, the world was confronted with a missile war between Iran and Iraq. At about the same time, other regional powers such as India and Israel, for reasons of their own, publicized major rocket and missile launches. Disclosures in the press revealed other potentially destabilizing rocket developments in every region of the world, from South America and South Africa to East Asia.

In the eyes of many, missile proliferation symbolizes the anarchy prevailing after the cold war. The problem appeared just as the superpower confrontation was receding. Not since the West learned of the Soviet atomic bomb in August 1949 has a major threat to international security appeared so abruptly. The discovery that dozens of regional actors possessed or were experimenting with large rockets was especially chilling. Potentially armed with anything from conventional explosives to thermonuclear warheads, these new weapons threatened to recreate the balance of terror from which the world had just escaped.

Despite the apparent novelty of the issue, regional powers have been trying to acquire long-range rockets for decades. Their interest in long-range rockets, for both military and civilian purposes, can be traced back to the 1950s. The launch of Sputnik in October 1957 was the catalyst for increased spending on rocket development and space research, not only in the United States but nearly everywhere. Although many of the earliest regional efforts looked clumsy to some and silly to others, a few prescient observers saw their long-term potential. As early as 1961 a major industry publication identified 'a total of 28 countries now acquiring rocket power'.[1] Had he wished, the author could have noted that another 40 countries were already involved in space research or other aspects of rocketry. Most of the missile projects of greatest concern today can be traced back to that time.

Recognition of missile proliferation has been an on-and-off affair. In a cycle that has occurred repeatedly for over 35 years and will undoubtedly be repeated in the future, dramatic and well-publicized events have raised public and official awareness, but such widespread concern has invariably proved to be temporary. Egyptian efforts to develop long-range ballistic missiles in the mid-1960s forced Western officials to deal with the issue for the first time. In the repercussions of the 1973 Middle East War the issue emerged again. A series of revelations of interest in rockets among emerging powers in the late 1970s, and other disclosures in the late 1980s, also triggered spasmodic Western attention. Each time, however, missile proliferation disappeared from the headlines within months, replaced by more immediate concerns of international security. The dramatic Scud missile wars over Israel and Saudi Arabia in 1991 gave the issue an unprecedented urgency, but it was not long before public attention shifted to the disintegration of the Soviet Union and the civil wars in Somalia and the former Yugoslavia.

The world has been fortunate that missile proliferation could be temporarily forgotten. Despite steady interest and the gradual accumulation of capabilities, nothing has emerged comparable to the Soviet–US nuclear confrontation that dominated global security politics for 40 years. Most observers would agree, however, that unless vigorous steps are taken to reverse regional proliferation trends, it is only a matter of time before ballistic missiles dominate global security politics again.

Long-range ballistic missiles pose a special threat to international stability, especially when nuclear-armed. They are unsurpassed as symbols of power, threatening potential adversaries with almost instant and uncontrollable attack. They are also extremely provocative, threatening to escalate conflict from the battlefield to unprotected cities, transforming local conflicts into regional or intercontinental maelstroms and forcing the world to treat every local dust-up as a potential global cataclysm. Yet rocket development can also be very sensitive to disruption and vulnerable to outside control. Indeed, ballistic missile proliferation is probably more amenable to control than any other proliferation problem.

---

[1] Poirer, B., 'Rocket power ranks abroad rapidly increasing', *Missiles and Rockets*, 7 Aug. 1961, pp. 48–50.

This study stresses that missile proliferation is sufficiently alarming to warrant strong international action—that the spread of rocket technology is difficult but far from impossible to control. Two major schools of thought challenge these propositions about the nature of missile proliferation. The *technological and political determinists* view missile proliferation as a phenomenon largely beyond the influence of policy making. The *irrelevance school* maintains that whether or not anything can be done about missile proliferation is a minor question because there is little to become excited about in the first place. This and the following chapter examine these two perspectives in order to ascertain the nature of the threat posed by missile proliferation and to establish its amenability to outside influence and control.

II. Technological determinism

One of the oldest arguments about the development and spread of new weapons is that the process is virtually unstoppable—that it is so far beyond the reach of normal policy making that only the most extreme measures can bring it under control. The specific arguments that weapons are out of control are not new, nor have they been confirmed by experience. Just as experience shows that policy makers have almost always retained great latitude over the development and deployment of major weapons in the past, there is every reason to believe that the same is true regarding the spread of ballistic missiles today.

The belief that advances in military technology are beyond control goes back at least to the late 19th century. Then, as now, advocates of new weapon projects argued that technological forces supported their conviction that there was no sensible alternative but to invest in the most advanced weapons of the day—battleships, dreadnoughts, submarines, poison gas, bomber aircraft, and so on.[2] Identical arguments have been used by disarmament advocates ever since the time of the 1899 and 1907 Hague Conferences to maintain that the only solution to armaments competition is to ban whole categories of weaponry, if not the entire armaments process altogether.[3] Both sides shared the premise that technology itself creates an all-or-nothing situation in which governments have little choice but to act comprehensively or yield the game entirely.

Technological determinism has usually been an implicit assumption. In the words of the physicist Ralph Lapp, 'when technology beckons, men are helpless'.[4] Only in the late 1970s did scholars try to clarify the concept directly. Much of the inspiration for this came from the more general discontent with commonplace belief in autonomous technological forces, with 'technology out of control', previously identified by scholars and radical activists. They

---

[2] See, e.g., Massie, R. K., *Dreadnought: Britain, Germany, and the Coming of the Great War* (Ballantine: New York, 1991), pp. 468–69, 487–89.

[3] Among the most prominent examples are Noel-Baker, P. J., *Disarmament* (Harcourt Brace: New York, 1926); and Myrdal, A., *The Game of Disarmament* (Pantheon: New York, 1976).

[4] Lapp, R. E., *Arms Beyond Doubt: The Tyranny of Weapons Technology* (Cowles: New York, 1970), p. 173.

emphasized the deleterious effects of modern technology in society as a force out of control, potentially undermining democratic values, weakening social bonds and harming the environment. Their pessimistic assessments mocked the healing effects of modest political reforms. Instead, their recommendations tended to stress radical measures such as abandoning industrial economics in favour of returning to pastoral and communal ways of life.[5]

Similar convictions animate the belief that military technologies develop through their own internal logic. They may sometimes be shaped by the bureaucratic or economic interests of the organizations responsible for them, but they stand largely beyond the influence of national policy making. Once a programme has reached a certain critical size, according to this argument, it is impossible to control it. Other forces may affect the rate of progress but not its certain end. In the words of Marek Thee, 'no matter how contemporary arms races are conceived in theory and however they are described in their multicausal complexity, we must recognize the central role of the running drive of military R&D . . . Military R&D has become the crucial variable in armament dynamics'.[6]

A blind force, then, compels governments to acquire major weapons regardless of whether or not they best serve the national interest. The process has been described variously as 'a self-sustaining technological momentum', 'the technical imperative' or 'technology creep'. It dictates that once a military–industrial project reaches a critical size, once its success becomes essential to the success of a major firm or government agency, it is extremely difficult and often impossible to stop. The determinist perspective is inherently pessimistic. If it is correct, the threat of ballistic missile proliferation can be reduced only by eliminating all work on large rockets, everywhere on the planet.

Individual arms control measures are unlikely to have much effect from this perspective. Instead of ending military competition the most they can be expected to achieve is to channel it into other paths, typically even more dangerous. The only way to cope with the effects of the technological imperative is to end all development of potentially destabilizing weapons. 'Purely technical restrictions and control measures, as well as ethical and moral exhortations, are not enough, however', writes Thee. 'It is indispensable that the underlying structural issues should be addressed as well'. The only meaningful controls are prohibitions on entire areas of destabilizing technology. 'There is no way to halt armaments and reverse the arms race unless we seriously address the problem of military technology and check military R and D'.[7]

---

[5] This perspective owes much of its authority to the writings of the German philosopher Martin Heidegger. A valuable assessment is given by Winner, L., *Autonomous Technology: Technics-out-of-Control as a Theme in Political Thought* (MIT Press: Cambridge, Mass., 1977). An uncompromising presentation of this perspective is given by Cooper, B., *Action into Nature: An Essay on the Meaning of Technology* (University of Notre Dame Press: Notre Dame, Ind., 1991).

[6] Thee, M., 'Science-based military technology as a driving force behind the arms race', eds N. P. Gleditsch and O. Njolstad, *Arms Races: Technological and Political Dynamics* (Sage: London, 1990), p. 119.

[7] Thee, M., *Military Technology, Military Strategy and the Arms Race* (Croom Helm: London, 1986), pp. 127, 130.

Faith in technological determinism leads to the assumption that regional rocket programmes will develop along a predictable path towards possession of long-range ballistic missiles. Borrowing from liberal models of economic development and previous studies of regional arms industries, this approach maintains that countries will gradually ascend a ladder of development. From this perspective, a typical emerging missile power is expected to progress incrementally. It will start by importing small battlefield weapons, advance through several stages of progressively greater technical and industrial sophistication, and culminate the process with domestic production of long-range rockets.

The ladder model undoubtedly has heuristic value. It is certainly useful for comparing the relative capabilities of different countries. As a description of how countries actually perform, however, it bears little resemblance to reality. Few countries progress smoothly up development ladders, in this or any other field. As Keith Krause noted in a related context, few if any regional countries reach the highest level of military–industrial capability, producing advanced weaponry of their own design. The conventional arms industries of these countries usually ascend only to the middle rungs, where they stagnate or struggle to keep from falling behind.[8]

In retrospect, it is clear that no country's military research and development (R&D) resembles the self-perpetuating process described by determinists. The history of the Strategic Defense Initiative (SDI) in the United States, from President Ronald Reagan's 1983 Star Wars speech until the programme's end in 1993, illustrates the uncertainty in the process. Dogmatic technological determinists can point out that SDI work continues in other forms, but the elaborate space-based defences they feared most are nowhere to be seen. As for rocket programmes in the regional countries, these are far from robust enterprises propelled by ineluctable technical forces. Time and again, experience has revealed that regional rocket programmes are sensitive to a wide variety of political, organizational, economic and technological factors. Disruption in one of these areas is often sufficient to bring a project to a halt. Serious problems in several areas usually spell the end of an entire programme. These vulnerabilities create numerous opportunities for restraint. External efforts, even modestly conceived ones, have great potential as agents of control.

One of the repercussions of the many barriers to mastering rocket technology is the rise of a covert market in ballistic missiles. Countries unable to build their own missiles naturally try to buy finished missiles from others. At various times almost every rocket-making country has sold its technology to others. Today only China and North Korea still try to export whole missiles. Yet countries often find it impossible to buy the missiles they want. Technological forces undoubtedly make rockets available, but they do not ensure that emerging powers can acquire the items they want.

---

[8] Krause, K., *Arms and the State: Patterns of Military Production and Trade* (Cambridge University Press: Cambridge, UK, 1992), pp. 171–74.

III. Political determinism

A more nuanced approach to the study of weapon procurement argues that no single factor can explain why nations acquire advanced military equipment. A major weapon programme rather is promoted by a wide variety of mutually supporting political forces. The most important of these lie entirely within the nation, because many organizational and industrial interests combine to make major programmes unstoppable. From this perspective weapon procurement is only remotely a reaction to foreign adversaries. Instead it is internal interests that explain weapon decisions.

In the most sophisticated statement of this argument, Dieter Senghaas described weapon procurement as an *Eigendynamik,* a self-generating mechanism whereby weapons develop through the interaction of their technology with the domestic politics of the innovating state. By serving the economic needs of industry and organized labour, the tactical requirements of the armed services and the prestige requirements of national leaders, weapons generate 'self-centred imperatives of national armament'.[9] There is a basic harmony of interest among major national institutions which ensures that they will support each other on major weapon programmes. Without anything to interfere with this mutual support, without institutions prepared to say otherwise, the political process is unable to stop military innovation. Variations of this argument have been especially appealing to analysts trying to explain the origins of controversial weapons such as the hydrogen bomb, MIRVs (multiple independently targetable re-entry vehicles), long-range ballistic missiles or the deployment of cruise missiles in Europe.[10]

Viewed with hindsight, it is clear that all-or-nothing arguments based on the assumptions of political determinism mostly express anxiety over the particular political circumstances of the day rather than any ineluctable process. Recent history is replete with examples of weapon projects that stop or even shift into reverse. Following the signing of the INF Treaty in 1987, many of the weapons that seemed most alarming in the 1980s were destroyed. START I and START II (Strategic Arms Reduction Treaties), signed in 1991 and 1993, respectively, commit the United States and the Soviet successor states to destroy two-thirds of their strategic nuclear forces, including most of the MIRVed ICBMs that overshadowed arms debates in the 1970s. Under the 1990 Treaty on Conventional Armed Forces in Europe (CFE Treaty), the armies of the cold war protagonists are being rapidly reduced as well. In each case choice prevailed over necessity. Political determinism is less reductionist than purely technical arguments, but not much more can be said for it. In the light of such

---

[9] Senghaas, D., *Rüstung und Militarismus* [Arms and militarism] (Suhrkamp: Frankfurt, 1972). A similar concept is developed by Krell, G., *Rüstungs-dynamik und Rüstungskontrolle: Die gesellschaftlichen Auseinandersetzung um SALT in den USA, 1969–1975* [Arms dynamic and arms control: the domestic debate over SALT in the USA, 1969–1975], 2nd edn (Hagg und Herchen: Frankfurt, 1978).

[10] Examples include Shapely, D., 'Technology creep and the arms race', *Science*, 22 Sep. 1978, pp. 1102–105; and Zuckerman, S., 'Science advisors and scientific advisors', *Proceedings of the American Philosophical Society*, Aug. 1980, pp. 241–55.

events any arguments based on deterministic assumptions appear to be anachronistic and misleading.

Regional powers retain the same margin for choice as other countries. In 1987–88, for example, a series of disclosures created sudden concern that Argentina, Brazil and India would quickly deploy their own fleets of nuclear-powered submarines.[11] By the early 1990s, however, it was clear that the threat had been grossly exaggerated. Although genuinely interested, these countries were only prepared to finance small R&D programmes. None is willing to pursue full-scale development of prototype naval reactors, much less actual deployment. Although all three countries have domestic interests strongly in favour of such a step, it will take considerable political change to make that possible.

Similar conclusions can be drawn from the failure of many countries to develop nuclear weapons, despite mastery of the essential technology. Having all the prerequisites—facilities, finances and talent—was not enough to lead most nuclear-capable countries to build nuclear armaments. Instead of the 25, 30 or 40 nuclear weapon states anticipated in the early 1960s, today there are only five declared plus Israel and possibly North Korea and Pakistan. Some countries, such as Canada, Japan, the Netherlands and Sweden, clearly could develop nuclear weapons but choose not to do so.[12] Others, such as Egypt, South Korea and Taiwan, have serious security concerns yet no longer show any serious interest in a nuclear option.[13] More recently Argentina, Brazil and South Africa surrendered their own elaborate nuclear weapon endeavours after years of aggressive R&D—in the case of South Africa, after actual deployment of six nuclear bombs which have since then been destroyed.

IV. Arms racing

A more sophisticated version of the determinist position emphasizes arms racing as the basic engine of weapon creation and spread. The sudden appearance of dozens of regional ballistic missile projects in the late 1980s might suggest that arms racing is at work. The process was formally identified by Samuel Huntington as 'a progressive, competitive peacetime increase in armaments by two states or coalitions of states resulting from conflicting purpose and fears'.[14] Despite common use of the term 'arms racing', it is fraught with troublesome ambiguity, especially about the intentions, speed and type of equipment involved. Must weapons be procured by two nations specifically to deal with

---

[11] Goldblat, J., 'Submarine proliferation', *Bulletin of the Atomic Scientists*, Sep. 1988; and Sanders, B. and Simpson, J., *Nuclear Submarines and Non-Proliferation*, PPNN Occasional Paper 2 (Mountbatten Centre for International Studies, University of Southampton: Southampton, UK, July 1988).

[12] Cowen Karp, R. (ed.), SIPRI, *Security Without Nuclear Weapons?* (Oxford University Press: Oxford, 1992); and Reiss, M., *Without the Bomb* (Columbia University Press: New York, 1988).

[13] The best study of Egypt's failure to pursue nuclear weapons is Bhatia, S., *Nuclear Rivals in the Middle East* (Routledge: London, 1988).

[14] Huntington, S. P., 'Arms races: prerequisites and results', *Public Policy,* 1958, reprinted in Art, R. J. and Waltz, K. N. (eds), *The Use of Force*, 2nd edn (University Press of America: Lanham, Md., 1983), p. 439.

each other, or is it enough if these weapons can be used against each other? Must weapon procurement decisions by nations caught in an arms race follow each other quickly—by weeks or months—or can they follow by years or even decades? Must nations invest in comparable weapons or is it enough generally to improve their arsenals?

A more specific definition by Colin Gray sees an arms race as 'two or more parties perceiving themselves to be in an adversary relationship, who are increasing or improving their armaments at a *rapid* rate and structuring their respective military postures with a *general* attention to the past, current, and anticipated military and political behaviour of the other parties'. A clear definition turns arms racing into something distinct and unusual, not vague and normal. Gray's emphasis on rapid counter-arming would narrow the confirmable occurrence of arms racing to only a few countries and regions, leaving the rest of the world in less dangerous forms of arms competition. Barry Buzan goes further to clarify the exceptional nature of an arms race when he argues that 'it implies a notably intense process of military competition that contrasts with whatever passes for normality in military relations between states'.[15]

In contrast to the implied meaning of an arms race, most regional rocket programmes have been gradual and deliberate. Although several programmes were revealed in the late 1980s, most of these were started at least 10 or 20 years before or even earlier. Nor were all these programmes directed at specific adversaries. Rather, some are expressions of a general process of national military expansion, with only weak links to the action–reaction cycle that George Rathjens saw at the heart of arms racing.[16] Others are essentially commercial endeavours in which profit motives are paramount. A few are primarily civilian space launch projects with secondary military potential. Ballistic missile proliferation is undoubtedly part of a vague and amorphous international arms dynamic which makes ballistic missiles increasingly attractive to regional leaders. However, the international spread of missile capabilities is too varied to be explained through any approach that does not emphasize the special characteristics of individual missile programmes themselves.

The idea that the spread of ballistic missiles is also the result of forces beyond the control of any one state has great appeal to some observers on both sides of the issue. It leads one prominent US analyst to conclude that: 'The question is no longer whether industrializing countries will develop and deploy advanced missiles but when'.[17] Semi-official Indian and Chinese spokesmen often argue that the international dynamics of missile technology make it impossible for their countries to restrain their missile development or exports independently. More important than missile control, they say, is resolution of regional conflict; international conflicts are an important motive for missile

[15] Gray, C. S., 'The arms race phenomenon', *World Politics*, vol. 24, no. 1 (Oct. 1971), p. 40; and Buzan, B., *Introduction to Strategic Studies: Military Technology and International Relations* (Macmillan and the International Institute of Strategic Studies: London, 1987), p. 72.

[16] Rathjens, G. W., 'The dynamics of the arms race', *Scientific American*, Apr. 1969.

[17] Nolan, J. E., *Trappings of Power: Ballistic Missiles in the Third World* (Brookings Institution: Washington, DC, 1991), p. 10.

acquisition and they also make the use of such weapons feasible. Alternatively, these spokesmen favour a global ban prohibiting the possession of ballistic missiles by all countries.[18] The latter position has also found increasing favour among Western critics of existing control arrangements, who believe that the only serious hope for controlling missile proliferation is a universal ban on all ballistic missiles.[19]

V. Missile proliferation trends

The pace of missile proliferation in the 1980s leaves little doubt that many regional powers believe that these weapons are worth their price. A comprehensive list of major rocketry projects world-wide is presented in appendix 1. This compilation shows that, in addition to the 5 declared nuclear weapon states—Britain, China, France, Russia and the United States—at least 36 countries have experimented with the development of major rockets, and dozens of others have some relevant technology. Some are clearly trying to develop advanced and long-range ballistic missiles, while others are probably interested only in space launch applications, and a few merely flirted with a technology they were not prepared to pursue aggressively.

The symbolism of large rockets obscures the actual trends of missile proliferation. For many observers, the public discovery of missile proliferation in the late 1980s was a shock that encouraged exaggeration of the problem. Press reports contributed to the confusion by revealing dozens of previously obscure regional rocket projects, typically implying that these had only recently started and were close to establishing complete strategic forces. Commentators in emerging powers, proud of their nations' accomplishments, often did everything possible to feed foreign panic. Concerned officials in the United States and elsewhere wove these tales into a lurid picture of rockets out of control. This extreme concern made it easy to overlook the fact that most of these projects had started years or decades previously and few showed signs of rapid progress.

The intervening years have helped to winnow the wheat from the chaff. There can be no doubt that missile proliferation poses a grave threat to international peace and stability. However, it is misleading to view it as a uniform threat: the challenge of missile proliferation varies considerably from country to country. Few countries have seen rapid or direct progress, many have stumbled, and several are no longer seriously interested.

Missile proliferators can be divided into three categories or tiers, depending on their technical capabilities: those with substantial indigenous technical

---

[18] Bu Ran, 'Missiles: proliferation and control', *Beijing Review*, 2–8 Dec. 1991; and Hu Yumin, 'Proliferation of guided missiles and control over missile transfer', *International Strategic Studies* (Beijing), Dec. 1991.

[19] Frye, A., 'Zero ballistic missiles', *Foreign Policy,* no. 88 (autumn 1992), pp. 3–20; and 'Revisiting zero ballistic missiles Reagan's forgotten dream', *F.A.S. Public Interest Report*, May/June 1992. A similar argument is used to advocate a global INF Treaty in Bailey, K. C., 'Can missile proliferation be reversed?', *Orbis*, winter 1991.

Table 2.1. Three tiers of ballistic missile proliferators, 1994[a]

First tier: Developing indigenous long-range ballistic missiles	Second tier: Capable of developing long-range missiles with foreign assistance	Third tier: Dependent on foreign-supplied ballistic missiles
India	Argentina	Afghanistan
Israel	Brazil	Algeria
North Korea	Egypt	Chile
	Indonesia	Cuba
	Iran	Libya
	Iraq (pre-1991)	Pakistan
	South Korea	Syria
	Serbia	Yemen
	South Africa	Iraq (post-1991)
	Taiwan	

[a] A comprehensive list of countries capable of developing ballistic missiles would have to include in the rank of the first tier more distant possibilities, starting with Japan, whose M series space launchers could be adapted as IRBMs within a few months, although high-performance guidance and re-entry vehicles would require a few years for full development. Japan's liquid-fuel N and H series launchers could be adapted into ICBMs, but with greater difficulty. Canada, Germany, Italy and Ukraine have industries capable of developing large rockets within as few as 5 years; and Australia, Belgium, the Netherlands, Poland, Romania Spain, Sweden and Switzerland could do so in about 10 years.

resources, which are capable of creating their own strategic missile forces with or without outside assistance; those which have sufficient resources to conduct rocket development but are able to develop long-range missiles only with large-scale foreign help; and those which are dependent on foreign suppliers for entire missile systems (see table 2.1).

The *first tier* is very exclusive. While no emerging power is capable of developing long-range rockets entirely on its own, three have reached a point where they no longer rely on foreign assistance. Their programmes are slow and their capabilities are less than they would prefer, but they can continue to make progress without outside help.[20]

Of all the emerging regional powers, only Israel has both developed and deployed its own long-range missile forces. Israel has invested in missile R&D systematically since the early 1960s, culminating in the current Jericho-2/ Shavit series which appears to be fully integrated into its strategic forces. Israel relied extensively on foreign technology, mainly from France, in the early years. Today it is the only country among all the emerging powers with its own truly indigenous rocket programme, with little need for foreign assistance.

The only other regional power with comparable technical capabilities is India. The Indian research programme is almost as old as Israel's and considerably larger in scale, although it has not demonstrated equal coherence. With

[20] A similar conclusion is reached in a 1993 CIA analysis. See Lippman, T. W., 'CIA says threat of missile strike on U.S. is slight', *International Herald Tribune*, 27 Dec. 1993, p. 3.

resources divided among several competing civilian and military projects, India has been unable to bring any but the smallest projects to completion.[21] Nor has India made strategic decisions establishing clear goals for these projects. Instead, India's rocket programmes exhibit the symptoms of a vague experiment. Despite several test launches of large civilian and military rockets since 1980, little has been accomplished beyond showing long-term potential. Such demonstrations are not without impact; with the first launch of the PSLV (Polar Space Launch Vehicle) booster in September 1993, India marked its ability to develop ICBMs.

North Korea is the other regional power known to be developing a strategic rocket force on its own. Although its resources are more limited than those of Israel and India, North Korea stands out for its goals, which appear to be as much economic as military. Work started in the early 1970s, but little progress was made until the early 1980s when the programme was wedded exclusively to Scud technology. By 1987 Scud copies were in series production and were being sold to Iran. An extended-range version was transferred to Syria and Iran in 1992 and assembly was arranged for Iran and possibly Egypt. With a 1000-km version under development, North Korea has reached the limits of Scud technology and seems unlikely to make further advances unless a new source of technology can be found. Authorities in Pyongyang may dream of 2000- or even 3000-km range missiles, but realization of such ambitions depends on foreign help.

After these countries come a *second tier* of others that have experimented with large-scale rocket technology but, for one reason or another, have not extended this work beyond the prototype stage. All rely extensively on foreign assistance and have had great problems since it became difficult to acquire such assistance in the late 1980s. Several countries discontinued their programmes before the metal-cutting stage, at which expenses rise swiftly. Others were probably never committed to the idea of full-scale development and abandoned it after some initial experiments, as appears to have been the case with Indonesia and Taiwan. A few, such as Argentina, Brazil and South Africa, downgraded their programmes as regional tensions eased and to avoid antagonizing outside powers, especially the United States. Still other countries, such as Iran and Libya, tried to build their own missile systems in the past but now find it much easier to rely on missiles purchased from willing suppliers such as China or North Korea. Finally, one second-tier country, Iraq, was forced to stop its missile programmes by UN military intervention and joined the third tier.

Many of the countries in the second tier have impressive technical and industrial resources. With sufficient motivation and access to foreign technology they can undoubtedly co-produce foreign missiles, especially weapons based on

[21] Current Indian projects include 3 space launchers (ASLV, PSLV and GSLV) and 2 ballistic missiles (Agni and Prithvi), as well as many other smaller missiles. The largest system actually approaching deployment is the Prithvi, a tactical missile for the Indian Army and technically the least ambitious of all Indian rocketry projects. Based on a propulsion system borrowed from the Soviet SA-2 Guideline surface-to-air missile (SAM), it comes in 150-km and 250-km versions and could be fully operational in the mid-1990s.

relatively simple Scud-type technology. A few are certainly capable of becoming first-tier proliferators by changing policies and developing their own long-range rockets. From this pool will emerge some of the most serious proliferation threats of the future.

For second-tier countries with moribund rocket programmes, the overwhelming question is: Which technology and what interest remain? Can they still develop long-range rockets within a decade or so, or must they start virtually from scratch? One of the most daunting problems in assessing quiescent missile programmes is determining whether a project has been ended permanently, whether technical resources have been shelved for future applications, or whether design and development work is actually continuing. In countries where the armed forces and other agencies have substantial autonomy, it is entirely possible for relevant work to continue in extreme secrecy, even without the knowledge or consent of the central government.[22]

The *third tier* includes those countries relying entirely on foreign-supplied missiles. Although they may be able to modify foreign-supplied rockets, they cannot develop entirely new ones on their own. These countries are both the most susceptible to outside control and the most volatile: without foreign help there is little they can accomplish, but one shipment can give them a strategic capability overnight.

The most extreme example is Iraq. Fifteen years of R&D gave Iraq great notoriety but failed to generate a single usable missile throughout its long war with Iran and up to the time of the 1991 Persian Gulf War. President Saddam Hussein relied on foreign suppliers for all the hundreds of missiles that Iraq actually deployed, including over 800 Scud missiles. With its most advanced programmes disassembled by the United Nations Special Commission on Iraq (UNSCOM), Iraq has been stripped of its second-tier capabilities and reduced to third-tier status; its only hope for acquiring missiles in the foreseeable future is from a foreign supplier.

In addition to Iraq, there have been a few other special cases of countries able to buy missiles in considerable quantities or of impressive quality. Afghanistan received a huge number of missiles, possibly as many as 2000 Scuds, from the Soviet Union. China supplied Saudi Arabia with DF-3 IRBMs, by far the largest missiles deployed anywhere outside the major nuclear weapon states. These cases appear to be exceptional. More typically, the international arms market has been a capricious supplier. Ordinary recipients received only token numbers of missiles during the cold war. The small missile forces of such countries as Algeria, Cuba and Yemen appear to be historical accidents, not harbingers of future trends. More portentous is the emergence of new suppliers guided only by profit. With the help of new suppliers a few third-tier missile

---

[22] An extreme example of this ambiguity is the Argentine Condor-2, which the Menem Government declared at an end in Apr. 1990. The decision prompted a tug of war with the Argentine Air Force, which kept the project alive covertly—a dispute which also concerned the question of who controls the Argentine military. After many conflicting announcements, in Feb. 1992 the remnants of the project were formally transferred to a civilian agency. The saga seems doomed to continue so long as Argentina still has some rocket technology left to fight over.

proliferators, such as Pakistan and Syria, have been able to purchase missile systems of the sort they were denied during the cold war.

VI. Forces against missile proliferation

As recently as 1989, William Webster, then Director of US Central Intelligence, testified before the US Congress that there were likely to be 15–20 Third World countries building their own ballistic missiles by the year 2000.[23] In fact, the pace of ballistic missile proliferation has slowed remarkably since the mid-1980s. Instead of the virtually unlimited spread of missiles, there are not likely to be more than six regional actors producing ballistic missiles in the early years of the next century.[24] Clearly this is not a threat so small that one can afford to ignore it, but it is also not so overwhelming that one must abandon hope of bringing the problem under control.

Regional progress in long-range rocket technology is limited almost entirely to first-tier proliferators. Today only two of these countries—Israel and North Korea—have manufactured complete missile forces. India has seen its programme slow considerably because of a variety of problems, although it is beginning to deploy its first fully functional missile, the Prithvi. No second-tier country can be expected to accomplish as much within the next 10 years. The Iraqi programme is lost in the nation's rubble, although it almost certainly survives in the dreams of Saddam Hussein. The second-tier countries with the strongest motives to build their own ballistic missiles—such as Egypt, Iran and possibly Taiwan—are heavily dependent on the cooperation of foreign suppliers. No other regional actor currently has active programmes or the technical resources to develop long-range rockets on its own.[25]

For all missile proliferators, domestic development and production are highly preferable to buying finished missiles from abroad. Not only is the symbolic and political weight of an indigenous weapon much greater, but reliance on imports can be crippling with such a sensitive item. In lieu of domestic programmes, imports—the international trade in finished missiles—become the key to proliferation. Even in this arena, however, one sees far fewer countries trying to buy or sell than might be expected.

The failure of missile proliferation to proceed as anticipated cannot be fully explained; too many of the reasons lie hidden in the idiosyncrasies of national programmes and specific projects. Even so, several general forces can be seen as militating against faster missile proliferation. Some are fundamental and unlikely to change quickly. Others are more delicate and could yield to permit a

---

[23] Speech before the Town Hall of California, Los Angeles, 30 Mar. 1989.

[24] Other analyses have reached similar conclusions. See, e.g., Odom, W. E., *et al.*, *The Emerging Ballistic Missile Threat to the United States* (The Proliferation Study Team: Washington, DC, Feb. 1993), p. 22.

[25] Clarke, R., Testimony before the Subcommittee on Technology and National Security, Joint Economic Committee, US Congress, 23 Apr. 1991; and Karp, A., 'Ballistic missile proliferation', *SIPRI Yearbook 1991: World Armaments and Disarmament* (Oxford University Press: Oxford, 1991), chapter 9.

new surge of missile development in regional countries. The most important impediments include the following factors.

1. *Ballistic missile development is more difficult than many regional actors have appreciated.* Although it is the basic force making missile proliferation possible, the spread of technology does not lead automatically to coherent and successful projects. The quantity and complexity of equipment and technology that must be imported, even for development of a liquid-fuel missile comparable to the 1950s-vintage Soviet Scud, are substantial. The extent of this technology offers many opportunities for control. More advanced and longer-range missiles require even more foreign technology, creating ever more opportunities for supplier controls.

2. *Ballistic missile proliferation rose higher on the international agenda* in the late 1980s and early 1990s. As a result, statesmen—led by Washington—have been more concerned about the issue and more willing to support control policies with aggressive diplomacy. This was clearest in the case of the Argentine–Egyptian–Iraqi Condor-2 missile project, which was brought to a halt in 1989–90; in international pressure on China, which may prevent additional exports of M-series missiles; and in the work of UNSCOM, which systematically disassembled and destroyed much of Iraq's missile establishment.

3. *There are specific technologies which must be acquired to produce ballistic missiles,* making export controls relatively easy to implement and highly effective. Control efforts can be tailored to focus on fuels, engines, guidance systems, re-entry vehicles, simulation and test technology. The brevity of the MTCR (Missile Technology Control Regime) Equipment and Technology Annex[26] clearly illustrates this simplicity, especially when it is contrasted with the mammoth length of the Chemical Weapons Convention or the START I Treaty.

4. *Export controls won greater international support than could have been anticipated.* This was clearest in the development of the MTCR, which grew from 7 original members in 1987 to 25 formal members and several informal adherents at the end of 1994. However, export controls could be much stronger. Alternative suppliers, such as North Korea, greatly weaken its effectiveness, China remains profoundly ambivalent about export controls, and even more committed governments often fail to enforce controls effectively.

5. Despite wars in the Middle East and domestic conflict elsewhere, *the threat of interstate warfare abated during the 1980s.* Even if the late 1980s did not mark the end of history, there is less fear of countries going to war against each other. The dangers of domestic conflict may be greater than ever—the chaos in the former Yugoslavia leaves no doubt—but fewer independent countries fear foreign attack or demonstrate aggressive intentions against their neighbours. The 1990 Iraqi invasion of Kuwait does not appear to portend

---

[26] The MTCR Guidelines for Sensitive Missile-Relevant Transfers were originally agreed in 1987 and revised in 1992. The attached Equipment and Technology Annex consists of 2 categories of equipment and technology whose transfer is to be controlled by national governments.

greater international instability so much as the lingering persistence of old dangers.[27]

On balance, the forces inhibiting proliferation grew stronger than those encouraging it. The result was to undercut some of the most important justifications for many ballistic missile projects. This is clearest for Argentina, Brazil and South Africa, where security motives evaporated.[28] Even in tense regions such as South Asia, where the danger of war has not disappeared, there is less immediate fear of full-scale conflict.[29] Weak justifications also slowed missile programmes in Egypt and Taiwan and eradicated previous interest in South-East Asia. Even in these more secure countries, symbolic and economic motives often remain, but they do not appear to be enough to make rocket technology an urgent national priority.

VII. How can missile proliferation be controlled?

The uneven experience of rocket development in regional countries shows that there is nothing inevitable about missile proliferation. The further spread of ballistic missiles is likely, and strenuous efforts will be required to halt some of the most worrisome projects. Few of these programmes, however, are entirely beyond the influence of outside powers. Experience also teaches the importance of acting quickly to restrain weapon programmes; proliferation is not inevitable, but it is far easier to stop the development of new weapons than to reverse their deployment after they have been issued to the troops in the field.

Contrary to the expectations of technological determinism, the spread of ballistic missiles is a delicate process, vulnerable to outside pressure and sensitive to changing circumstances. The ageing and increasing availability of rocket technology make ballistic missile proliferation possible and increasingly likely, but never unavoidable or immutable.

In these circumstances export controls will remain a fundamental and essential instrument for proliferation control. Political and technical factors are together responsible for proliferation problems, but only the latter tend to lie within the immediate influence of outside powers. While the discriminatory nature and uneconomic side-effects of export controls are to be regretted, it is difficult to envisage a reliable alternative. Broader measures such as a global ban on all ballistic missiles or regional conflict resolution would have obvious advantages for proliferation control. They may be the only mechanisms capable of removing the ballistic missile forces already deployed in regions such as the Middle East and South Asia. Broader measures would also be valuable for the goals they establish, but they seem too elusive and probably too distant to con-

---

[27] Mandelbaum, M., 'The Bush foreign policy', *Foreign Affairs*, vol. 70, no. 1 (1991), especially pp. 10–12.

[28] Stanley, R., 'Co-operation and control: the new approach to nuclear non-proliferation in Argentina and Brazil', *Arms Control*, vol. 13, no. 2 (Sep. 1992), pp. 191–213.

[29] Thomas, R. G. C., 'The growth of Indian military power', eds R. Babbage and S. Gordon, *India's Strategic Future: Regional State or Global Power?* (Macmillan: London, 1992), chapter 3.

trol missile proliferation in the near future. Even if successfully implemented, moreover, universal bans and conflict resolution are not a sufficient response to the problem. Control will rely for many years on the support of other restraints to deal with possible violators and enhance confidence.

In the long run, alternative approaches may hold greater promise for even stronger restraint of missile proliferation by addressing its motives. Do any of these offer another way of dealing with missile proliferation that is so promising as to replace export controls altogether? Although the range of proposals that have been suggested is very diverse, they can be reduced to four general categories: unilateral initiatives, negotiated arms control agreements, conflict resolution and export controls.[30] All are potentially worthwhile and deserve careful consideration. Every approach, however, is burdened with serious flaws.

Unilateral initiatives have a poor reputation, being associated with starry-eyed idealism and the glorification of weakness. This caricature obscures the fact that countries periodically abandon major military programmes, including ballistic missiles, when they believe that they are unnecessary or harm national interests. The list of ballistic missile programmes cancelled or scaled back (see chapter 4, section IV) should leave no doubt that nothing in the rocket business is certain.

The factors that contribute to unilateral decisions to drop major military programmes are diverse, ranging from improvements in the regional political environment to technical problems with the programme itself or more general national economic difficulties. Having seen how forces like these led to a dramatic series of cancellations and cut-backs in Europe in the wake of the cold war, some analysts have suggested that similar forces could lead to unilateral decisions to drop programmes in other regions.[31]

Some regions have been especially vulnerable to this logic, recognizing that some programmes serve no sensible end and should be mothballed or allowed to die. Egypt gave up on its German-designed missiles in the mid-1960s. Algeria retired its small force of Soviet-supplied FROG rockets in the mid-1980s. Around the same time Greece and Turkey mothballed their stocks of US-supplied Honest John rockets.[32] More recently, Kuwait has shown no interest in replacing the FROG missiles stolen by the Iraqi Army during the 1990 invasion. The most likely candidate for unilateral restraint in the near future may be Saudi Arabia, whose force of Chinese-supplied DF-3 IRBMs is very costly to maintain and serves no clear strategic role.[33]

---

[30] The author develops this typology more fully in: Karp, A., 'Ballistic missiles in the Middle East: realities, omens and arms control options', *Contemporary Security Policy*, vol. 15, no. 3 (winter 1994/95).

[31] Sadowski, Y. M., *Scuds or Butter? The Political Economy of Arms Control in the Middle East* (Brookings Institution: Washington, DC, 1993).

[32] Karp, A., 'Ballistic missile proliferation', *SIPRI Yearbook 1989: World Armaments and Disarmament* (Oxford University Press: Oxford, 1989), pp. 291, 302.

[33] Navias, M. S., *Going Ballistic: The Build-up of Missiles in the Middle East* (Brassey's: London, 1993), p. 57.

Other countries may make similar decisions, but the process is too irregular and too easily offset by the acquisition of alternative weapons to have much overall effect. Economic forces, for example, offer the clearest explanation of why North Korea has not sold more Scud missiles in the Middle East than it actually has. Economic constraints also explain the inability of Russian firms to find new clients for SS-21 ballistic missiles despite aggressive marketing efforts.[34] So far, however, these forces have not been strong enough to convince a regional government to drop long-range ballistic missiles already in service. Nor is there a clear method for structuring such steps into a systematic process for regional restraint.

Negotiated control of ballistic missiles has greater potential to bring about systematic control and cuts in regional missile forces. The arms control experiences of the United States and the Soviet Union in the 1972 SALT I Interim Agreement and the subsequent INF, START I and START II Treaties offer tempting precedents for regional arms control. In all of these cases, ballistic missiles were the primary—but not the exclusive—target of control efforts.

With these examples in mind, a wide variety of proposals have been advanced to restrict missile proliferation. Among the most prominent are proposals for specific regional arms control regimes, confidence-building measures like declaration and inspection of regional missile forces, globalization of the INF Treaty, an international ballistic missile test ban or an outright ban on ballistic missiles.[35] What all these ideas have in common is the core concept of a negotiated agreement between antagonists, a political commitment to restrain a threatening technology.

While the many negotiated proposals all have individual strengths and weaknesses, one problem they share is their dependence on the willingness of regional adversaries to overlook their immediate disputes and agree on a more important common interest. From this point of view, a technology is ripe for control only when all sides agree that the disadvantages of its possession outweigh any advantages. They also must agree that consideration of this one technology can be separated from other issues inhibiting regional conflict resolution. Clearly this is not the case in most regions of the world. In the Middle East, South Asia or North-East Asia, by comparison, key regional powers appear to be convinced that missiles are essential. All too often they continue to be appreciated as a deterrence force, an instrument of international influence or a symbol of the state.

---

[34] Martin Navias argues that a revitalized sense of self-interest made Moscow less willing to sell ballistic missiles such as the 300-km range Scud-B or the 500-km SS-23. See note 33, p. 69. The SS-21 is a unique case, however—a 120-km missile that Moscow clearly would like to export but has had no luck finding takers. Zaloga, S., 'The Tochka tactical ballistic missile system', *Jane's Intelligence Review*, Jan. 1994, pp. 6–10.

[35] Examples include Bailey, K. C., 'Can missile proliferation be reversed?', *Orbis*, winter 1991; Frye, A., 'Zero ballistic missiles', *Foreign Policy*, no. 88 (fall 1992); Morel, B. F., 'Proliferation of missile capability', *Disarmament*, vol. 14, no. 3 (fall 1991); and Schelb, U., *Raketenzielgenauigkeit und Raketenteststop* [Rocket accuracy and rocket test ban] (Interdisziplinären Arbeitsgruppe Friedens-und Abrüstungsforschung, Universität Marburg: Marburg, 1988).

Viewed from the presidential palace, the advantages of missile possession tend to be clear, while their disadvantages are obscure. Few governments appear to regard ballistic missiles as an inherently destabilizing technology. Instead they tend to view only the other guy's missiles as destabilizing. Like opponents of gun control in the United States, regional leaders often tend to see the technology of long-range rockets as something essentially desirable, tainted only by the irresponsibility of a few outlaws. The outlaws should be disarmed, not honest citizens. If one starts with this attitude, it is easy to conclude that any agreement to control or abolish ballistic missiles costs more than it is worth.

Arms control, as many observers have noted, tends to put the technological cart before the political horse. As the superpower experience showed, it was only after the political relationship had improved in the mid-1960s that even modest caps on current programmes became possible. Actual reductions and disarmament were possible only after the coming of Soviet General Secretary Mikhail Gorbachev and the evaporation of decades of mistrust.[36] Any regime to control regional ballistic missiles presupposes a degree of mutual acceptance that is still rarely found; Argentina, Brazil and post-apartheid South Africa are examples where negotiated controls may be feasible. Elsewhere, negotiated restrictions will be feasible only after a general framework for regional conflict resolution is firmly established.

General conflict resolution would undoubtedly be the most effective basis for control of ballistic missile proliferation. The clearest lesson of the disarmament experiences of the superpowers, countries in Europe or that between Argentina and Brazil is the overwhelming importance of political accommodation. Once adversaries abandon their conflict and distrust, arms control and disarmament measures can be negotiated with amazing ease. The completion of the Argentine–Brazilian nuclear accords of the early 1990s or the 1993 START II Treaty illustrate how rapidly the process can move. Even so, a general settlement does not guarantee any progress on a specific issue like missile proliferation. Argentina and Brazil, for example, have ended their nuclear weapon programmes and agreed to abide by the terms of the MTCR, but neither has shown much interest in submitting its rocketry programmes to the same kind of restrictions.[37]

There are three fundamental difficulties with reliance on general conflict resolution. Above all, it makes settlement of individual issues depend entirely on resolution of the total conflict. Only after a comprehensive settlement can issues like ballistic missile proliferation be tackled. Regardless of the immediate dangers it may pose, missile proliferation has to wait. Controls on ballistic missiles are less likely to emerge as a special case for regional arms control than as one aspect of a comprehensive regional settlement. Second, there is not much that outside actors like the United Nations or the United States can do to accelerate the process except to offer encouragement and support. Ultimately, it

---

[36] Booth, K. and Wheeler, N. J., 'Beyond nuclearism', in Cowen Karp (note 12), chapter 2.

[37] Redick, J. R., *Argentina–Brazil Nuclear Non-Proliferation Initiatives,* PPN Issue Brief no. 3 (Mountbatten Centre for International Studies, University of Southampton: Southampton, Feb. 1994).

will be broad political negotiations, domestic political change and acts of bold leadership that will make such settlements possible. Third, as shown by the Argentine–Brazilian example (which has not led to agreements on missiles or conventional forces), there is no guarantee that general progress will lead to similar progress on specific issues like missile proliferation.

In the regions where missile proliferation is especially worrisome, the outlook for a general political settlement is most remote. In North-East Asia ballistic missile proliferation is a secondary or tertiary issue, widely acknowledged but forced to wait behind the uncertainties of nuclear issues and resolution of Korean unification. In South Asia repeated efforts by Washington and Moscow to start a regional peace dialogue have met with little success. In the Middle East progress towards a general peace settlement continues to inch along, but the peace process does not reach to many of the countries of greatest concern, nor do the states in the region show much interest in restrictions on their ballistic missile forces even in the event of a settlement.

Export controls and the MTCR seem certain to remain the most important barrier to missile proliferation for the foreseeable future. As other arms control methods gain salience, the role of export controls will naturally recede. Until that day, however, their utility will remain unrivalled. Even after other—more politically oriented—forms of arms control come into effect, export controls will still be necessary to ensure compliance.

The advantages of export controls derive from their immediate power over essential technologies. They alone have the strength of being based in technological certainties. Their weaknesses are real and serious but more easily minimized than the weaknesses of other approaches. Although export controls have little effect on missiles already in regional hands, they can be highly effective in preventing or slowing the introduction of additional and more advanced systems. Most importantly, they make it very difficult for countries to develop the means to manufacture ballistic missiles of their own, narrowing the most immediate missile proliferation problem to one of controlling the trade in finished missiles.

Since its creation in 1987, the MTCR has evolved into an increasingly popular and effective body for coordinating national export controls. From its narrow base of six Western countries plus Japan, its membership has consistently grown. Today, virtually every potential supplier of advanced missile technology adheres to the same restrictions unilaterally. The only exceptions are North Korea—the only country that continues to make routine sales of ballistic missiles—and several Arab countries with large missile inventories which they could use for second-hand transfers.

The export standards of the MTCR have become much more severe since they were initially promulgated in 1987. Originally restrictions applied only to ballistic missiles capable of lifting a payload of 500 kg to a distance of 300 km. In 1991 the payload restriction was reduced so that in effect the regime now covers any surface-to-surface missile with a range of over 150 km. An exception in the original wording permitted technical assistance for most work on regional space launch rockets. An obvious loophole, this has been narrowed through informal diplomacy. Today it is widely accepted among adherents to the MTCR that the regime prohibits transfers of space launch technology to any country simultaneously working on ballistic missile development.[38]

The problem of fairness

As a technologically oriented tool, export controls are especially vulnerable to political criticism. The greatest problem confronting export control as the key instrument against missile proliferation is not its effectiveness but its inability to create an image of fairness. Although the MTCR is a multilateral regime that promotes cooperation among its members, its basis in an adversarial delineation against would-be proliferators makes it more like an alliance in operation. In a world hungry for a new world order based on cooperative international politics, this is not very appealing. From the perspective of key regional spokesmen, of which India is the most vocal, the whole approach discriminates against the right of governments to arm themselves as they please. Ballistic missiles, they note, are fully accepted among other nations, which have made only partial efforts to get rid of them. The critique is especially important because it casts doubt on the legitimacy of anti-proliferation export controls in general.

The challenge ultimately is a question of world order: Will future international security affairs be dominated by the pursuit of distinct national interests organized through us-against-them alliances, or will they give a greater role to collective security organizations based on universal principles? Most supplier governments are divided on such issues, willing to sacrifice some of their own self-interests to appease the demands of others, but not if this means providing potential adversaries with long-range ballistic missiles.

Ultimately, if ballistic missile proliferation is to be arrested once and for all, it will be necessary to create just such a universal norm. This process will have to include some of the approaches touched on above, such as regional peace settlements and a comprehensive ballistic missile ban. In the meanwhile, self-interest alone is leading to wider and wider acceptance of the principles of the MTCR. It is encouraging to see former adversaries of the regime becoming supporters. Among the European governments, including the former communist states of Eastern Europe and the ex-Soviet republics, support for the MTCR is complete. In Latin America, South Africa and East Asia as well, support is growing.[39] In the Middle East, Israel is the only adherent (although it is not a formal member). Egyptian officials maintain that Egypt is not opposed to the

---

[38] Ozga, D. A., 'A chronology of the Missile Technology Control Regime', *The Nonproliferation Review*, vol. 1, no. 2 (winter 1994), pp. 66–93.

[39] Ozga (note 38).

MTCR but would prefer that its work be opened to permit wider consultation.[40] Even in India there is growing appreciation of the benefits of joining.[41]

The growing acceptance of the MTCR is an important victory, leaving its critics increasingly isolated, but it leaves normative objections to the regime unresolved. In practice, officials involved in the effort to extend the MTCR acknowledge its shortcomings privately but emphasize the larger principle of non-proliferation in public. In the long run, it would be ideal to see export controls reduced to an appurtenance supporting a system of comprehensive security building. In the near term, however, there is no obligation to provide countries with the technics of long-range rockets.

Beyond contributing to acceptance of the goal of comprehensive security, criticism of the discriminatory nature of export controls has not had much impact. Western leaders, for example, may feel some regret, but not enough to reconsider their policies, which maintain broad, non-partisan support. Some regional observers have suggested that targeted countries will react by accelerating their rocketry programmes simply to spite foreign control efforts.[42] Their anger may be genuine, but large rockets are far too costly to pursue so frivolously. No country is developing rockets just to show its contempt for others, childishly insisting on doing what outside powers say is forbidden. As the following chapters show, a successful programme requires much better justifications.

---

[40] Discussions with Mahmoud Karem, Director of Disarmament Affairs, Egyptian Ministry of Foreign Affairs, and Mounir Zahran, Egyptian Ambassador to the United Nations, in Geneva, 14–15 Feb. 1994.

[41] E.g., Adhikari, G., 'Requiem for non-alignment', *Times of India* (New Delhi), 26 May 1992; and Mukerjee, C., 'The nuclear option: ambiguity difficult to maintain', *Times of India,* 9 June 1992.

[42] Mazari, S., 'Missile development in India and Pakistan', eds G. Neuneck and O. Ischebeck, *Missile Proliferation, Missile Defense, and Arms Control* (Nomos Verlagsgesellschaft: Baden-Baden, 1993), pp. 257–63. See also Chellaney, B., *Nuclear Proliferation: The U.S.–Indian Conflict* (Sangam Books: London, 1993), pp. 280–89; and Hussain, M., 'The role of advanced weaponry', eds W. T. Wander and E. H. Arnett, *The Proliferation of Advanced Weaponry* (American Association for the Advancement of Science: Washington, DC, 1992), pp. 21–22.

3. Does missile proliferation matter?

I. Introduction

Even if missile proliferation is something that policy can restrain, it may not be worth the cost. A second important challenge to rising concern about missile proliferation questions the gravity of the problem. There is an argument that if ballistic missiles do not introduce new or greater military capabilities—if they do not increase a proliferator's ability to inflict death and destruction—it is of no great consequence whether or not new countries are trying to acquire them.[1] If this is true, instead of focusing on militarily trivial ballistic missiles, greater attention should be devoted to the control of other weapons with greater military capability, especially manned aircraft and cruise missiles.

From this perspective one of the greatest dangers of missile proliferation is over-reaction. The risk is that over-emphasizing ballistic missiles will lead to wasteful or counterproductive diplomatic offensives and defensive investments. The drama of ballistic missiles can overshadow recognition of other weapon systems with greater overall strategic capability. To some observers the priority of missile proliferation appears genuinely quixotic:

Missiles do not offer significant advantages for surprise attack or delivery of weapons of mass destruction. Indeed, for the delivery of conventional munitions, aircraft can offer distinct advantages. The offensive potential of counter-airfield operations by attack aircraft may pose greater threats to crisis stability than missiles. And dual-role combat aircraft certainly offer greater operational flexibility than single-mission missiles.[2]

Sceptics emphasize that in most circumstances manned aircraft are more effective delivery systems than missiles, carrying greater conventional payloads with greater accuracy through all but the most hermetic air defences. Regional ballistic missile forces tend to be too small and too inaccurate seriously to threaten neighbouring countries, let alone countries farther away. Their military threat is minimal and can be dismissed in all but the most specific circumstances.[3] From this point of view, ballistic missiles are, like the horse cavalry or

---

[1] On the importance of the ability to inflict death and destruction as the basis for strategic assessment, see Schilling, W. S., 'U.S. strategic nuclear concepts in the 1970s', *International Security*, autumn 1981, pp. 49–79.

[2] Pike, J. and Bolkcom, E. C., 'Prospects for an international control regime for attack aircraft', eds H. G. Brauch *et al.*, *Controlling the Development and Spread of Military Technology* (VU University Press: Amsterdam, 1992), p. 314.

[3] Lumpe, L., Gronlund, L. and Wright, D., 'Third World missiles fall short', *Bulletin of the Atomic Scientists*, Mar. 1992, pp. 30–37.

the battleship after World War I, weapons that receive far more attention than they deserve.[4]

A less extreme position agrees that 'the military effectiveness of ballistic missiles has been exaggerated'. When armed with conventional or chemical warheads they are unlikely to be more efficient than manned aircraft. Nevertheless, with their ability to hit targets with little or no warning and to penetrate air defences, 'longer range regional ballistic missiles may pose an increased threat to the major powers'. However, their capabilities are decisive only when they carry nuclear weapons.[5]

Here as in most strategic disputes, politics is responsible for much of the confusion. Arguments regarding the military importance of ballistic missile proliferation have been polarized by the political aspects of the debate. Advocates of SDI have been among the most forceful voices describing the worst dangers of missile proliferation. Since the end of the cold war weakened the outlook for the SDI programme, it has been redirected to defend against missile proliferation, principally through permutations such as Global Protection Against Limited Strikes (GPALS). Challenges deriding the importance of missile proliferation have been especially vigorous from the opponents of SDI, hoping to undermine the programme by explaining away the threat. If there is no serious missile threat from regional powers, there is much less justification for building elaborate defences.[6]

Chinese spokesmen have also been sympathetic to the argument that missile proliferation has little strategic importance. In this case the argument has emerged not out of domestic debates but to refute the arguments of foreign audiences, especially Western governments trying to restrain Chinese missile exports. With the new ballistic missiles under development primarily for export, the Chinese Government has a hard-currency interest in presenting ballistic missiles as benignly as possible. Justifying missile exports leads semi-official spokesmen to plead that: 'The impact of missile proliferation, on the one hand, should not be exaggerated. In fact missile weapon systems occupy a very small place, compared to combat aircraft, in the arsenals of most countries, and are by no means the backbone of their military force . . . Missiles played only a very limited military role in past regional conflicts.'[7]

Other Chinese analysts reiterate similar themes: 'Why should ballistic missiles be singled out from other kinds of delivery vehicles?'[8] From this perspec-

---

[4] On the inter-war fascination with the battleship, see O'Connell, R. L., *Sacred Vessels: The Cult of the Battleship and the Rise of the U.S. Navy* (Westview Press: Boulder, Colo., 1991).

[5] Barker, J. *et al.*, *Assessing Ballistic Missile Proliferation and its Control* (Center for International Security and Arms Control, Stanford University: Stanford, Calif., Nov. 1991), p. 5.

[6] Pike, J. and Stambler, E., 'Constraints on the R&D and transfer of ballistic missile defence technology', in Brauch *et al.* (note 2), p. 61.

[7] This apparently became an official Chinese position, reappearing in virtually identical form in many semi-official statements. See, e.g., Bu Ran, 'Missiles: proliferation and control', *Beijing Review*, 2–8 Dec. 1991, p. 9; Hu Yumin, 'Proliferation of guided missiles and control over missile transfer', *International Strategic Studies* (Beijing), Dec. 1991, p. 32; and Zhuang Maocheng, 'Proliferation of ballistic missiles and regional security', *Disarmament*, autumn 1991, p. 50.

[8] Hua Di, quoted in ed. D. W. Tarr, *The Global Diffusion of Military Technology* (Center for International Cooperation and Security Studies, University of Wisconsin–Madison: Madison, June 1992), p. 53.

tive it is senseless to control ballistic missiles while leaving sales of other delivery vehicles unfettered. Rather than focus attention on missiles, the only weapon category in which Chinese exports are especially prominent, China insists that Western governments first act to restrain other aspects of the arms trade, especially their own sales of tactical aircraft, and promote regional conflict resolution.

How important is ballistic missile proliferation? Are ballistic missiles militarily critical weapons and, if not, should they be dismissed or at least given less prominence on the international disarmament agenda? There are few reliable guides to resolving the question of when ballistic missiles matter. The two best developed approaches are strategic analysis and historical assessment based on actual experience, each of which is considered below.

II. Strategic analysis

The obvious way to evaluate any new problem in international security is to study it through the lenses of classical strategic analysis. Formal methods of strategic assessment apply tools developed by operations research in the 1940s and analysis of superpower nuclear forces in the 1950s to establish the most efficient methods of achieving military objectives.[9] The strengths of this approach arise from reliance on orthodox concepts and analytical methods inherited from classical nuclear strategy, stressing the dominance of the international system, the salience of rational, value-maximizing behaviour, and the decisive relationship between capabilities and missions.

Classical strategy rests on the expectation that all states, as rational, power-maximizing entities, will strive to acquire the greatest feasible forces to maximize their military capability and as instruments of diplomatic influence. When applied to proliferation, this approach reiterates the assumptions of US strategic theory enunciated in the 1950s to cope with the Soviet Union, applying identical concepts to regional contexts of greater contemporary importance.[10] This is seen most clearly in the tendency to evaluate emerging missile forces on a country-by-country basis, stressing their strategic implications as determined by geography and missile characteristics such as quantity, range, armament, accuracy and targeting.

Much of the best research on ballistic missile proliferation borrows heavily from classical nuclear strategic analysis. Classical strategic analysis has the virtue of facilitating elegant assessments of general trends involving dozens of countries and scores of projects. It also generates a useful guide to capabilities

---

[9] Wohlstetter, A., 'Strategy and the natural scientists', eds R. Gilpin and C. Wright, *Scientists and National Policy Making* (Columbia University Press: New York, 1964).

[10] The implicit models for such studies of proliferation are the pioneering works of US nuclear strategy, especially Wohlstetter, A. J. *et al.*, *Selection and Use of Strategic Air Bases*, R-266 (Rand Corporation: Santa Monica, Calif., 1954); and Goldhamer H. and Marshall, A. W., *The Deterrence and Strategy of Total War, 1959–1961: A Method of Analysis*, RM-2301 (Rand Corporation: Santa Monica, Calif., 1959).

of individual countries based on limited information about their forces and strategic intentions.

Sharing many of the strengths of classical strategic theory, however, formal methods cannot escape its major shortcomings. The approach has great general utility for outlining the potential dimensions of missile proliferation and setting independent standards for evaluating its significance. However, it cannot account for the diverse trends in ballistic missile proliferation since the mid-1980s; although a few regional powers are clearly maximizing their missile capabilities as anticipated, others seem ambivalent or have lost interest altogether. The inability of strategic analysis to explain this diversity stems from the narrowness of its basic concepts, above all deterrence. Although routinely used as an abstraction easily applied to country after country, the characteristics of deterrence depend on specific attitudes, culture, institutions and geography.[11] Consequently, the incentives for missile proliferation and procurement policies cannot be uniformly generalized as classical strategy might lead one to think.

Nor can strategic analysis resolve fundamental debates over the implications of missile proliferation. As was the case with operations research in the 1940s and systems analysis in the 1950s and 1960s, strategic assessments of proliferation are easily skewed towards the political disposition of the analyst. The same analytical techniques used by some authors to argue that missile proliferation presents only discrete and distant threats can also be used to support the worst-case conclusion that missile proliferation poses an overwhelming and immediate threat to North American and European security.[12] While this approach has made valuable contributions to the understanding of missile proliferation, it quickly exposed its own shortcomings. Another method of analysis is needed to explain the missile programmes of regional powers.

Aircraft ambiguities

Strategic assessment has been used to argue that ballistic missiles introduce few or no new capabilities that cannot already be met by manned aircraft. Aircraft can almost always be loaded with greater quantities of conventional, chemical or biological weapons, carry them greater distances and deliver them with greater accuracy. The advantages of aircraft are magnified by their reusability. Most analysts following this line of analysis conclude that ballistic missiles lack strategic significance, that their military impact has been exaggerated

---

[11] Jervis, R., *The Meaning of the Nuclear Revolution* (Cornell University Press: Ithaca, N.Y., 1989), p. 66.

[12] See, e.g., Payne, K. B., *Missile Defense in the 21st Century: Protection Against Limited Threats* (Westview Press: Boulder, Colo., 1991). An early but still highly informative critique stressing the artificiality of the assumptions of strategic analysis is Green, P., *Deadly Logic* (Ohio State University Press: Columbus, 1966). A more general analysis is given by Quade, E. S., 'Pitfalls of systems analysis', ed. E. S. Quade, *Analysis of Military Decisions* (American Elsevier: New York, 1970).

except in very specific situations and that they become meaningful only when armed with nuclear warheads.[13]

Other comparative assessments go further, to maintain that aircraft are superior delivery systems with nuclear weapons as well. Aircraft have the advantage of being more reliable, versatile and recallable. 'In other words,' writes Uzi Rubin, 'ballistic missile proliferation has little to do with nuclear proliferation'.[14] The only unique advantage of ballistic missiles, from this point of view, is the difficulty of interception. Everyone agrees that it is more difficult to shoot down a missile, but this is not enough to make them more cost-effective than aircraft in any but the most extreme situations.

There are two major faults with this kind of comparison which should be examined more closely. First, there is usually not a balanced comparison between missiles and aircraft, overlooking many of the serious weaknesses of aircraft in warfare. This problem can be corrected, however, by considering additional variables. Second, and more troublesome, is the inherent weakness of strategic analysts in dealing with governments with complex and changing motives.

The effectiveness of conventionally armed missiles undoubtedly depends on too many factors to permit facile generalization. Manned aircraft and cruise missiles, however, are hardly more predictable. The meagre results of massive strategic and tactical bombing in the Korean and Viet Nam wars are well known.[15] One conclusion on which assessments of the 1991 Allied campaign against Iraq agree is that aircraft bombardment achieved only some of its objectives. Although the successes of the Allied air operations cannot be gainsaid, they required considerably greater effort and were far less dramatic than its architects expected. The ineffectiveness of the air campaign was often the result of self-imposed rules of engagement, but in many cases aircraft accuracy was far less than anticipated and the results of the Allied effort virtually nil.[16]

Manned aircraft are capable of delivering ordinary unguided ordnance with accuracies (circular error probable, CEP) of 35 metres or better, far better than most ballistic missiles. Such performance, however, is far from routine: it requires great pilot skill, appropriate atmospheric conditions, and a clearly identified and undefended target. In reality, such perfect 'milk runs' are rarely possible anywhere but on the practice range. In typical experience, targets are obscured by cloud, smoke and camouflage; the aircraft is approaching at maxi-

[13] Fetter, S., 'Ballistic missiles and weapons of mass destruction', *International Security*, vol. 16, no. 1 (summer 1991), pp. 4–42; Mandeles, M. D., 'Between a rock and a hard place; implications for the U.S. of Third World nuclear and ballistic missile proliferation', *Security Studies*, vol. 1, no. 2 (winter 1991), pp. 235–69; and Ottenberg, M. A., 'Operational implications of Middle East ballistic missile proliferation', *Defence Analysis*, vol. 7, no. 1 (1991).

[14] Rubin, U., 'How much does missile proliferation matter?', *Orbis*, winter 1991, p. 33.

[15] Clodfelter, M., *The Limits of Air Power: The American Bombing of North Vietnam* (Free Press: New York, 1989); and Tilford, E. H., *Setup: What the Air Force did in Vietnam and Why* (Air University Press: Maxwell Air Force Base, Ala., 1991).

[16] Munro, N. and Opall, B., 'Survey questions U.S. air efficiency in Desert Storm', *Defense News*, 25 Jan. 1993, p. 3; and 'Tactical bombing of Iraqi forces outstripped value of strategic hits, analyst contends', *Aviation Week & Space Technology*, 27 Jan. 1992, pp. 62–63.

mum release speed and manœuvring to survive; and the air crew find their concentration affected by fatigue and by men on the ground trying to kill them. It is no surprise that a large proportion of ordinary bombs miss their targets completely—roughly 50 per cent of the time, even under the relatively favourable conditions of Operation Desert Storm.[17] The disappointing performance of subsequent Allied air raids on Iraq in January 1993 did even less to strengthen the image of air power, destroying less than 50 per cent of the Iraqi radar and missile sites they attacked.[18]

Better performance with manned aircraft requires that pilots take great risks or that they use precision guided munitions (PGMs). Either approach raises the cost of aerial bombing to levels that can make ballistic missiles more efficient by comparison.[19] The dangers of flying long aiming-runs over defended targets to improve accuracy were made clear when five British Tornado bombers were lost in the first few days of Operation Desert Storm. Far from being able to go anywhere, any time, manned aircraft must be husbanded carefully to survive against modern air defences. The attrition rate of fighter aircraft in modern warfare has varied from a high of about 30 per cent per sortie for the Syrian Air Force against Israel in 1982, to 20 per cent losses for Egypt in 1973 and 15 per cent per mission for Argentina in 1982, down to 1.5 per cent for Israel in 1973 and perhaps 0.01 per cent for Allied aircraft over Iraq in 1991.[20]

Even the lowest attrition rates do not always indicate effectiveness. Many of the air forces with the lowest loss rates deliberately avoided high-risk attacks on high-value targets. They often preserved their aircraft by restricting attacks to safer targets. The Israeli Air Force in 1973, for example, suffered alarming losses in its early attacks on Egyptian air bases and Syrian air defence installations. Its commanders had no choice but to change tactics quickly to emphasize more vulnerable targets.[21] The great successes of the Allied bombing of Iraq in 1991 should not be allowed to conceal similar inhibitions. US air policy was guided by the rule that 'no target is worth an airplane'. Every time an aircraft was lost the mission was altered or abandoned.[22] The British Command made a similar switch after experiencing unanticipated losses of Tornado bombers in the first few days of Desert Storm.[23] Subsequently, the British forces avoided

---

[17] Smith, R. J. and Richards, E., 'Half of some bombs missed targets, officials say', *International Herald Tribune*, 23–24 Feb. 1992, p. 5.

[18] Fairhall, D., 'Pentagon confirms pilots are not always entitled to fire', *The Guardian*, 26 Jan. 1993, p. 4.

[19] On the sensitivity of comparisons of the attrition rates of ballistic missiles and aircraft, see Fetter (note 13).

[20] Brown, N., *The Strategic Revolution* (Brassey's: London, 1992), pp. 78–79.

[21] Herzog, C., *The Arab–Israeli Wars*, revised edn (Vintage: New York, 1984), pp. 309–10. According to Nordeen, L. O., Jr, *Air Warfare in the Missile Age* (Smithsonian Institute: Washington, DC, 1985), pp. 147, 163, Israel admitted losing 115 out of 380 tactical aircraft available when fighting broke out on 6 Oct. 1973. Of these, 50% were lost in the first 3 days of the 18-day war.

[22] Cohen, E. A., 'The air war in the Persian Gulf', *Armed Forces Journal*, June 1993, pp. 10–14.

[23] US News and World Report, *Triumph Without Victory: The History of the Persian Gulf War* (Times Books: New York, 1992) p. 258.

risks but saw accuracy deteriorate considerably, leading to unintended strikes on civilians.[24]

It becomes clear that aircraft can be only dubious substitutes for ballistic missiles, requiring an attacker to risk considerable losses to achieve success. Conventionally armed missiles may be inefficient compared to aircraft under ideal circumstances, but in the face of active defences the differences between the two are much finer.

The use of precision guided munitions provides a partial solution, increasing the lethality while reducing the vulnerability of manned aircraft. In the most famous example, the defences protecting North Viet Nam's Paul Doumer bridge, which carried most of Hanoi's rail traffic from China, withstood repeated bombing attacks by the US Air Force and Navy, at a cost of several US aircraft. On 10 May 1972 the bridge was raided again by US aircraft in one of the first missions using PGMs (in this case laser- and television-guided bombs). This time the bridge was knocked out for several months.[25] The mission was an unquestionable success for PGMs, celebrated and routinely cited as proof of what such munitions can do.

Although the mission was a clear success, it was neither cheap nor simple. References to the Paul Doumer raid typically overlook the total size of the force involved: 32 strike aircraft and 85 support aircraft for defence against MiG aircraft, electronic countermeasures, command and control, and refuelling. Even so, two F-4 fighters involved in the raid were lost and three crewmen were killed. Recovering the surviving crewman required repeated sorties by 119 aircraft, several of which came close to destruction themselves.[26] Nineteen years later, in Desert Storm, Allied air forces flew equally high ratios of support missions. From this perspective, precision guided munitions are far from cheap. Their basic contribution has been to keep manned aircraft viable, enabling them to perform missions which otherwise would be impossible.

These weapons themselves are not without cost. Relatively simple laser-guided bombs cost about $65 000 each, a Maverick air-to-ground missile costs $180 000 and a HARM (High-speed Anti-Radiation Missile) anti-missile defence weapon $280 000. The most expensive PGMs in service today are probably those for the US–Israeli Have Nap air-to-surface missile (ASM), at about $1 million each, and the Tomahawk cruise missile, costing some $1.8 million each.[27] Typically, several weapons are needed to destroy a target. As the January 1993 Allied raids on Iraq showed, even the best designed and

[24] Hallion, R. P., *Storm over Iraq: Air Power and the Gulf War* (Smithsonian Institute: Washington, DC, 1992), pp. 213–15.

[25] Lavelle, A. J. C. (ed.), *The Tale of Two Bridges and the Battle for the Skies over North Vietnam*, USAF Monograph Series (Office of the Historian, United States Air Force: Washington, DC, 1976), pp. 160–64.

[26] Eschmann, K. J., *Linebacker: The Untold Story of the Air Raids Over North Vietnam* (Ivy: New York, 1989), pp. 49–51.

[27] Nicholas, T. and Rossi, R., *Military Cost Handbook 1992*, 13th edn (Data Search Associates: Fountain Valley, Calif., 1992), pp. 3-1/2, 9-6.

most effective guided weapons can go astray.[28] The cost of munitions and the need for redundancy reduce the comparative advantage of aircraft over missiles. All but the very largest and most advanced air-launched ordnance individually still cost less than a Scud missile, exported for about $1.5 million each. However, the advantage of manned aircraft is not as great as a superficial analysis might suggest.

Mutable motives

Some of these weaknesses can be overcome. The quality of strategic analysis can be improved by adding previously overlooked variables, such as the willingness to expend aircraft and the cost of munitions and support aircraft. Another, equally significant, weakness is inherent in the approach and virtually impossible to overcome.

Formal strategic analysis, comparing missiles and other weapon systems in terms of cost-effectiveness, is especially poor at capturing the motives most important in regional rocketry programmes. Scientific assessment relies on nothing more than quantitative measurement of the relationship between military ends and means. It is dependent on unambiguous understanding of the goals a weapon serves. If the goals are not clear, if they change capriciously, formal models become misleading simplifications. This was not a great problem in analysing US and Soviet nuclear forces; the goal of deterring superpower nuclear war and conventional war in Europe was something almost everyone could agree on. Compared to the relatively stable dynamics of superpower deterrence, regional strategic goals tend to be much less formal, more flexible and often obscure.

Iraq's ballistic missile programme provides an illuminating example. Over the years its motives shifted from pure symbolism to war fighting, deterrence and finally escalation. President Saddam Hussein's first 12 Scud missiles were acquired from the Soviet Union in the mid-1970s as purely *symbolic* weapons, enhancing Iraqi prestige and the political strength of the Soviet Union's commitment. By the mid-1980s Iraq was firing hundreds under a *war-fighting* strategy in an effort to force Iran to abandon the Iraq–Iran War. In 1990 Saddam Hussein spoke of Iraqi missiles as a *deterrent* against Israel and the United Nations force. When they were used in January 1991, it was not primarily to win or deter but to *escalate* the conflict by drawing in Israel.[29]

The importance of prestige and symbolism is especially difficult to include in strategic analysis. Orthodox strategic analysis overlooks its importance in part for methodological reasons; it is difficult to quantify prestige. Exceptional strategic thinkers—Bernard Brodie is a notable example—readily acknowl-

---

[28] 'Pentagon admits U.S. missile hit hotel in Baghdad', *International Herald Tribune*, 19 Jan. 1993, p. 7.
[29] Some of this ambiguity is captured by Karsh, E., 'Rational ruthlessness', eds E. Karsh, M. S. Navias and P. Sabin, *Non-conventional Weapons Proliferation in the Middle East* (Clarendon Press: Oxford, 1993), chapter 3.

edged the importance of prestige as a strategic factor, one that can help a country avoid wars and help bring fighting to a rapid close. Even Brodie's work, however, leaves the impression that prestige and symbolism can be incorporated only on a case-by-case basis.[30]

Symbolic factors have also been overlooked for political and ideological reasons. Today it is often forgotten that formal strategic analysis was developed by US economists and mathematicians connected with the Rand Corporation, for whom prestige alone was not a valid reason for buying a new weapon.[31] Their analytical techniques were developed largely to oppose prestige projects such as the US Air Force's B-70 Mach-3 bomber and encourage investment in inconspicuous developments such as aerial refuelling and missile hardening. This predisposition against prestige weapons is not shared in other regions of the world, where the value of a weapon such as a ballistic missile as a symbol of power is more tangible and compelling.

Rather than refuting the significance of ballistic missile proliferation, comprehensive strategic analysis will tend to confirm its importance. Regional decision makers are not fools; they have limited procurement budgets and must make careful choices. Their interest in a particular weapon may be entirely intuitive, but rarely are their choices made without judgement, experience and awareness of opportunity costs.

III. Historical assessment

A second technique for establishing the significance of ballistic missiles is historical assessment. It is sometimes forgotten that the primary justification for quantitative strategic analysis of superpower nuclear forces was to overcome the almost total lack of relevant experience. Scientific methods were developed to compensate for the lack of actual experience and make strategic planning more than just a matter of hypothetical judgement. When it comes to the use of conventionally armed ballistic missiles in war, however, there is sufficient experience for limited concrete comparison. Ballistic missiles have been fired in at least eight conflicts, under different situations and with a variety of results. The most important of these experiences was the first.

More than 50 years after its first test flight in 1942, the Nazi German V-2 rocket remains the leading example of the use of ballistic missiles in warfare. Not only was it the first successful long-range rocket, and the first fired in anger, but it was also built and used in greater numbers than any other large rocket. Probably the most thoroughly studied of all ballistic missile projects, it also serves as an example of the scale and scope of the effort required to develop and build long-range rockets.

[30] Brodie, B., *War and Politics* (Macmillan: New York, 1973), pp. 160–63, 201–3, 491–93.
[31] Enthoven, A. and Smith, W., *How Much is Enough: Shaping the Defense Program, 1961–1969* (Harper & Row: New York, 1971); and Kaufman, W., *The McNamara Strategy* (Harper & Row: New York, 1964).

Figure 3.1. A V-2 rocket

A German V-2 (A-4) rocket being prepared for launch during British tests at Cuxhaven shortly after World War II. (Photograph: Smithsonian Institution)

The V-2 was developed in a programme that began with a group of amateur scientists in 1929, before they won army sponsorship in 1932.[32] By the late 1930s it was Germany's largest single R&D programme and would later grow to a scale rivalling the Allied Manhattan Project. Weighing 14 tonnes and standing 14 metres high, the rocket could carry a payload of 750 kg over a maximum distance of 320 km. In practice it was rarely fired farther than 220 km because of its poor accuracy. Although consistently supported by the Army, only after the defeat at Stalingrad did Hitler and the Nazi Party emphasize the weapon as a key to victory.[33]

The decisions by Hitler and Nazi Party functionaries in 1943 to mass-produce the V-2 were encouraged by the promise of low cost. In these decisions they

---

[32] Although known throughout its development and service in the German Army as the A-4, the missile is best known by its Nazi Party propaganda designation, the V-2.

[33] The best general introduction is the book by the programme's military commander, Dornberger, W., *V-2: Der Schuss ins Weltall: Geschichte Einer Gross-Erfindung* [V-2: the shot into space: the history of a great invention], (Bechte Verlag: Esslingen, 1952). The technical aspects of the V-2 are examined in great detail in Kooy, J. M. J. and Uytenbogaart, J. W., *Ballistics of the Future* (Technical Publishing Company H. Stam: Haarlem, the Netherlands, 1946), pp. 280–400.

also had to consider the weapon's poor accuracy and conventional explosive warhead, hoping that sheer numbers could compensate for other shortcomings. The final production contract awarded to Nordhausen-Mittelwerk called for 12 000 V-2s. Over 5700 were produced by the end of the war.[34] This was achieved despite the most active opposition any rocket project has had to face, including a massive British bombing attack on the Peenemünde Research Station on 17–18 August 1943 and subsequent US raids, which probably set the programme back several months.[35] Despite delays, the programme continued to make adequate progress. Production reached a height of 600 missiles a month in November 1944. This manufacturing accomplishment was achieved through remarkable improvisation, necessitating enormous human suffering and considerable distortion in much of the rest of Germany's military–industrial effort.[36]

The total expense of the enterprise can only be estimated: while all cost data on the V-2 are vague and incomplete, some tentative evaluations of the financial burden of the project are essential to put the endeavour in perspective. V-2 production costs have been reported by programme participants and historians with access to production contracts as $38 000–$60 000 per missile.[37] These estimates, however, cover only light manufacturing and final assembly from components at the Nordhausen-Mittelwerk underground production facility. Manufacturing also involved hundreds of suppliers, apparently with separate contracts. Although final assembly could be performed largely by semi-skilled slave labour, this was not a viable option for production of precision components. Production of highly sophisticated sub-systems such as the turbo-pump, guidance package, control systems and the numerous actuators and servo-motors, as well as less complicated elements such as the warhead and fuse, must have rivalled or surpassed the cost of final assembly. The total average cost of producing the missile remains uncertain, but an estimate of $70 000–$90 000 per missile is more comprehensive ($280 000–$360 000 in 1990 US dollars).[38]

To this must be added the R&D investment that constituted at least 60 per cent of the total costs of the programme. Construction and operation of the

[34] The only other ballistic missile built in comparable numbers is the 280-km range Soviet Scud B. Some 2500 were deployed by the Soviet Army between 1965 and the end of production in the early 1980s. Cochran, T. B. *et al.*, *Nuclear Weapons Databook, Vol. IV: Soviet Nuclear Weapons* (Harper & Row: New York, 1989), pp. 220–22. A similar number may have been built for evaluation, training and foreign sales, making some 5000 in all.

[35] Middlebrook, M., *The Peenemünde Raid* (Penguin: London, 1988), p. 222.

[36] According to Milward, A. S., *The German Economy at War* (Athlone Press: London, 1965), p. 106, compared to a single V-2, '[f]or the money and effort at least six high-performance fighters could have been turned out. The complex electrical equipment of V-2 retarded the production of vital electrical equipment for U-boats, and the development of a more efficient radar system'.

[37] From the production contract of 19 Oct. 1943, David Irving estimates the average cost of production at Nordhausen-Mittelwerk at $48 000 each, including overheads. Dornberger gives a figure of $38 000 per missile, while Speer recalls a cost of 250 000 Reichsmarks, or $60 000. Irving, D., *The Mare's Nest* (William Kimber: London, 1964), pp. 298–304; Dornberger, W., 'The German V-2', ed. E. M. Emme, *The History of Rocket Technology* (Wayne State University Press: Detroit, Mich., 1964), p. 39; and Speer, A., quoted in Milward (note 36).

[38] This estimate owes much to discussions with Michael J. Neufeld, curator in the Department of Aeronautics, National Air and Space Museum, Smithsonian Institution, Washington, DC.

German Army Experimental Station at Peenemünde, where most of the development work was undertaken, cost approximately $262 million. After the war, US specialists estimated the total cost of German R&D work on the V-2 at $750 million (approximately $3 billion in 1990 US dollars).[39]

Once R&D costs are included, the total value of the V-2 programme reaches at least $1.1 billion in then-current dollars ($4.6 billion in 1990 dollars). The value of each V-2 missile rises to approximately $200 000 in then-current dollars ($800 000 each in 1990 dollars). This is about half the cost of modern missiles with similar range and payload (but much better accuracy), such as the Soviet Scud-B or Chinese M-11. To these cost figures should be added the cost of crews, training, and launch and support vehicles; the production of propellants, especially liquid oxygen; and the construction of two vast underground launch facilities in north-eastern France.[40] Unfortunately there is no basis for accurately estimating the cost of these items.

Even after all identifiable costs are included, the V-2 was a great manufacturing success. Industrial successes, however, cannot conceal its disappointing military performance. Despite considerable delays in the original Wehrmacht plan, the missile was put into operation prematurely. Starting on 8 September 1944, a total of some 4300 V-2 missiles were fired operationally, all against cities in Western Europe. The effect of the missiles was reduced not only by their conventional armament but also by their poor reliability; approximately 25 per cent of them blew up on the launch stand or in the air, and others simply disappeared without a trace.[41] Although the exact number remains in doubt, about 1500 were fired at London and other British cities; about 2100 at Antwerp, the site of major Allied docks; and the other 700 at other cities in France and the Low Countries. Of the missiles launched, some 3165 are believed to have reached the area of their targets—1115 in Britain and 2050 on the continent.[42]

For this effort, the V-2 attacks delivered about 2400 tonnes of high explosive and killed a total of about 7000 men, women and children. The effects of the attacks on the Allied war effort cannot be separated from those of the simultaneous bombardment by some 15 000 V-1 'buzz bomb' cruise missiles. The two

[39] Hölsken, H. D., *Die V-Waffen* [The V-weapons] (Deutsche Verlags-Anstalt: Stuttgart, 1984), p. 19, estimates the construction and operating budget of the Peenemünde station at 1.1 billion Reichsmarks, or $262 million at the pre-war exchange rate of RM 4.2/$1. The $750 million figure is from a US Army press release dated 4 Dec. 1945, cited in Bower, T., *The Paperclip Conspiracy: The Battle for the Spoils and Secrets of Nazi Germany* (Michael Joseph: London, 1987), p. 229. The latter refers to the amount the USA would have had to spend during the war to achieve similar results. Actual costs for Nazi Germany were much less because of lower wage scales and the extensive use of slave labour.

[40] Michael J. Neufeld arrives at a total programme cost of $5 billion (in 'early 1990s dollars') or approximately $880 000 each. Neufeld, M. J., *The Rocket and the Reich: Peenemünde and the Coming of the Ballistic Missile Era* (Free Press: New York, 1995), p. 273. On the Watten and Wizernes underground launch facilities (never used), see Henshall, P., *Hitler's Rocket Sites* (St Martin's: New York, 1985).

[41] Launch reliability figures are cited in Baker, D., *The Rocket: The History and Development of Rocket and Missile Technology* (Crown Publishers: New York, 1978), p. 60.

[42] Dornberger (note 37), p. 42; Irving (note 37), p. 306; and Jones, R. V., *Most Secret War: British Scientific Intelligence 1939–1945* (Hamish Hamilton: London, 1978), p. 459. The only precise figures on V-2 attacks are Allied talleys of missile hits. Only participants' estimates are available for the total number launched.

threats undoubtedly dislocated some aspects of Allied planning; large numbers of fighter and bomber aircraft had to be allocated to the destruction of V-weapon infrastructure and launch sites and the interception of V-1s. The military impact, however, never lived up to the worst fears of British planners who, in 1943–44, understanding only the scale of the German R&D programme, assumed that the missiles would be far larger and more accurate and would carry a warhead five times as big.[43] In the end, the military effect was sufficiently negligible to be safely disregarded in leading historical assessments of World War II.[44]

The dislocations to civilian life were greater: during the heaviest V-1 'buzz-bomb' attacks in August 1944, almost 1.5 million London residents evacuated the city and almost as many fled again when V-2 attacks reached their height in November and December. The misfortunes of the V-weapon attacks were small, however, compared to the effects of Allied bombing on Germany. By the end of 1944 Luftwaffe opposition was negligible and the Allies had perfected long-range bombing into a reliable tool for the destruction of entire cities. With radar navigation, long-range fighter escorts and incendiary bombs, conventional aircraft could achieve levels of destruction rivalled only by nuclear weapons. Conventional raids on Dresden and Tokyo are well remembered for causing greater destruction than either of the atomic bombs dropped on Japan.[45]

Often overlooked is how commonplace massive conventional bombing had become. The scale and efficiency of the Allied bomber campaign were so great that individual raids more destructive than all the V-weapon attacks combined became virtually routine. A typical example is the bomber attack on the commercial town of Pforzheim (population then 80 000) in south-western Germany on 23 February 1945, an attack now forgotten by all but local residents. The town was targeted by a medium-sized force of 361 British Lancaster bombers, which dropped 1571 tonnes of bombs in just 22 minutes. The bombs and subsequent fire killed 17 000 people and destroyed three-quarters of the city.[46] Without any exceptional effort, this single, modest raid produced more than twice the destruction inflicted by all the V-2s combined. For the British people, already inured by the experience of the Blitz and increasingly confident that

---

[43] In their early intelligence estimates, British experts such as R. V. Jones and Duncan Sandys initially conjured up a much better missile, one they thought would justify an effort of such proportions. See Jones (note 42), pp. 342–43.

[44] An extreme case is the posthumously published volume: Liddell Hart, B. H., *History of the Second World War* (G. P. Putnam: New York, 1970), which makes only one passing reference to the V-2, on p. 677. A slightly more generous treatment is that of Gerhard L. Wienberg, who devotes 2 out of 1100 pages to Germany's V-weapons but accepts the view that it was too little, too late. Weinberg, G. L., *A World at Arms: A Global History of World War II* (Cambridge University Press: Cambridge, 1994) pp. 561–63.

[45] The refinement of conventional bombing is described by its greatest tactician in LeMay, C. L. with Kantor, M., *Mission with LeMay: My Story* (Doubleday: Garden City, N.Y., 1965), pp. 319–91.

[46] Zier, H. G., *Geschichte der Stadt Pforzheim* [History of the city of Pforzheim] (Konrad Theiss Verlag: Stuttgart, 1982), pp. 345–52; Schmalacker-Wyrich, E., *23 Februar 1945: Augenzeugenberichte vom Fliegerangriff auf Pforzheim* [23 February 1945: eye witness accounts of the air raid on Pforzheim] (J. Esslinger: Pforzheim, 1963), especially pp. 118–27.

victory was drawing near, the far less destructive V-2 attacks were not sufficient to undermine public morale.[47]

In retrospect, it has been argued that the entire programme was misconceived and that Germany would have been better off investing the same resources in conventional manned aircraft. More typical was the assessment of Prime Minister Winston Churchill, who respected the V-2 as 'an impressive technical achievement' but concluded that 'it was fortunate that the Germans spent so much effort on rockets instead of bombers'. Ordinary bombers, he pointed out, were better suited for attacks using the conventional ordnance of the day: they carried more and were more accurate, cheaper and reusable. Even the German Minister of War Production, Albert Speer, whose support was essential to the programme, later repudiated his actions, writing that: 'The whole notion was absurd . . . I not only went along with this decision on Hitler's part but also supported it. That was probably one of my most serious mistakes'.[48]

The most incisive argument against the V-weapons was made by German fighter commander Adolph Galland, who went so far as to suggest that, had the same resources been invested in jet and rocket-powered fighter aircraft, Germany could have kept air supremacy throughout the war, possibly making the Normandy invasion impossible.[49] This misses the point that by the winter of 1943/44 Germany was losing the war on every front and dimension; no single weapon could save the crumbling Reich—no number of V-2s, no number of fighters.

Despite competition from the V-weapon effort, production of German fighter aircraft actually accelerated tremendously through 1944, creating an outright surplus of aircraft by the end of year. As Galland himself understood only too well, hundreds of machines were grounded for lack of crews and fuel.[50] Earlier introduction of jet fighters might have dramatically affected the war, but their introduction was not slowed by competition with other R&D programmes; the jet aircraft had a priority equal to that of the V-weapons. Political factors, if anything, hindered their rapid introduction, especially Hitler's perverse insistence that all but a handful of the new aircraft be used as bombers.[51] Even if more jet fighters had been available, Germany lacked the pilots and fuel to operate them to great effect, as Galland himself clearly understood.[52]

---

[47] This was the judgement of Churchill, W. S., *The Second World War, Vol. 6: Triumph and Tragedy* (Houghton Mifflin: Boston, Mass., 1953), pp. 43.

[48] Churchill (note 47), pp. 52, 54; and Speer, A., *Inside the Third Reich*, transl. R. Winston and C. Winston (Macmillan: New York, 1970), p. 365.

[49] Galland, A., *The First and the Last: The German Fighter Force in World War II*, transl. M. Savill (Methuen: London, 1955), p. 328, cited approvingly in Rubin (note 14), p. 36.

[50] Galland (note 49), pp. 260, 314.

[51] Galland (note 49), pp. 334–46.

[52] Galland (note 49), pp. 279, 281, 296. Elsewhere in his memoirs (p. 310), Galland seems more ambivalent about the contribution of the V-weapons, criticizing the programme, but noting that it aided Germany by soaking up about one-quarter of all the Allied bombs dropped in mid-1944.

Figure 3.2. A V-2 rocket being prepared for launch

Note the large number of vehicles and personnel (the 'travelling circus') required to operate the system. These include rocket and fuel transporters, electrical generators, launch facilities, guidance facilities, spare parts and crew transport. The complexity of the V-2 made it difficult to use successfully and, combined with its poor reliability and accuracy, greatly reduced its potential effectiveness. Many contemporary systems like the Scud missile require a smaller but still troublesome baggage train. (Photograph: Smithsonian Institution)

Some Allied leaders were more impressed with the V-2. Many field commanders shared the impression of Curtis LeMay, who believed that earlier use of the V-2 could have changed the course of the war.[53] In the judgement of Philip Joubert de la Ferté, responsible for designing Britain's defences against the V-weapons, 'If the planned production of V1 and V2 had been available in the winter of 1942–43 I doubt the invasion of Europe would have been feasible'. Because it could not be intercepted, the V-2 was especially troubling in his view.[54] Supreme Commander General Dwight D. Eisenhower seems to

---

[53] LeMay (note 45), p. 397.
[54] Joubert de la Ferté, P. J., *Rocket* (Hutchinson: London, 1957), pp. 115, 120.

have been especially impressed, going so far as to write later: 'I feel sure that if he [Hitler] had succeeded in using these weapons over a six-month period, and particularly if he had made the Portsmouth–Southampton area one of his principal targets, Overlord might have been written off'.[55]

After the D-Day invasion, however, the missiles presented no overwhelming danger to Allied military operations. The only direct effect was temporarily to close the port of Antwerp, possibly slowing the already ponderous British advance. By the autumn of 1944, destroying V-2 launch capabilities was, by Eisenhower's own description, only an 'incidental' Allied objective.[56] As president during the 1950s, his lack of interest in ballistic missiles would become legendary.

These perspectives on the V-2 are not necessarily contradictory. The impact of the programme was highly contingent on a variety of events. Had the programme progressed closer to the original schedule—if its priority had been higher in the late 1930s and early 1940s, if secrecy had been able to save it from Allied bombing and if development problems had been slightly less severe—some 600 missiles a month could have been fired at D-Day invasion preparations, enough to overcome their miserable accuracy. Although this almost certainly would not have won the war, it could have changed its course. The Western Allies might have been forced to cancel Operation Overlord in favour of a slower attack on Germany from the south.

As events unfolded, however, the V-2 arrived too late to strike more than terror, and this was insufficient under the circumstances. Contingency explains why men such as Speer and Galland could support the V-2 in 1943 and perceive it as a blunder later. As a weapon, the V-2 was neither a panacea nor a frivolity. Rather it was an opportunity that failed.

IV. Modern experience

Other national leaders have tried to employ conventionally armed ballistic missiles in exactly the same way as the V-2 was used as a terror weapon. None was on the scale of the Nazi German missile campaign. Some of these attempts were futile gestures, evidence not of capability but of weakness. In no case were missile attacks alone enough to change the course of a war, although some were more consequential than others:

1. The Egyptian and Syrian attacks on Israel with Scud and FROG missiles during the 1973 Middle East War were too small and inaccurate to have any tactical effect, involving no more than a few dozen weapons. Israel minimized the public impact by censoring reports.[57] Nevertheless, a prominent Israeli analyst later argued that the Scud missiles were 'the most significant weapons

---

[55] Eisenhower, D. D., *Crusade in Europe* (Doubleday: Garden City, N.Y., 1948), p. 250.

[56] Eisenhower (note 55), p. 258.

[57] Bermudez, J. S., Jr, 'Ballistic missiles in the Third World—Egypt and the 1973 Arab–Israeli War', *Jane's Intelligence Review*, Dec. 1991, pp. 531–37.

system sent to Egypt', that they greatly inhibited Israeli strategy in the war and made Israeli leaders more willing to accept US diplomatic initiatives that brought the war to a close after three weeks.[58]

2. On 16 April 1986 Libya responded to the US bombing of Tripoli by firing two Scud missiles at a US Coast Guard station on the Italian island of Lampedusa. The missiles fell short and were regarded by the Pentagon as a useless gesture, but they had a cautionary effect on other governments in the region.[59]

3. After six years of intermittent missile attacks, Iranian cities were subjected to about 190 Iraqi missile strikes during the 1988 War of the Cities. The attacks killed some 2000 people, drove half the people of Tehran out of the city and damaged public morale. The Iranian Government contributed to the effects by publicizing the attacks to win international sympathy, inadvertently helping to terrorize its own demoralized people. Other events, including reverses on the battlefield and the rising opposition of the United States, also contributed to Iran's capitulation.[60] Iraq revealed little about the 90 or so missile strikes on Baghdad and rode them out with little effect.[61]

4. In Afghanistan, between November 1988 and the war's end in May 1992, the Soviet Union and the Afghani Government in Kabul fired perhaps as many as 2000 Scud missiles at rebel targets, in much the same way that the United States used B-52 strikes in the final stages of the Viet Nam War. The attacks occasionally caused serious destruction, inhibiting the insurgents from concentrating their forces.[62] It is feasible that this helped the Afghani Government survive temporarily.

5. At the beginning of the civil war in Bosnia in October 1992, it was reported that Bosnian Serb forces launched roughly 10 FROG missiles in an attack against Bosanski Brod. The reports were unconfirmed, although it is known that the Serbian Army possessed FROG missiles and may have released some to Serbian forces in Bosnia. The effect of the attacks—if they occurred— is impossible to gauge, although the city fell to Serbian forces later that month.[63]

6. Iraq fired at least 81 Scud missiles during Operation Desert Storm in 1991, including at least 38 directed at Israel. For Iraq, the attacks greatly improved

---

[58] Evron, Y., *The Role of Conventional Arms Control in the Middle East*, Adelphi Paper no. 138 (International Institute for Strategic Studies: London, 1977), pp. 6, 11. This view was shared by Chief of Staff David Elazar, according to Cohen, E. A. and Gooch, J., *Military Misfortunes: The Anatomy of Failure in War* (Free Press: New York, 1990), p. 102.

[59] Various interviews with US Defense Department and Italian Ministry of Defence officials.

[60] Accounts vary. Hiro, D., *The Longest War: The Iran–Iraq Military Conflict* (Paladin: London, 1990), a book sympathetic to Iran, attributes virtually no effects to the missiles.

[61] McNaugher, T., 'Ballistic missiles and chemical weapons', *International Security*, autumn 1990.

[62] Isby, D. C., 'Soviet arms deliveries and aid to Afghanistan 1989–91', *Jane's Intelligence Review*, Aug. 1991, pp. 348–54.

[63] *Jane's Defence Weekly*, 7 Nov. 1992, p. 15. Croatian Radio allegations that Serbian forces used Scud missiles in Dec. 1992 in the battle for Gradacac were denied vehemently by the Serbian news media. *Nonproliferation Review*, vol. 1, no. 2 (winter 1994), p. 188. These later reports indeed seem less credible; the Scuds were controlled by the Yugoslav (Serbian national) Army and are too few and too powerful to be delegated to any ally. Tactically their use is senseless in a theatre where enemy cities are in easy range of artillery and mortars.

public morale and support for Saddam Hussein.[64] In Israel the missiles caused widespread destruction (but only one direct death) and their threat was enough to seriously disrupt Israeli public life. For several days Israeli leaders debated whether and how to retaliate against Iraq. Their most likely response would have been a combination of land and air attacks, exactly what Saddam Hussein probably wanted, possibly wrecking the Allied coalition and permanently changing the nature of the war. As Allied countermeasures took effect, and the greatly feared chemically armed missiles failed to materialize, these anxieties diminished.[65]

Other effects were more permanent. Despite Israel's inaction, its strategic priorities were permanently altered. Previously ambivalent, Israeli leaders now agreed on the need for extensive investment in missile defences and satellite intelligence.[66] The effects of a similar number of Scud attacks on Saudi Arabia were far less dramatic, because of geographic considerations and the better performance of Patriot defences. Scud suppression still absorbed 25–30 per cent of the enormous Allied air war effort. The failure to end the Scud threat is widely regarded as one of the greatest Allied failures of the war.[67]

7. There is greater certainty regarding missile attacks in the Yemeni Civil War in May 1994. Reports indicate that Southern forces based near the South Yemen capital of Aden launched roughly 20 Scud missiles against the Northern capital of Sana'a in an unsuccessful effort to undermine public support there for the war. Later in the conflict North Yemeni forces apparently unleashed missiles against Aden after surrounding and besieging the city, with much greater effect on the already demoralized population. The Northern missiles may have been Scuds or FROGs, but more likely were short-range artillery rockets.[68]

The clearest theme running through these cases is the uncertain effect of conventionally armed missiles. Missile attacks with high explosives are seldom decisive in and of themselves. Their impact is highly contingent on numerous considerations, mitigated by their unreliability and inaccuracy, by targeting

[64] Dilip Hiro, who questioned the missiles' impact in the Iran–Iraq War, was ready to acknowledge their importance in 1991. Hiro, D., *Desert Shield to Desert Storm* (Paladin: London, 1992), pp. 323–24, 442–44.

[65] Barber, L., 'Israelis seek US permission to strike Scud sites', *Financial Times*, 29 Jan. 1991, p. 1; and Tyler, P. E., 'The riposte that never was: Israel planned to invade Iraq in reply to Scud attacks', *International Herald Tribune*, 8 Mar. 1991, p. 3. The US Army also fired roughly a dozen 135-km ATACMS in ground-to-ground attacks on Iraqi radars and communications sites. How they fit into the overall Gulf missile war is obscure, but they should be acknowledged.

[66] Interview with Moshe Arens, *Jane's Defence Weekly*, 8 June 1991, p. 992; interview with Major-General Avihu Ben-Nun, *Defense News*, 30 Sep. 1991, p. 54; Fisher, S., 'Iraqi missile attacks spur backing for Israeli military satellites', *Armed Forces Journal* (Apr. 1991), p. 29; and Opall, B., 'Israel debates lasting effects of nonretaliation in Gulf War', *Defense News*, 9 Sep. 1991, p. 38. This consensus does not extend to the controversial Arrow programme in particular.

[67] Navias, M., *Saddam's Scud War and Ballistic Missile Proliferation*, London Defence Studies 6 (Centre for Defence Studies: London, 1991).

[68] Watkins, E., 'Hundreds wait to quit Yemen as fears grow that war will worsen', *Financial Times*, 13 May 1994, p. 4; 'Secessionists in Southern Yemen names heads of new government', *New York Times*, 23 May 1994, p. A2.

choices, geography, numbers, and an opponent's morale and ability to take countermeasures. Chemical or biological weapons may change this, but only nuclear warheads make ballistic missiles decisive weapons with certainty. Consequently, there is a natural tendency to view missile proliferation as a hand-maiden of nuclear proliferation, to believe that missile proliferation does not matter as much if the nuclear proliferation problem is dealt with first.[69]

Several of these examples illustrate another aspect of conventionally armed missiles. While their military effect is contingent on particular circumstances, their political impact is largely independent of circumstance. Even when their direct contribution to destruction or defeat is questionable, they invariably become an overwhelming concern to those who must face them. In part this is due to their potential as carriers of chemical, biological or nuclear weapons, a potential which must be disproved by experience before it will be disbelieved. But more intrinsic considerations are also at work. Ballistic missiles have another quality, one which leads ordinary people and their political leaders to react with the greatest anxiety, even after they are certain that the missiles will reach them with conventional explosives alone.

V. Why do ballistic missiles matter?

The contingency of ballistic missiles narrows the most serious military threats they pose to particular situations. Armed exclusively with conventional explosives, their effects are strategically significant only under highly specific circumstances. The most common of these circumstances are tight regional military balances where countries face each other with vigorous air defences that excessively raise the cost of attack by manned aircraft. For countries facing an adversary with impressive air defences—as do North Korea, Pakistan and Syria—ballistic missiles may be a cost-effective investment. In great numbers, even conventionally armed missiles can play havoc against large targets such as cities, airfields or infantry concentrations. Conventionally armed missiles, moreover, may be a sign of a country's intent to deploy its missiles later with chemical or nuclear warheads.[70]

The examples above demonstrate that ballistic missiles are rarely, if ever, decisive on their own, but that they can have effects that are disproportionate to their actual destructiveness. Ballistic missiles have a symbolic significance that is potentially much more important than their military effects. Even small numbers of conventionally armed missiles can be highly significant politically. Symbolic attacks in war can be of great moment: one need only recall the militarily trivial 1942 Doolittle raid on Japan, or the Allied raid on Dieppe that

---

[69] The author advocated this position in earlier articles, although he now believes it to be seriously misleading. See, e.g., Karp, A., 'Space technology in the Third World', *Space Policy*, vol. 2, no. 2 (May 1986), pp. 157–68.

[70] Bailey, K. C., *Doomsday Weapons in the Hands of Many: The Arms Control Challenge of the '90s* (University of Illinois: Champaign, Ill., 1991), pp. 5–6, 103–7. A more nuanced statement is made by Carus, W. S., *Ballistic Missiles in Modern Conflict* (Praeger: New York, 1991), chapter 3.

same year.[71] Virtually every nation has in its history the revered memory of a military act—often a small raid or an otherwise unsuccessful or unimportant action—that symbolizes national decisiveness, determination and heroism. At a minimum such actions prove that the enemy is not invulnerable and that one's own cause is not lost. In similar situations where conventionally armed ballistic missiles are too few or too small to matter on the battlefield, they gain their importance from their psychological effects.

Why do ballistic missiles matter so much in subjective perceptions of warfare? Ballistic missiles may be unique among weapons for their ability to affect perceptions in great disproportion to their actual ability to cause death and destruction. In evaluating the V-2, R. V. Jones, chief of British Royal Air Force scientific intelligence during World War II, later recalled his feeling that 'our own politicians had been carried away with the threat: for some psychological reason they seemed far more frightened by one ton of explosive delivered by rocket than by five tons delivered by aircraft'.[72] Why did missiles affect the minds of both their designers and their victims so unlike other weapons? Writing with remarkable prescience *before* the first missiles struck Britain, Jones saw the reason for their effect in basic human fears and myths:

The answer is simple: no weapon yet produced has a comparable romantic appeal. Here is a 13 ton missile which traces out a flaming ascent to heights hitherto beyond the reach of man, and hurls itself 200 miles across the stratosphere at unparalleled speed to descend—with luck—on a defenceless target. One of the greatest realizations of human power is the ability to destroy at a distance, and the Nazeus [*sic*] would call down his thunderbolts on all who displease him.[73]

It is a point that has been intuitively appreciated by national leaders facing the threat of missile attack ever since. During his April 1963 meeting with President John Kennedy, Shimon Peres—then Israeli Defence Minister—felt compelled to explain why his country viewed Egyptian ballistic missiles as an extreme danger, telling the dubious Kennedy that: 'A conventional warhead is very different from a bomb released from a plane. The main feature of a missile is that it is unmanned. It sows terror and enhances the sense of power of those who employ it, because there are no effective means of defence against it'.[74]

It is the certainty of attack that gives ballistic missiles their fundamental importance. Even in situations where they only marginally affect the quantitative destruction of war, they have an immense effect on perceptions of the quality of the dangers. The feeling of utter defencelessness is among the most horrifying man can confront. It is the basis for military establishments and, if

---

[71] Even an authority normally as sceptical (and dismissive of the V-2) as Liddell Hart accepts the significance of the Doolittle raid. See Liddell Hart (note 44), pp. 344–46. A more extensive treatment of the raid and its effects is given by Doolittle, J. H. with Glines, C. V., *I Could Never Be So Lucky Again: An Autobiography by Gen. James H. 'Jimmy' Doolittle* (Bantam: New York, 1991), pp. 213–71.

[72] Jones (note 42), p. 455.

[73] Jones' Sep. 1944 report is quoted in Jones (note 42), pp. 455–57.

[74] Golan, M., *Shimon Peres: A Biography* (Weidenfeld and Nicolson: London, 1982), p. 116.

one accepts the argument of Hobbes' *Leviathan*, for the state itself. The greatest power of the ballistic missile is to nullify our efforts to create a structured and predictable world.

Critics who insist that conventionally armed missiles are merely psychological weapons that can be dismissed by sensible military planners miss the point that much of warfare is psychological, too. This point verges on the obvious, yet prominent strategists find it necessary to go to great lengths time and again to remind their readers of its importance.[75] The essence of warfare is not measured purely in terms of destruction but in the ability to use force and threats to achieve political goals. Weapons that intimidate or panic an adversary have a military significance that is different from, but not necessarily any less than, that of weapons more efficient in killing and destroying.

VI. Conclusions

The proper significance of ballistic missiles is not easy to appreciate, with perceptions often driven to extremes. All too often, observers feel compelled by their practical needs or unbound emotions to minimize or exaggerate the truth. Two examples show how this polarization affects even highly insightful participants.

As the possibility of war with Iraq grew increasingly likely in the autumn of 1990, Allied leaders and analysts watched closely for signs that Saddam Hussein was preparing to unleash Scud missiles and debated their likely impact. Typical of official opinion before the war were the views of General Norman Schwarzkopf, who maintained that the missiles did not pose a serious threat; Saadam Hussein's Scuds were too few and too lightly armed to disrupt Allied operations.[76] This was a conclusion shared by well-known strategic analysts and some experts on missile proliferation as well.[77] Their views were militarily unassailable in terms of the effect of the Scud missiles on Allied ability to liberate Kuwait and defeat Iraqi forces. In terms of the missiles' political effects, however, they seem weirdly myopic.

One of the first Americans to witness the launch of a ballistic missile saw the nature of missile attack much differently. In November 1944, William Liscum Borden was piloting a US bomber back from a mission over the Netherlands when he saw a V-2 lifting off to attack Britain. Although he felt inured by the experiences of that war, he realized that this was something entirely different. He was seized by an intuitive sense that international security had been changed forever. 'I became convinced', he wrote after the war, 'that it was only

---

[75] The classic statement is made by Schelling, T. C., *Arms and Influence* (Yale University Press: New Haven, Conn., 1966), chapters 1–2. Twenty-five years later the same point was made more forcefully in van Creveld, M., *The Transformation of War* (Free Press: New York, 1991), chapter 6.

[76] *U.S. News and World Report* (note 23), p. 260.

[77] Luttwak, E. N., 'The Saddam threat has been grossly exaggerated', *International Herald Tribune*, 14 Jan. 1991, p. 8; and Rubin, U., 'Iraq and the ballistic missile scare', *Bulletin of the Atomic Scientists*, Oct. 1990, pp. 11–13. Schwarzkopf changed his opinion after the Scud attacks began and authorized the massive Allied Scud suppression campaign.

a matter of time until rockets would expose the United States to direct, transoceanic attack . . . The truth is that an air corps based primarily on planes flown by men became obsolescent on the day the first V-2 streaked from Holland to London'.[78] Borden's judgement errs in the opposite direction from Schwarzkopf's; his insight is politically profound, but militarily questionable regarding conventionally armed missiles.

The true nature of ballistic missiles lies somewhere between these extremes. The effects of ballistic missiles are uncertain and ultimately depend less on their own capabilities than on surrounding circumstances. Armed only with conventional warheads, they can be effective weapons under peculiar circumstances, but they cannot be decisive in any but the most specific situations. To be certain of affecting the course of a war, they must carry nuclear warheads or possibly other weapons of mass destruction. Yet even without the ability to inflict massive destruction they can affect the political decision making surrounding the conduct of the conflict.

Balanced appreciation of the capabilities of ballistic missiles must consider the specific forces and countries involved. Where large quantities of short-range missiles can reach major targets, even with conventional armament they can potentially be militarily significant. But longer-range missiles are too costly to be deployed in such quantities. They are unlikely to be militarily effective without nuclear—or possibly chemical or biological—warheads, although they may have great symbolic clout regardless. More specific assessments of regional capabilities must consider not only the characteristics of the missile forces and the geography but also the operational doctrine of their armed forces, the goals of government policy, the resolve of national leaders and the morale of their victims.

Those on both sides of the debate over ballistic missile effectiveness make valid points: the symbolic salience of ballistic missiles is peerless among modern weapons, especially as instruments of terror and political tools in peacetime; but in wartime other weapons, such as manned aircraft and cruise missiles, must be taken no less seriously. On balance, conventionally armed ballistic missiles are mostly political weapons, but their military effects cannot be disregarded. National leaders must deal with both aspects of the problem.

[78] Borden, W. L., *There Will Be No Time: The Revolution in Strategy* (Macmillan: New York, 1946), pp. ix, 54–55.

4. The soft technology: managing missile programmes

I. Introduction

In coming to grips with missile proliferation, one naturally emphasizes the role of physical technology—the bits and pieces of equipment required to build large rockets. For any government trying to develop large missiles, however, the essential technology includes a long catalogue of invisible items as well. There is much more to any major R&D project than just assembling metal and plastic. Easily overlooked are the necessary skills, experience and judgement required of engineers and programme managers. Also behind every missile programme are conceptual, organizational, financial, and command and control factors, each imposing its own problems for ballistic missile development.

The factors discussed in this chapter as part of the technics of rocketry go far beyond the usual meaning of technology. Such factors as personnel, organization and finance are the 'software', the 'invisible technology', of innovation. In some respects they are more important than the hardware or physical equipment usually associated with weapon development. They are included here as elements of technology in its broadest sense, meaning the means of creation. This broadening of the meaning of technology may seem arbitrary, but it is neither capricious nor unprecedented.[1]

From this perspective, the technics of missile development are virtually endless. They stretch from arcane equipment to the structure of government and society itself. This chapter examines the most important political and economic elements of a missile programme, those most likely to cause serious problems for a country trying to develop its own ballistic missile or space launcher. The emphasis throughout is not only on the obstacles to be overcome but also on the choices and trade-offs that must be made before progress can be made with the physical technology, choices that must be made long before large missiles can be ready on the launch pad or in the silo.

Once we accept the proposition that there is no blind technical imperative forcing new weapons upon us, we must also acknowledge a spectrum of other forces that affect their procurement. The role of sociological forces in the process of technical development is widely recognized by scholars of technology. Even when physical laws and military priorities make certain weapons potentially worthwhile, social factors will determine how aggressively they are pursued.[2] Studies of weapon procurement have emphasized the importance of

---

[1] A pioneering study is Price, D. K., *The Scientific Estate* (Harvard University Press: Cambridge, Mass., 1965).

[2] This theme is developed in Morison, E. E., *Men, Machines, and Modern Times* (MIT Press: Cambridge, Mass., 1966), especially chapter 2, 'Gunfire at sea'.

politics and bureaucratic processes in determining how weapon decisions are made by the major powers.[3] This approach has been applied with great success in studies of how the United States acquired ballistic missiles during the 1950s, especially to explain why some programmes progressed much faster than others.[4] Oddly, domestic politics have been all but ignored in studies of weapon procurement by regional powers, despite the fact that most are relatively open to study. If we are to cope with the threat of weapon proliferation, however, these broader aspects of weapon procurement must be appreciated and addressed as well.

The challenge of rocket development is getting a whole spectrum of factors right at the same time and place. Not only must the physical wherewithal be collected and assembled, but the political and managerial structures must be firmly established. The problems for emerging missile powers are different from those faced by the superpowers which invented the long-range rocket, but only by a matter of degree. For would-be proliferators trying to emulate the technological accomplishments of the established powers, many of the problems imposed by the technology of rocketry are the same. It is no surprise that most of their efforts never get beyond the drawing board, while many die in development and others linger for years, incomplete and eventually forgotten. When so many factors are necessary for success, a programme can be stopped by shortcomings in almost any of the areas explored below.

II. Goals: the dual-use dilemma

By its very nature, rocket technology is equally suitable for civilian and military applications. This technical fact, the basis of the most difficult controversies over missile proliferation, has influenced the development of rocketry almost since its invention. While there are differences between space launch rockets and ballistic missiles, the essential similarities between the two make it impossible to separate them completely or permanently. The particular goals guiding an individual rocket project may affect its adaptability for other applications but never completely rule out switching them from one role to another. All civilian rocket programmes raise possibilities for missile development.

The first modern rocket research was motivated by the promise of space flight. From the time that the Russian visionary Konstantin Tsiolkovsky pioneered the principles of advanced rocketry in the 1890s, rocket scientists naturally aimed their efforts at the moon. The first practical study of rocket

---

[3] Allison, G. T. and Morris, F. A., 'Armaments and arms control: exploring the determinants of military weapons', *Daedalus*, vol. 104, no. 3 (summer 1975), pp. 99–129; Evangelista, M., *Innovation and the Arms Race* (Cornell University Press: Ithaca, N.Y., 1988); and Kaldor, M., 'The weapons succession process', *World Politics*, vol. 38, no. 4 (July 1986), pp. 577–95.

[4] Armacost, M. D., *The Politics of Weapons Innovation: The Thor–Jupiter Controversy* (Columbia University Press: New York, 1969); Beard, E., *Developing the ICBM: A Study in Bureaucratic Politics* (Columbia University Press: New York, 1976); and Sapolsky, H. M., *Polaris System Development* (Harvard University Press: Cambridge, Mass., 1972), all of which examine US missile procurement in the 1950s.

dynamics, Hermann Oberth's *Die Rakete zu den Planetenräumen*, was dedicated to this goal.[5] Working independently and in ignorance of each other during the 1920s and 1930s, small groups of rocket experimenters in Germany, the Soviet Union and the United States as well as individual researchers in Britain, France and Italy all were attracted to the rocket by the idea of space travel.[6]

In each case, however, the initial interest in space exploration soon yielded to an even more compelling devotion to rocketry itself. As if mesmerizing all who saw it with its conceptual elegance and raw power, the tool conceived as a vehicle for space exploration became an end in itself. Practical forces also intervened to change the nature of the investigations; none of the research groups could afford anything beyond experiments with very small rockets.[7] Determined to continue development of their ideas, the scientific and engineering communities consistently volunteered their talents to military sponsors. Robert Goddard, for example, tried unsuccessfully to win Army support during World War I. Like his Russian counterparts, Goddard devoted his work during World War II to military rockets.[8]

It was German researchers who established not only the technical prototype of the modern rocket outlined in the previous chapter, but also the path of its development. For the small band of enthusiasts who began rocketry development at a disused ammunition dump outside Berlin in 1929, the only justification for their work was space flight. Yet when the Ordnance Office of the German Army offered to sponsor their work in 1932, the German enthusiasts accepted without compunction. In the years since 1945 it has been debated whether the Nazis used the scientists or the scientists used the Nazis. Some biographers have argued that the rocket engineers were politically naive in allowing their talents to be misused.[9] There is no evidence, however, that the civilian scientists and engineers led by Wernher von Braun and General Walter Dornberger ever objected to serving military ambitions. As loyal Germans, they saw no conflict; rockets capable of attacking distant targets were equally suitable for launching into space and intellectually of equal interest.[10]

[5] Oberth, H., *Die Rakete zu den Planetenräumen* [Rocket to celestial space] (R. Oldenberg: Munich, 1923), better known through the 1929 edition, *Wege zur Raumschiffahrt* [Path to space travel].

[6] General works include Emme, E. M. (ed.), *The History of Rocket Technology: Essays on Research, Development and Utility* (Wayne State University Press: Detroit, Mich., 1964); Hall, R. C. (ed.), *Essays on the History of Rocketry and Space Flight*, 2 vols (National Aeronautics and Space Administration: Washington, DC, 1977); and Winter, F. H., *Rockets into Space* (Harvard University Press: Cambridge, Mass., 1990).

[7] The most successful early rocket scientist, Robert Goddard, received private financial support from the Guggenheim Foundation, enabling him to develop a series of rockets culminating in a rocket of 275 kg (600 lb) thrust in 1938. An impressive accomplishment under the circumstances, this was less than 2% of the thrust of the German V-2 in 1942.

[8] The literature on Goddard is vast but mostly for the specialist. The best survey of his technical accomplishments and financial difficulties are his research notes, published as Goddard, R. H., in eds Goddard, E. C. and Pendray, G. E., *Rocket Development: Liquid-fuel Research, 1929–1941* (Prentice-Hall: New York, 1961).

[9] A prominent book arguing this theme of 'innocent scientists' is Ordway, F. I., II, and Sharpe, M. R., *The Rocket Team* (Crowell: New York, 1979).

[10] Dornberger, W., *V-2: Der Schuss ins Weltall: Geschichte Einer Gross-Erfindung* [V-2: shot into space: history of a great invention] (Bechte Verlag: Esslingen, 1952); Hölsken, H. D., *Die V-Waffen* [The V-weapons] (Deutsche Verlags-Anstalt: Stuttgart, 1984); and Neufeld, M. J., 'The guided missile and the

Only a few months after the first V-2 rocket was launched on 3 October 1942, the German Army suffered its first decisive defeat of the war at Stalingrad. As the German war effort deteriorated from that point on, weapons previously on the periphery of German planning became increasingly important to the Nazi leadership and to Hitler himself. Even so, von Braun's Rocket Team at Peenemünde was able to continue some purely scientific work, including launching several V-2s into space as sub-orbital sounding rockets. Until the advancing Soviet Army forced them to abandon Peenemünde in February 1945, the Rocket Team devoted considerable effort to designing the two-stage A-9/10, a potential ICBM or satellite launcher.[11]

This prototype effort to build a major rocket demonstrated that there is no essential difference between military and civilian rockets.[12] Any rocket capable of carrying a destructive payload can be used to launch scientific payloads into the upper atmosphere or outer space. Large rockets can carry nuclear weapons thousands of kilometres or place satellites into orbit. There are physical differences between civilian and military rockets, especially in guidance and re-entry technologies. In practice, however, the problem of converting a rocket from one role to another has never been an insurmountable one; large rockets have been used interchangeably for civilian and military missions. When pressed to comment on the difference between ballistic missiles and space launchers, President John Kennedy allegedly responded 'attitude'. Apocryphal or not, the comment sums the matter up neatly.

The scientists and engineers responsible for large rockets everywhere have displayed the same ambidexterity as their predecessors at Peenemünde. It is no accident that almost every country able to build large rockets has used its early models interchangeably for military and civilian roles. The Soviet Union relied upon its first ICBM, the SS-6 (or R-7), to launch the world's first orbital satellite, Sputnik, into orbit in 1957, and the first astronaut, Yuri Gagarin, in 1961. Over 35 years since it was first launched, and long after it was retired from the Strategic Rocket Forces, the SS-6 remains in production, serving today as one of Russia's most important space launchers. Alan Shepard, the United States's first astronaut, was launched into space by a Redstone rocket developed from the V-2. John Glenn was lifted into orbit by an Atlas rocket originally designed as an ICBM.

Similar observations could be made about the early rocket projects of Britain and France which were used interchangeably in military and civilian roles. China still launches satellites on boosters originally designed as ballistic missiles. India and Israel have also used most of their rocket types interchange-

---

Third Reich', eds M. Renneberg and M. Walker, *Science, Technology and National Socialism* (Cambridge University Press: Cambridge, Mass., 1994).

[11] von Braun, W., 'Survey of development of liquid rockets in Germany and their future prospects', *Journal of the British Interplanetary Society*, Mar. 1951, pp. 75–80.

[12] The terms civilian and military rockets are used here as synonyms for space launch vehicles and ballistic missiles. This common usage should not obscure the importance of satellite launch vehicles for lifting military reconnaissance satellites and other military payloads into orbit. Stares, P., *Space and National Security* (Brookings Institution: Washington, DC, 1987), chapter 3.

ably for military and civilian missions. The biggest exception to this trend is Japan, the one rocket builder seemingly—thankfully—oblivious to the military relevance of its creations.

For most rocket builders, the specialization of civilian and military rockets comes only over time. After using the same basic rockets for all their needs, emerging missile powers gradually do develop specially designed vehicles for each task. Typically, this process is more bureaucratic than anything else; the military has its own rockets and the civilians theirs. This division evolved in the United States in the 1960s, in France in the 1970s and in the Soviet Union in the 1980s. Yet in almost every case civilian rockets could still be militarized and vice versa.

The inherent similarity of civilian and military rocket technology makes it impossible for outsiders to be certain about a newcomer's goals by examining its rocket work alone. Early experiments with engine designs, fuel combinations, airframe configurations, and safety and operating procedures tend to follow well-trodden paths. The technology itself limits the options that newcomers are likely to pursue. Even after national decision makers have chosen which direction to emphasize, their true course can be concealed with ease for several years. The differences between the two paths lie not in the external characteristics of a rocket but in the components within—especially the high-accuracy guidance, control and re-entry technologies characteristic of long-range missiles. Such components do not have to be designed for a rocket at the start. In most cases they can be developed and fitted later, long after a rocket has been introduced for civilian use.

The dual-use reality of the rocket makes it easy for proliferators to conceal their military intentions behind civilian appearances. Almost all missile proliferators targeted by Western export controls have pleaded that their work is exclusively for peaceful scientific research and civilian space launch. Even when bellicose political statements, leaked documents or investments in obvious military sub-systems left no doubt about the real military goals of their projects, countries such as Argentina, Egypt, Iraq and South Africa have claimed that they were not working on ballistic missiles. From a technical perspective, there is always an element of truth to such claims: the rockets *could* be used for civilian undertakings. The differences are not in the rockets so much as in the minds of the policy makers.

The differences between military and civilian rockets, marginal in the early years of any country's rocketry programme, tend to become more significant as the programme matures. Had von Braun's Rocket Team, for example, been allowed to concentrate exclusively on its original goal of space flight, it undoubtedly would have emphasized a rocket much larger than the V-2 and put more effort into the engine rather than other sub-systems. Over time, military programmes tend to develop rockets of smaller size than space launchers, using solid fuels and highly refined sub-systems, easing problems with concealment, sheltering and readiness.

Such differences are not essential, however. Even after several decades of rocket development, China's ballistic missile force relies on rudimentary technologies such as 1950s-vintage liquid fuels and strap-down guidance—technologies better suited for less demanding civilian space launch missions. In the same way, Israeli space launchers appear to be unnecessarily sophisticated for their ostensible mission, employing technologies usually associated with ballistic missiles.

The most advanced space launchers, such as the US Pegasus and Icarus, may converge back towards ballistic missiles. By emphasizing features such as solid fuel and high reliability for rapid operation, these state-of-the-art boosters could easily be converted to ballistic missiles. Such similarities among advanced technologies may not be relevant to emerging missile powers today. Twenty or thirty years from now the situation could be very different.

III. Size: the critical choice

The most important factors governing a country's progress in rocketry are the goals it sets and the strategies it uses to reach them. The policy decisions made in the early years of rocket development strongly influence not only its ability to achieve initial goals but also the potential for moving beyond them later. No goal is more important than size; from the physical dimensions of the rockets that a programme aims to develop follow the minimum personnel, managerial, financial and technical requirements the project must meet. Choices made regarding size, range and payload affect the kinds of technology acquired and kinds of domestic capability developed. By establishing the general parameters of rocket activity, early decisions on rocket size will affect the emergence of a country's overall capabilities. These early commitments will shadow decision making for years, often for decades, constraining the ability to pursue new and more ambitious goals later.

As a rule, the smaller the rocket, the easier it will be to develop it domestically or purchase it from a foreign supplier. The smaller the rocket, moreover, the greater its dual-use potential for both military and civilian applications. Larger rockets are more costly and difficult to develop, and converting them for other applications requires progressively greater effort and risk. Comparing the four major types of rocket shows the importance of a country's initial goals and procurement strategies. The four types are illustrated by typical examples in table 4.1.

Sub-orbital sounding rockets and artillery rockets

The smallest rockets are often distinguished exclusively by 'attitude'. The two groups of smaller rockets most relevant to ballistic missile proliferation both have distinct origins and very different applications. Sounding rockets are used mostly by civilian space agencies for scientific research in the upper atmo-

Table 4.1. Characteristics of typical contemporary rockets

Type/ Name	Country	No. of stages	Max. range (km)	Length (m)	Launch weight (kg)	Typical payload (kg)	Guidance	Fuel
Artillery rocket								
Oghab	Iran	1	40	4.8	360	70	None	Solid double-base
Sounding rocket								
Rohini-560	India	2	(140)	8.4	1 350	100	None	Solid double-base
Ballistic missile								
M-9/DF-15	China	1	600	(11.0)	6 200	500		Strap-down Solid composite
Jericho-2	Israel	2	1 450	(12.0)	(7 000)	(800)	Inertial	Solid composite
Space launcher								
ASLV	India	4	3 000	23.5	39 000	400	Strap-down & radio	Solid composite
CZ-3	China	3	12 000	43.9	202 000	3 200	Inertial	Liquid

Data in parentheses are author's estimates.

Sources: Clark, P. S., 'Chinese launch vehicles—Chang Zheng 3', *Jane's Intelligence Review*, Aug. 1992; Foss, C. F. (ed.) *Jane's Armour and Artillery, 1992–93* (Jane's: Coulsdon, Surrey, 1992); Lewis, J. W. and Hua Di, 'China's ballistic missile programs', *International Security*, fall 1992; and Wilson, A. (ed.), *Jane's Space Directory, 1993–94* (Jane's: Coulsdon, Surrey, 1993).

sphere. They started big and complex, gradually becoming small and simple. The first sounding rockets were converted in the 1940s from the largest ballistic missiles then existing. Smaller, more specialized designs were developed later to meet the specific requirements of sub-orbital research. Artillery rockets are used to attack ground targets at ranges beyond the reach of howitzers and other artillery. They have matured in an opposite path, beginning as very small and simple weapons during World War II, later evolving into the considerably larger and more versatile systems they are today.

Concealed by these seemingly extreme differences are essential similarities. By the early 1960s the two types had merged into a single set of rockets, sharing everything but payload and launching methods. In many ways they are indistinguishable and they are often used interchangeably. They are often manufactured by the same firms on the same production lines with the same tooling and equipment. They use the same casings, fuels, engines and igniters. Among established rocketry powers these similarities are little more than an engineering curiosity, an otherwise overlooked fact that permits a few dual-use applications, enabling organizations to stretch their budgets. For would-be proliferators the similarities are of much greater significance, creating a source of rockets which can be converted directly to artillery rockets or ballistic missiles. More generally, sounding rocket programmes enabling civilian organizations to acquire technologies and facilities essential to the development of military rockets, while building rocketry skills that are easily transferred to military operations.

Today most sounding rockets are solid-fuel, unguided rockets capable of carrying a small payload (typically less than 200 kg) to high altitudes during a short sub-orbital flight. They might carry equipment to study the upper atmosphere, test new instrumentation or for zero-gravity experiments. Their chief virtues are low cost, high reliability and easy operation.[13] This was not true of the first sounding rockets, which were based on the largest systems available in the 1940s. The United States fired several dozen captured V-2s for its first major upper-atmospheric experiments beginning in 1947.[14] In the Soviet Union the V-2 was copied for domestic production beginning in the late 1940s—some as the R-1 ballistic missile, others as the Soviet V-1 and V-2 scientific sounding rockets.[15] In the United States there was considerable unhappiness with the V-2 in this role. The rocket was difficult and costly to launch. About 40 per cent of launches were unsuccessful. Even among the successes there were serious performance problems. After its engine had burned out, but still less than half-way into its ascent, the rocket would usually begin to tumble uncontrollably as it coasted up, ruining much of the data it collected. Most importantly, there just were not enough of them.[16]

In response to these problems several second-generation sounding rocket programmes were started. Some, like the Jet Propulsion Laboratory's Corporal and the US Navy Viking, were no less difficult to use than the V-2 they replaced. The first practical sounding rocket was a much smaller vehicle, the Aerobee. Weighing only 685 kg when empty, this liquid-fuel vehicle could carry a scientific payload to an altitude of 120 km. Unlike previous sounding rockets, the Aerobee was unguided, as would be all future sounding rockets.[17] They now depend exclusively on aerodynamic refinement and rapid acceleration to ensure a proper flight. When improvements in solid propellants were transferred to sounding rocket work in the mid-1950s, the technology was complete. The Nike-Cajun, a two-stage solid-fuel rocket developed by the University of Michigan in the mid-1950s, perfected the sounding rocket. It could reach altitudes as high as 180 km or lift payloads weighing up to 100 kg for a cost of $3150 per vehicle.[18] Other sounding rockets in widespread use are the

[13] The best review of the subject is Corliss, W. R., *Sounding Rockets, 1958–1968: A Historical Summary*, NASA Historical Report Series SP-4401 (National Aeronautics and Space Administration: Washington, DC, 1971).

[14] Newell, H. E., Jr., *High Altitude Rocket Research* (Academic Press: New York, 1953).

[15] Stache, P., *Sowjetische Raketen* [Soviet rockets] (Militarverlag der DDR: Berlin, 1987), pp. 35–48.

[16] Rosen, M. W., *The Viking Rocket Story* (Faber and Faber: London, 1956), pp. 36–37.

[17] Miller, J., 'The Aeojet General X-8A Aerobee', *The X-Planes* (Aerofax Publishers: Arlington, Tex., 1988), chapter 12; and Smith, C. P., *Summary of Upper Atmosphere Rocket Research Findings,* Upper Atmosphere Research Report no. 21 (Naval Research Laboratory: Washington, DC, Feb. 1954).

[18] Hansen, W. H. and Fishbach, F. F., *Final Report: The Nike-Cajun Sounding Rocket* (Engineering Research Institute, University of Michigan: Ann Arbor, Mar. 1957). Inflation and more elaborate ground

British Skylark, French Centaure, Dragon and Eridan, and the Japanese Kappa series. All of these have been exported, often to emerging rocket powers.[19]

These changes gradually transformed the sounding rocket from something large and extraordinary to something relatively small and uninteresting. The net effect was to render the sounding rocket a commonplace technology, one which Wernher von Braun could dismiss with justification as 'the unromantic drudges of rocketry.'[20] Unlike space launch vehicles or ballistic missiles, sounding rockets are cheap enough to launched regularly and in great quantity. By the time the Aerobee was retired in 1985, for example, over 1500 of several versions had been launched. The total number of sounding rockets based on Nike missile engines is unknown but probably reaches over 5000.[21]

Within the banal routine of sounding rocket operations are greater implications. At a minimum, any sounding rocket can be used to carry explosives, instantly transforming it into an artillery rocket. The similarities between large sounding rockets and artillery rockets are so strong that they are easily confused, even by trained observers.[22] A greater risk is that these civil programmes will be used to facilitate related military projects. Some countries use their sounding rocket programmes to acquire capabilities with obvious military implications. For several countries—Israel, Japan and Pakistan are typical examples—sounding rockets were an introduction to modern rocketry.[23] From these modest beginnings with these simple rockets they mastered operational procedures and solid fuel handling, preparing them to graduate to full-scale ballistic missiles or space launchers.

Specific manufacturing technologies also arrived through sounding rocket work. India and Brazil, for example, mastered solid-fuel mixing and casting through co-production of foreign-designed sounding rockets.[24] They and other countries like Argentina and South Africa developed their first sophisticated

procedures have brought the cost of a Nike-Cajun launch up to an average of $20 000 in the mid-1990s. The experiments they carry often cost 10 times as much. Author's discussions with NASA officials, Nov. 1994 and Mar. 1995.

[19] Ellis, J. A., 'Skylark sounding rockets—past and present,' *Journal of the British Interplanetary Society*, vol. 45, no. 4 (Apr. 1992), pp. 179–80; and Pirard, T., 'A review of space programmes in Japan, part one', *SpaceFlight*, Mar. 1976, pp. 99–108.

[20] Wernher von Braun and Frederick I. Ordway, III, *Space Travel: A History*, 3rd edn (Harper and Row: New York, 1985), p. 152.

[21] Discussions with NASA officials, Wallops Flight Facility, Wallops Island, Va., 18 Mar. 1995.

[22] A revealing incident occurred on 25 Jan. 1995, when a sounding rocket launched from Norway's Andoya Rocket Range towards an impact on Spitzbergen was detected by Russian early-warning radars. This initiated a partial strategic alert involving President Boris Yeltsin. Norwegian authorities maintain that they warned the Russian Government a month before of the launch, but apparently the warning did not reach the Russian Strategic Defense Forces. Another factor in the affair may have been the rocket itself, a US NASA Black Brant-12, the largest ever launched from Andoya and probably the first to rise high enough to be detected on Russian radars. 'Peaceful rocket makes waves', *Aftonposten* (Oslo), 26 Jan. 1995, p. 1 (translation by the Norwegian Royal Ministry of Foreign Affairs); and 'Yeltsin tests missile theory,' *Financial Times*, 27 Jan. 1995, p. 2.

[23] Fellows, L., 'Israel announces research rocket,' *New York Times*, 6 July 1961, p. 1; Itokawa, H., 'Project Kappa,' *First Symposium (International) on Rockets and Astronautics, Tokyo 1959 Proceedings* (University of Tokyo: Tokyo, 1960), pp. 188–97, from the Frederick I. Ordway, III, collection at the US Space and Rocket Center, Huntsville, Alabama; and *U.S–Pakistan Cooperate in Space Experiments*, release no. 62-129 (National Aeronautics and Space Administration: Washington, DC, 7 June 1962).

[24] 'Rocket propellant plant starts production,' *Nuclear India*, vol. 8, no. 1 (Sep. 1968), pp. 1–2.

test ranges—later essential for ballistic missile development—as part of their sounding rocket activities.[25] More important than any particular technology, however, sounding rocket work brings familiarity with modern rocketry. Would-be rocket powers typically emerge from their first few years of sounding rocket experiments feeling more competent, ready to undertake more ambitious projects.

Sounding rockets do not have to be small. The largest and most sophisticated, employing three or four stages and standing 15–20 metres in height, may reach altitudes of 2500 km. In one relatively common application, this permits 5–10 minutes of zero-gravity for experimental purposes. These large sounding rockets are created by combining stages and sections from other rockets, typically rocket engines recycled from decommissioned military systems. One of the largest in regular use today is NASA's Black Brant-12. This consists of a recycled Talos first stage and a Taurus second stage, both originally built as first-stage engines for surface-to-air missiles, and purpose-built Black Brant third and fourth stages. This creates a surprisingly simple system able to carry a payload of 136 kg to an altitude of 1500 km. The largest sounding rocket currently used by the United States is the Aries, which carries a payload of 1134 kg. This is based on the second stage of a decommissioned Minuteman ICBM, a rocket readily available after strategic arms reductions.[26]

The easy substitutability between sounding rockets and other rockets, even ballistic missiles, creates broad opportunities for would-be proliferators. It is only too likely that emerging rocket powers will take advantage of this substitutability, using the cover of sounding rocket operations to defend what actually are ballistic missile programmes, just as other ballistic missile programmes like Otrag and Condor have been defended as space launch projects.

The relationship between sounding rockets and military systems is inherent in the technology; any country capable of fielding the former will have the ability to deploy the other. The connection is a permissive one; it need not be pursued. A few countries, like Canada, Germany, Indonesia, Norway and Sweden, support major sounding rocket programmes that have never led to anything more. India offers an important example of a country with substantial sounding rocket expertise—enough to make it one of the world's most advanced actors in the field—which it has not applied to military projects. Work began with imported Nike-Cajun and French Centaure rockets in the mid-1960s, switching to domestic production by the early 1970s.[27] Twenty years later the Indian Space Research Organization (ISRO) continues regular sounding rocket launches stressing two domestic vehicles, the Rohini-200 and Rohini-560.[28]

---

[25] A well-documented example is Ricciardi, H. J., and Estol, C. J., *Chamical Sounding Rocket Range* (Comision Nacional de Investigaciones Espaciales, Secretaria de Aeronautica: Buenos Aires, 1963) from the Frederick I. Ordway, III, collection at the US Space and Rocket Center, Huntsville, Alabama.

[26] *Expendable Launch Vehicles* (NASA Goddard Space Flight Center: Greenbelt, Maryland, n.d. [1994?]), pp. 2–3, 6.

[27] *Jane's All the World's Aircraft, 1972–73* (Jane's: London, 1972), p. 611.

[28] Government of India, *Department of Space Annual Report, 1993–94* (Indian Space Research Organization: Bangalore, 1994), p. 44.

Indian sounding rockets could provide the basis for a significant artillery rocket or ballistic missile capability. The Rohini-560 uses a large engine (0.56 metre in diameter) that could be used with minimal alterations to propel a single-stage ballistic missile with a range of 80–150 km, even more in a two-stage version. Such a weapon might complement the country's growing military rocketry capabilities. The option to militarize the Rohini series has been available for over 20 years, but it has not been pursued. Civilian control may partially explain the failure to militarize the sounding rocket programme, which belongs entirely to the ISRO, not its military counterpart, the Defense Research and Development Organization. Even so, this explanation is not totally convincing; civilian control has not prevented the military from using the first-stage engine from the SLV-3/ASLV space launchers in the Agni ballistic missile demonstrator. A more likely cause may be lack interest in the Indian Army and Defence Ministry. In lieu of other explanations, Indian restraint in this area deserves more recognition.

Although artillery rockets had different origins, they have become progressively more like sounding rockets over the years. Today the two often are almost completely identical. Simple artillery rockets were used by China as early as the 13th century. In modern times they have been developed as alternatives to traditional howitzer artillery, starting with the British Congreve rockets used against Copenhagen in 1804. It took over a century to transform the weapon into something sufficiently accurate, powerful and reliable for routine use. The first fully acceptable artillery rocket was the Katyusha, employed by the Soviet Army in World War II.[29]

Although its significance is not easily appreciated in a world that has long since grown bored with rockets the size of the Saturn-5, perfecting the artillery rocket was the most important achievement of rocketry engineering until the introduction of the V-2. The artillery rocket also stands out as the most important accomplishment of Soviet rocketry throughout the war. If not for Stalin's personal intervention, it never would have assumed the importance it did. His decision was adamant and involved the arrest and purging of many of the engineers and scientists associated with long-range rocketry like the liquid-fuel engine expert Valentin Glushko and the rocket designer Sergei Korolev.[30] Comparable—albeit less powerful—weapons were developed in Britain, Germany and the United States, but only in the Soviet Union was the weapon's potential fully appreciated. It had a permanent effect on missile proliferation. By making artillery rockets into a key technology, and later making them available to all Soviet client states, Stalin made this basic rocket technology into something ubiquitous. The process it started whetted many countries' appetite for rocketry, accelerating a process of missile proliferation that otherwise might have been much slower.

---

[29] Bellamy, C., *Red God of War: Soviet Artillery and Rocket Forces* (Brassey's: London, 1986).

[30] Zaloga, S., *Target America: The Soviet Union and the Strategic Arms Race, 1945–1964* (Presidio: Novato, Calif., 1993), pp. 108–12. Both Glushko and Korolev were released during the war and later assumed commanding positions in the Soviet rocketry programme.

Figure 4.1. The Brazilian Astros SS-60 artillery rocket

Artillery rockets like the Brazilian Astros SS-60, shown here, are much larger and more costly than weapons like the basic Russian artillery rocket, the BM-21. These differ from ballistic missiles only in that they lack an active guidance and control system. Manufactured by Avibras and sold widely in the Middle East, this rocket has a range of 68 km. In the foreseeable future, weapons using similar technology are likely to be deployed with ranges of over 120 km. Whether such weapons can be procured in sufficient numbers to be militarily effective remains to be seen. (Photograph: Jane's Information Group)

Development began in the mid-1920s under the leadership of men like Vladimir Artemyev, B. S. Petropavlovsky and M. I. Tikhomirov, based after 1928 at the Gas Dynamics Laboratory in Leningrad. Their chief innovation was a solid fuel (trinitrotoluene-proxylin, or PTP) with double the energy of conventional black powder and very even burning characteristics. This allowed for much greater accuracy in flight than earlier solid-fuel rockets. After over a decade of work, in 1937–38 a team under the leadership of Georgiy Langemak invented an improved fuel, a combination of nitroglycerin and gun-cotton usually known as double-based fuel, which was much easier to manufacture for larger rockets and allowed much greater range.[31] The first truck-mounted Katyushas were deployed with Red Army artillery units in 1939. A more practical design, that of the BM-13 (also known as Katyusha), initially with a range of 8 km, was issued to fighting units in 1941 and remains in service in many countries.[32]

[31] Accomplishment was no guarantee of survival in Stalinist Russia. Soon after announcing his findings, Langemak was purged. Zaloga (note 30).
[32] Bolonkin, A., *The Development of Soviet Rocket Engines* (Delphic Associates: Falls Church, Va., 1991), pp. 10, 12–14, 26–31.

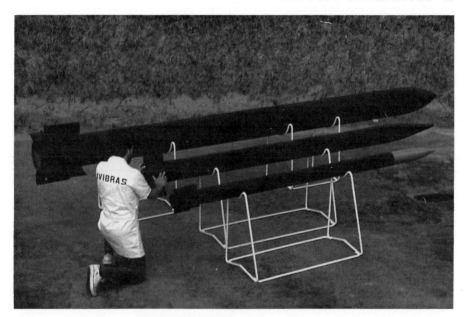

Figure 4.2. Brazilian Astros artillery rockets

Three rockets of the Brazilian Astros family—ranging from the Astros SS-30 to the SS-60—showing the dimensions of typical artillery rockets. All are based on designs adapted from civilian sounding rockets. (Photograph: Jane's Information Group)

By the late 1980s the Katyusha's successors, such as the BM-21, were part of most modern armies and many not-so-modern ones. The largest artillery rockets, such as the Russian FROG-7, which weighs 2500 kg and can travel 70 km, are usually considered as ballistic missiles although they, too, are unguided. In the 1980s countries like China and Iran were trying to develop artillery rockets capable of travelling 120 or even 200 km, but their efforts have not been fully successful.[33] Without active guidance, artillery rockets cannot be militarily effective beyond ranges of 90–120 km, nor can such large ones be bought in large quantities.

Interest in artillery rockets is heavily influenced by military doctrine and diplomatic relations. They are extremely common weapons among clients of China and the former Soviet Union. Orthodox Soviet military doctrine emphasized the importance of such 'shock' weapons; easy to use, they provided rapid and impressive support for ground operations. China adopted Soviet doctrine for its armed forces and became a leading manufacturer and exporter of artillery rockets as well. Both countries supplied them routinely to foreign clients as part of pre-configured armament packages for army brigades and divisions. The military doctrine of the United States or NATO never accorded equal impor-

[33] Bermudez, J. S., Jr, 'Iran's missile development', in eds W. C. Potter and H. W. Jencks, *The International Missile Bazaar* (Westview: Boulder, Colo., 1994), pp. 60–62.

Figure 4.3. French Centaure and Dragon sounding rockets

Two French sounding rockets being prepared for launch: in the centre a Centaure; a Dragon is in the bottom left corner. Designed for atmospheric research, sounding rockets can contribute to ballistic missile development in many ways. As noted, they can be converted directly. Potentially more important, they can start a process of technology transfer and domestic development. Both of the rockets shown here have been manufactured in India since the 1960s. Although India uses them exclusively for civilian research, the manufacturing experience introduced India to construction of modern rockets. (Photograph: Aérospatiale)

tance to shock tactics or artillery rockets, preferring more discrete use of regular artillery and air support. As a result, artillery rockets are much less common among Western nations and their arms clients, although this has changed to some degree since the introduction of a US multiple-rocket launch system (MRLS) in the early 1980s.

The dual-use link between sounding and artillery rockets was more evident at the beginning of the rocket age. In the 1940s and 1950s scientists and military men had few alternatives in their rocket work and used identical rockets in different applications. Since then the differences have become more explicit as specialized versions were developed for particular uses. Even so, some countries continue to use the same basic rocket designs interchangeably for military and scientific roles. This is most obvious in Brazil, where Sonda sounding rockets developed in the 1960s and 1970s are used in almost identical form as Astros artillery rockets. These were subsequently sold widely in the Middle East.[34] In another case, Pakistan apparently purchased large numbers of sounding rockets from France in the 1980s, some of which were deployed in 1988 as Hatf-1 and -2 missiles.[35]

The wide availability of smaller rockets is illustrated in appendix 1, which shows the number of countries with rockets in service or in full-scale flight-testing in 1994. Of the countries with some kind of rocketry capability, more than half have nothing larger than artillery rockets. Most of these only have 122- or 140-mm calibre weapons transferred from China or the Soviet Union. Larger artillery rockets have been available since the 1960s, but they remain rarer than smaller varieties. Intriguingly, sounding rockets are much less common than artillery rockets, despite their technical similarities. It would appear that, once again, pure science just does not sell as well as national defence.

Today, artillery rockets are among the most ubiquitous of major weapon systems. For many countries, artillery rockets were an introduction to ground-to-ground rocketry, a starting-point which leads many to long-range ballistic missiles. Even insurgents and terrorists have mastered artillery rockets, as did Lebanese militias and the Palestine Liberation Organization (PLO) in the mid-1970s and Afghan rebel groups in the mid-1980s. For most of their owners, however, this is not the start but the end of efforts to master rocket technology. Familiarity with small rockets permits and facilitates but does not inevitably lead to work with larger rockets. Less than half of the countries (and virtually none of the sub-state groups) operating artillery rockets go on to experiment with more advanced systems.

Ballistic missiles and space launch vehicles

In larger rockets the relationship between civilian and military applications becomes less immediate. A rocket designed as a space launch vehicle can almost always be adapted to military applications, but this may require modifying rocket stages, engine and airframe and providing better guidance and con

---

[34] Shuey, R. D. et al., Missile Proliferation: Survey of Emerging Missile Forces (Congressional Research Service: Washington, DC, 3 Oct. 1988), pp. 89–93.

[35] Discussions with US Defense Department officials and staff members at Lawrence Livermore National Laboratory; and Chandrashekar, S., 'An assessment of Pakistan's missile capability', Missile Monitor, no. 3 (spring 1993), pp. 4–11.

trol systems as well as a warhead and re-entry vehicle. A rocket like the Japanese solid-fuel M3 space launcher can undoubtedly be converted into an IRBM, but only after considerable time and effort have been expended to develop proper ground handling, guidance and re-entry systems. For India, adapting its SLV-3 launcher into the Agni IRBM 'technology demonstrator' required much of the nation's rocketry talent and resources and forced serious delays in the country's other large rocket projects.

Despite the difficulties which modification may pose, there is no way to eliminate the military potential of a civilian space launcher. The oldest, least efficient and most unreliable space launcher still retains the potential for use as a ballistic missile. Even a very poor ballistic missile—one crudely converted from a space launch rocket, vulnerable on the ground, difficult to launch and unreliable in flight—may be enough to meet the military requirements of an emerging power. Like the early ballistic missiles deployed by China, the Soviet Union and the United States, such improvisations might not win beauty contests, but they may have an adequate chance of carrying out their missions.

For all larger rockets, however, other factors make them progressively more demanding, ruling them out for most countries. The quantity and sophistication of the technology that must be integrated rise dramatically. The financial demands become more burdensome and the managerial and organizational problems quickly grow beyond the administrative experience of most governments. The scale of the undertaking can expand from the level of a single factory to the resources of the entire nation. Problems such as guidance and warheads that could be overlooked now become overwhelming. Not only do the impediments to domestic development rise, but the chances of finding foreign suppliers become fewer as well. The more ambitious a country's rocket goals, the less likely it is that they will be achieved.

The narrower availability of larger systems is equally clear from an examination of the geographic distribution of surface-to-surface weapons capable of carrying a significant warhead at least 40 km, as shown in table 4.2. While nearly 90 countries have at least rudimentary artillery rockets, only some 38 countries have rockets capable of travelling 40 km or more. Only 12 countries have long-range ballistic missiles capable of delivering major payloads over 600 km, and only 9 countries have systems capable of delivering significant payloads distances of 1500 km or more.[36]

The importance of development strategies

No decision plays so great a role in the development of long-range rockets as the choice of development strategies. The physics and engineering of rockets might lead one to expect that would-be missile powers will start small and

---

[36] The latter include 2 ex-Soviet republics (Kazakhstan and Ukraine) obligated under the 1992 Lisbon Protocol to the START I Treaty to eliminate their long-range missiles by 1997. Belarus had ICBMs as well until surrendering them to Russia in 1993.

Table 4.2. Distribution of ballistic missiles in operation in 1994

Country	Missile range (km)[a]					
	40–110	110–300	300–600	600–1500	1500–5 500	> 5500
China	X	X	X		X	X
Kazakhstan	X	X				X[b]
Russia	X	X			X	X
Ukraine	X	X				X[b]
United States	X	X			X	X
Britain	X	X			X	
France	X		X		X	
Saudi Arabia	X				X	
India		X			X	
Israel	X	X	X	X		
North Korea	X	X	X	?[c]		
South Africa				X		
Bulgaria	X	X	X			
Czech Republic	X	X	X			
Iran	X	X	X			
Slovakia	X	X	X			
Syria	X	X	X			
Algeria	X	X				
Belarus	X	X				
Belgium		X				
Egypt	X	X				
Germany	X	X				
Hungary	X	X				
Italy	X	X				
South Korea	?	X				
Libya	X	X				
Netherlands		X				
Pakistan	X	X				
Poland	X	X				
Romania	X	X				
Taiwan		X				
Yemen	X	X				
Brazil	X					
Cuba	X					
Greece	X					
Iraq	X					
Serbia	X					
Turkey	X					

[a] With normal payload.

[b] Scheduled for elimination under the 1992 Lisbon Protocol to the START I Treaty.

[c] North Korea is developing a 1000-km range missile, which was first tested in May 1993. There are reports of longer-range versions, but these are difficult to verify.

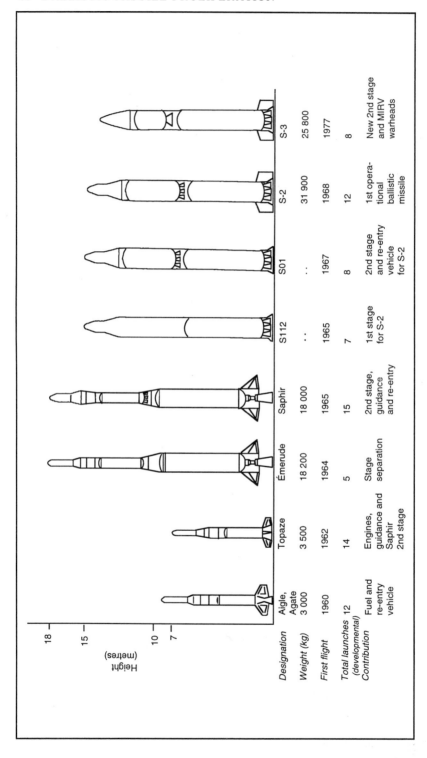

Designation	Aigle, Agate	Topaze	Émerude	Saphir	S112	S01	S-2	S-3
Weight (kg)	3 000	3 500	18 200	18 000	..	..	31 900	25 800
First flight	1960	1962	1964	1965	1965	1967	1968	1977
Total launches (developmental)	12	14	5	15	7	8	12	8
Contribution	Fuel and re-entry vehicle	Engines, guidance and Saphir 2nd stage	Stage separation	2nd stage, guidance and re-entry	1st stage for S-2	2nd stage and re-entry vehicle for S-2	1st operational ballistic missile	New 2nd stage and MIRV warheads

Height (metres)

Figure 4.4. Incremental missile development in France, 1960–77

slowly plan bigger systems. In reality, surprisingly few try to follow such a logical, step-by-step sequence. Countries often start not with modest steps but with huge leaps, trying to develop remarkably large and advanced systems in their first major effort. Some have initiated several similar projects simultaneously, hoping that at least one will show promise. Others seem to emphasize individual projects, conceived around specific characteristics with no obvious pattern or attempts to relate their needs and goals.

In the mid-1950s the United States began developing various classes of missiles not in sequence but simultaneously. This made it possible to create a comprehensive missile force in the early 1960s. At the same time, Britain began its ballistic missile development not with small rockets but by immediately leaping to the Blue Streak IRBM. Unlike Britain, India began its rocket programme with work on space launchers in 1973; not for another 10 years did the government in New Delhi authorize development of a short-range ballistic missile. When Brazil accelerated its rocket programme in the mid-1980s it tried to push everything at once, with six major projects from 150-km range missiles to an ICBM-sized space launcher.

Each country had reasons for the choices it made, but some came to regret their improvised arrangements: Brazil and Britain saw their programmes collapse, and India endured false starts and serious delays. Emerging powers today confront similar risks. With scarcer resources they will find it more difficult to recover from their mistakes. Their success will depend increasingly on the soundness of the development strategies they employ to tailor means to ends.

One strategy that minimizes both the burdens and risks of rocket development while opening a wide number of options is *incremental development.* Rather than concentrate exclusively on one particular rocket at a time, a programme can be designed to move in sequence through progressively larger designs, improving the performance of major components, and gradually introducing new ones. To be most effective, however, incremental development must be planned at the start of the programme. If imposed on a programme already under way, incremental development tends to have a degenerative effect; because any project can be justified for its potential contribution, incremental strategies can become an excuse for leaving questionable projects intact when they should be cancelled. If planned properly, however, such a strategy can make exceptionally efficient use of financial and technical resources.

France has shown how incremental development works at its best. All French ballistic missiles can trace their ancestry along a single path of development, shown in figure 4.4. This process started with a series of progressively larger and more complicated research rockets developed in the early 1960s. Each of these rockets required the development of key technologies, which were later integrated into major prototypes. This single line branched into three different but closely related paths in the mid-1960s: land-based ballistic missiles as illustrated here, space launchers beginning with the Diamant and submarine-launched missiles starting with the M-112. All three branches shared the same technical core. The Diamant space launcher was the same as the previously

Table 4.3. Incremental development of Chinese long-range rockets, 1960–84

Designation	First flight	No. of stages	Length (m)	Lift-off weight (t)	Maximum range[a] (km)
DF-1[b]	1960	1	17.6	20.4	590
DF-2	1964	1	20.6	32.0	1 050
DF-3	1966	1	24.0	64.0	2 650
DF-4	1970	2	28.0	80.0	4 750
DF-5	1979	2	32.6	183.2	12 000
DF-6[c]	1984	3	37.5	202.0	> 15 000

[a] Maximum range with normal payload.

[b] A copy of the Soviet R-2. All data refer to the Soviet version.

[c] The DF-6 was cancelled in 1973 and later developed as the CZ-3 space launcher, to which these data refer.

Sources: Clark, P. S., 'Chinese launch vehicles–Chang Zheng 1', *Jane's Intelligence Review*, Nov. 1991, pp. 508–11; Clark, 'Chinese launch vehicles–Chang Zheng 3', *Jane's Intelligence Review*, Aug. 1992, pp. 372–76; Lewis, J. W. and Hua Di, 'China's ballistic missiles programs', *International Security*, fall 1992, pp. 7–19; and Zaloga, S., *Target America* (Presidio: Novato, Calif., 1993), p. 253.

developed Saphir test rocket with a third stage added. Submarine-launched missiles were based on the second rocket stage pioneered in the S01. France has deployed an unbroken series of six different submarine- and ground-launched IRBMs. Development of new missiles never required more than 14 test-firings and never took longer than six years to reach deployment.[37]

China has used a similar strategy in its land-based rocketry (see table 4.3). After unsuccessful efforts in the mid-1950s to start their own large rocket, Chinese engineers built their entire programme around the Soviet SS-2, a 600-km missile received from Moscow in 1957. After this initial system was mastered it was stretched and stretched almost beyond recognition. Performance of the engines and other sub-systems improved gradually and additional stages were added. New technologies were developed and integrated, but only when unavoidable. Although its progress was elegant in an engineering sense, it was not especially rapid. In the early years China's rocket programme had to fend off repeated challenges by other projects and, like almost everything else in China, it slowed to a crawl during the worst of the 1966–71 Cultural Revolution. Yet in 1981 China was able to begin flight-tests of the DF-5 ICBM.[38] North Korea has used a similar approach more modestly and efficiently to

[37] Villain, J., *La Force de Dissuasion: génèse et évolution* [The deterrent force: creation and evolution] (Éditions Larivière: Paris, 1987), pp. 120–25, 211.

[38] Clark, P. S., 'Chinese launch vehicles', *Jane's Intelligence Review*, (Nov. 1991, Apr. 1992, May 1992 and Aug. 1992); and Wade, M., 'The Chinese ballistic missile program', *International Defense Review*, no. 8 (Aug. 1980), pp. 1190–92.

Figure 4.5. The Russian Scud-B missile

The Russian Scud-B (R-17) missile is the very symbol of ballistic missile proliferation. Scud technologies, relatively simple and widely available, pose the most serious challenge to international control of ballistic missiles in the post-cold war world. Essentially a perfected V-2 rocket, the Scud missile was developed in the mid-1950s for the Soviet Army and improved to reach its most successful form in the mid-1960s. Unlike the V-2, the Scud can be stored for years. It can be transported fully fuelled and set up and fired in 90 minutes. The Scud has been used in six regional conflicts since 1973. Currently deployed by at least 17 countries, it remains in production in North Korea. Despite its age and accuracy, it can be mastered by emerging powers, whether they seek merely to deploy it operationally, to modify its capabilities or to reverse-engineer it for local production. (Photograph: Jane's Information Group)

extend the range of its Scud versions, gradually extending the 280-km range weapon into a system with a reach of at least 1000 km.[39]

Incremental strategies are not a panacea for the dilemmas of ballistic missile development. As noted in chapter 2, there is no natural path of progress leading automatically from one stage of development to another. Countries reaching one rung on the ladder have no guarantee of reaching the next. Nor is there any rule forbidding countries from successfully leaping over stages in rocketry development, as did the United States and Israel. Step-by-step methods may not be essential, but they are the most efficient and reliable path of development.

For smaller powers and those with weak technological–industrial capabilities, however, any other approach is fraught with grave risks. Other would-be prolif-

[39] Bermudez, J. S., Jr, and Carus, W. S., 'The North Korean Scud B programme', *Jane's Soviet Intelligence Review*, Apr. 1989, pp. 177–81; and Bermudez, J. S., Jr, 'New developments in North Korean missile programme', *Jane's Soviet Intelligence Review*, Aug. 1990, pp. 343–45.

erators will undoubtedly try to reduce the cost and risks of rocket development by following the incremental strategy, as did France and China. They are the proliferators most likely to succeed.

IV. Design: the Faustian bargain

The most obvious element of any rocket development programme is also the most elusive. Design is a potentially endless process of trade-offs between the desirable and the feasible. A missile, more than most high-performance technologies, represents compromises between many conflicting or contradictory goals. Emphasizing performance raises costs and delays completion. Choices that would make a rocket strong and reliable tend to diminish its performance. Choices that would trim its cost tend to undermine reliability and performance as well. Accelerating its development tends to reduce its versatility and longevity in service. Raising the domestically produced content pushes cost and development time up while forcing most other parameters down.

To be sure, design dilemmas need not be as severe as they were when rockets were very new. More than 50 years after the first flight of the V-2, enough technology is available in the public domain for a newcomer to build a complete missile without engaging in any original research. Nevertheless, the burdens of rocket design and development should not be trivialized. It has been noted that the details and documentation of many early rocket designs, such as the US Army's Jupiter IRBM, are already easily available to the general public, to be copied at will.[40] It is equally revealing that no would-be missile proliferator has taken this route. Anything as complicated as a large rocket can be developed only in the context of a vast complex of supporting laboratories and industries. To build a 1950s US rocket today would require setting up the complete industrial infrastructure from that era—a feasible task but an absurd one.

Unless they are content with foreign-supplied missiles, emerging missile powers must select designs of their own, designs that reflect their own technical strengths and weaknesses. Although missile design is challenging, it is easier than design of other major weapons such as tactical aircraft or nuclear-powered submarines. The many proven rocket designs, even if they are not suitable for precise replication, provide useful models for emulation. Unlike most other weapons, ballistic missiles are in a sense ageless. Old designs remain useful long after other weapons of the same era have become totally obsolete. Ballistic missiles usually do not have to defeat an adversary's counter-weapon to succeed; they only have to reach a target to destroy it. This greatly simplifies their requirements and means that even the oldest relevant technology can be applied when desired. It also reduces scheduling pressures; a delay of five years or more need not undermine the missile's utility.

---

[40] Zimmerman, P. D., 'Bronze medal technology: a successful route to nuclear and missile proliferation', in eds G. Neuneck and D. Ischebeck, *Missile Technologies, Proliferation and Concepts for Arms Control* (Nomos: Baden-Baden, 1993), chapter 1. Zimmerman notes (p. 3) that this public availability does not extend to details of the V-2 or Jupiter guidance and controls, or the Jupiter re-entry vehicle.

Newcomers benefit not only from the proven viability of the ballistic missile but also from the failures of related technologies. As late as the mid-1960s the major powers felt compelled to invest heavily in a number of related concepts including intercontinental cruise missiles (the Navaho and Snark in the United States, and the Burya project in the Soviet Union), the manned ICBM (most prominently the US Dynosoar project), the Fractional Orbital Bombardment System (FOBS) and other systems involving stationing weapons in space, the Sänger space-plane proposal pursued at different times in the Soviet Union and West Germany and, until very recently, nuclear propulsion. All these dead-ends appeared to be viable rivals to the ballistic missile for many years. Today their shortcomings and outright failures are clear to all. Emerging powers can forget about them entirely and concentrate all their relevant resources on orthodox ballistic missiles alone.

The clearest sign of how missile design is growing easier is the continuous improvement in missile efficiency. The dimensions of a rocket required to carry a given payload over a specified range have declined tremendously since the 1950s. Since the early 1970s improvements in efficiency have come much more slowly and only after greater effort, but advances still continue. If a government really wants to do so, it can still invest endless sums by insisting on extreme technical specifications, as the United States did with the MX, Trident D-5 and the defunct Small ICBM (or Midgetman).[41] But this was due entirely to the Pentagon's decision to pursue the highest-performance technology feasible. Changes in technology also permit acquisition of missiles with lower capabilities, fully acceptable to countries with less demanding strategic requirements, at far lower cost.

By reducing the financial burdens of rocket procurement, efficient performance means that acceptable unit costs can be achieved with much smaller productions runs; where efficient procurement previously required production of hundreds of missiles, the economics of missile procurement now permit a country to seriously consider much smaller programmes, possibly involving only scores or dozens.[42] The price of rockets has not gone down sufficiently to make space flight cheap and easy, as was once prophesied, but it has gone down enough to reduce the barriers to acquiring ballistic missiles. This is the opportunity that countries are seizing as they try to enter the field.

Other factors make the design of ballistic missiles easier than the design of other major weapons. One is the unique nature of missile warfare. Most weapons are evaluated in terms of *relative* merits compared to similar systems. For a rifle, tank or naval vessel, what matters most is its ability to outperform other rifles, tanks or naval vessels. To be effective, ballistic missiles, on the other hand, must achieve only *absolute* levels of performance. How one ballis-

[41] Hampson, F. O., *Unguided Missiles: How America Buys its Weapons* (Norton: New York, 1989), chapters 5 and 6; and Evangelista (note 3), chapter 4.

[42] Based on traditional aerospace production learning curves. Large, J. P. *et al.*, *Production Rate and Production Cost*, R-1609 (Rand Corporation: Santa Monica, Calif., Dec. 1974); and Large, J. P., *Development of Parametric Cost Models for Weapon Systems*, P-6604 (Rand Corporation: Santa Monica, Calif., Apr. 1981).

tic missile compares to another is usually not consequential so long as it can reach its target. Unlike other weapons, they usually do not have to defeat other weapon systems to accomplish their missions.

In the future, progress on missile defences may alter this situation, but for many years to come attacking missiles will retain the same advantages they have had since 1944. It is enough to deliver a warhead sufficiently near a target. One result of this is to reduce the pressure for technical modernization and improvement. Fifty-year-old Lee-Enfield rifles, Sherman tanks and diesel submarines are virtually useless on the modern battlefield and today's counterparts must be updated continuously and replaced regularly to stay useful, but a 50-year-old ballistic missile design is just as deadly today as ever.

The need for absolute performance levels also creates special difficulties for ballistic missile development. To be viable, a ballistic missile must meet specific requirements for production cost, ease of production and maintenance, firing speed, range, payload and accuracy. Achieving these absolute levels of performance becomes more and more difficult as the size of the rocket increases. Although much of the technology for short-range missiles is already available on the civilian market or as part of the accepted trade in military technologies, longer-range weapons require technologies that are very difficult to acquire and even more difficult to master.

As a rule, larger rockets are less likely to be completed. Until recently, projects for short-range rockets, be they sounding rockets, artillery rockets or tactical missiles for other battlefield missions, were almost always carried through to completion, especially after reaching the prototype stage.[43] Larger projects are much more delicate. Not only is the progress of such projects uncertain, but it also often seems to be unlikely.

Every major power has cancelled ballistic missile and space launch projects, quickly withdrawn missiles after deployment or prematurely replaced them with something better. In almost every case, these projects were beset with fundamental problems of concept and design which no amount of brilliant engineering could overcome. Prominent examples include the following.

1. The *United States's* first operational ballistic missile, the 1950s Corporal, was too complicated for use under battlefield conditions. It was a failure of the kind the histories usually dismiss euphemistically as a learning experience. The Thor and Jupiter IRBMs deployed in the late 1950s were technically far more successful, yet they, too, were dismissed by President Eisenhower 'as little better than junk'. All were retired as soon as alternatives appeared.[44]

---

[43] The likelihood that short-range rocket programmes will be completed may be declining. With the end of the cold war, NATO collaborative missiles, such as ASRAAM (Advanced Short-Range Air-to-Air Missile) became tempting targets for cancellation, as did overly ambitious projects such as the US Air Force's Tacit Rainbow.

[44] On the Corporal, see Koppes, C. R., *JPL and the American Space Program* (Yale University Press: New Haven, Conn., 1982), pp. 38–61. The quotation on Thor and Jupiter is from Newhouse, J., *War and Peace in the Nuclear Age* (Knopf: New York, 1989), p. 123.

2. *Britain*, for reasons still hotly debated, announced its total commitment to missile weapons in 1957 and then gradually cancelled most of them anyway.[45] First to go was the Blue Streak IRBM, stopped in 1960, followed by the Blue Water short-range missile in 1962.[46] The country's only national SLV, the Black Arrow, was cancelled in 1971 after orbiting only one satellite. More recently, in 1993 the British Government abandoned plans to spend $5 billion on a new air-launched nuclear missile, the TASM, and cut its planned purchase of Trident D5 submarine-launched ballistic missiles by approximately one-third.[47]

3. *The Soviet Union* developed a series of disappointing ballistic missiles in the early 1950s and 1960s, few of which were deployed for more than a few years. Although the Soviet Union was the first to develop an ICBM, several attempts were required to produce one that was fully acceptable for military service. The first fully serviceable Soviet ICBM, the SS-9, was not deployed until 1966. Soviet designers continued to struggle in the 1970s with unsatisfactory ICBMs such as the SS-13 and SS-16. Overshadowed by an enormous propaganda campaign and deliberate secrecy, the space launch programme saw the spectacular failure of the N-1 moon rocket, while its costly Buran shuttle was allowed to wither on the vine in the 1990s.[48]

4. *China* built and abandoned several ballistic missile prototypes before settling on the DF-2 (CSS-1) IRBM. It was a troublesome and inadequate rocket, but it was also the first design minimally acceptable for China's strategic forces in the late 1960s. Several efforts to develop mobile and solid-fuel missiles failed during the 1970s.[49]

5. *France*, owner of what probably is the world's most efficient rocketry programme, decided in 1991 to drop its only land-based ballistic missile projects, halting the 480-km range Hadès, worth $2.3 billion, after building just 30 of a planned 120 missiles. The $5 billion S-45 IRBM with 4000-km range was cancelled outright. This left only submarine-launched missiles and the latest version of the Ariane space launcher still under development.[50] Even those are not

[45] Edmonds, M., 'The future of manned aircraft', ed. J. Erickson, *The Military–Technical Revolution* (Praeger: New York, 1966), pp. 170–86; and Rees, W., 'The 1957 Sandys White Paper', *Journal of Strategic Studies*, June 1989, pp. 215–29.

[46] Pardoe, G. K. C., *The Challenge of Space* (Chatto and Windus: London, 1964).

[47] Bates, S. and Fairhall, D., 'Defence cuts jar with MPs', *The Guardian,* 19 Oct. 1993, p. 1; White, D., 'Britain to drop project for new £3bn N-missile', *Financial Times*, 16–17 Oct. 1993, p. 1; and White, D., 'Britain to limit force of Trident nuclear missiles', *Financial Times*, 15 Nov. 1993, p. 1.

[48] Berman, R. P. and Baker, J. C., *Soviet Strategic Forces* (Brookings Institution: Washington, DC, 1982), pp. 38–55, 90–92, 98–105; Cochran, T. B. *et al.*, *Nuclear Weapons Databook, vol. IV: Soviet Nuclear Weapons* (Ballinger: New York, 1989), pp. 98–104; and Covault, C., 'Soviet Union reveals moon rocket design', *Aviation Week & Space Technology*, 18 Feb. 199), pp. 58–59.

[49] The most thorough sources on Chinese strategic missile development are Lewis, J. W. and Hua Di, 'China's ballistic missile programs: technologies, strategies, goals', *International Security*, vol. 17, no. 2 (autumn 1992), pp. 1–40; and Lewis, J. W. and Xue Litai, *China's Strategic Seapower: The Politics of Force Modernization in the Nuclear Age* (Stanford University Press: Stanford, Calif., 1994), pp. 129–205.

[50] Dawkins, W., 'France scraps plan for mobile missile', *Financial Times*, 22 Aug. 1991, p. 2; Riding, A., 'France drops plans to build new nuclear missile system', *New York Times*, 23 July 1991, p. 6; and Norris, R. S. and Arkin, W. M., 'French nuclear forces 1993', *Bulletin of the Atomic Scientists*, Oct. 1993, p. 56.

immune to cuts. In April 1994 the Balladur Government announced that deployment of the planned M5, an 8000-km range submarine-launched ballistic missile, would be delayed from the year 2005 to 2010. This action was interpreted by some to presage the eventual cancellation of the M5 project.[51]

None of these stillborn or cancelled projects was crippled by small technical problems of the sort that clever engineering can cure; it was basic assumptions and compromises essential to their design that made them untenable.

The experience of the major military powers demonstrates the great difficulty of developing an acceptable rocket the first time round, and the risks that must be faced later. It also shows that weaknesses in basic design are most likely to bring a project to a halt. Technical advances and the publication of a vast literature (which in effect permits newcomers to benefit from the experience of others) reduce some of the risks to missile proliferators. However, as in all other technical fields, the rule of trial and error remains the ultimate arbiter of success. Like their predecessors, new missile proliferators will encounter serious technical setbacks and some will witness the collapse of their programmes. Like their predecessors they are likely, especially at first, to deploy not the missiles they want to deploy but the missiles they can deploy.

V. Personnel: getting the job done

Contrary to the conventional wisdom, scientists rarely contribute directly to rocket development today. The role of scientists was limited even in the early years of rocketry, when the vast majority of rocketry scientists were physicists and chemists performing the applied work of engineers. By the end of the 1950s the great era of rocket research was over. Since then there has been little to learn about the physical principles of rocket dynamics, except in the most advanced areas of propulsion for interplanetary and interstellar space travel. With the conceptual catalogue essentially complete and the basic textbooks written, there is little or no basic research associated with contemporary chemically fuelled rocketry. Research and development have been replaced with the less speculative process of design and development.[52]

Today there is little or no place for scientists in regional rocketry. Men and women trained in scientific research work by the thousands on regional space launch and ballistic rocketry, but they are not advancing the state of human knowledge, not even by the most generous standard. Real scientific work occurs almost exclusively on specific applications such as atmospheric studies or research satellites. This could easily change with renewed interest in nuclear or other non-chemical propulsion for interplanetary exploration or the introduction of previously unknown physical principles. In the professional journals,

---

[51] Buchan, D., 'French strike N-weapons deal', *Financial Times,* 8 Apr. 1994, p. 14.

[52] Indeed, it has been a long time since a major new textbook on rocket design appeared. Such classics as George P. Sutton's *Rocket Propulsion Elements* have been reissued in numerous editions since the 1940s. The latest edition is the 6th (Wiley: New York, 1992).

scientists from Asia and Latin America have already made contributions to these fields, but it requires great imagination to see any country applying such concepts in a new missile in the near future, least of all a regional power. Their space launchers and missiles will undoubtedly rely on chemical fuels and other proven techniques for a long time to come.

Three different types of people are necessary to carry out a successful rocket programme: managers, engineers and technicians.

Programme management

Programme management is one of the most difficult things for an emerging proliferator to get right. Successful rockets do not emerge from routine bureaucratic processes. Consensus building and collective decision making may be possible after a country has a wealth of successful rocket development behind it, but such approaches tend to be disastrous if tried too early. Especially in the initial years of development, every successful rocket builder has found it necessary to rely on a single programme leader, one individual with the final say over all but the most important choices. Firm leadership and management are essential to allow sound designs to emerge, to preserve the integrity of the design as the work is delegated to individual teams and subcontractors, to resolve specific problems without creating worse ones elsewhere, and to get the endless tasks of rocket development completed in a thorough and systematic manner.[53]

Strong programme managers have been essential in the history of virtually every successful rocket development. The association between strong leadership and successful outcomes is too consistent to be accidental. In Germany the role of Wernher von Braun is well known. Less widely acknowledged is the role he played in the creation of the first generation of long-range rockets in the United States. In the Soviet Union, Chief Designer Sergei P. Korolev presided over nearly all his country's early launch vehicles and ballistic missiles through to the country's first ICBMs—the SS-6, SS-8 and SS-10. In China a similar role was played by the brilliant ex-US aerodynamicist from the California Institute of Technology, Tsien Hsue-Shen (Qian Xuesen).[54] British rocket development revolved around Geoffrey Pardoe of the de Havilland company; the weakness of his authority helps explain the failure of British rocketry. In India, for 20 years all major space launch and ballistic missile projects were the direct responsibility of A. P. J. Abdul Kalam, whose skill, authority and success reinforced each other. France, Israel and North Korea have not revealed the names

[53] The role of a successful project leader is identical to that of the 'bureaucratic innovator' identified in other contexts by Huntington, S. P., *The Common Defense* (Columbia University Press: New York, 1961), pp. 309–11.
[54] The importance of Tsien has been subject to some debate, in part because of a deliberate effort by the Chinese Government to conceal his role. His contributions are rehabilitated in Lewis and Xue Litai (note 49), pp. 130, 136, 177, 194, 254, 272, 294.

of their key managers, but it is likely that single geniuses have been at the helms of their most successful programmes, too.[55]

The importance of strong managers continues as rocket design work continues and the country progresses to more advanced designs, better suited to its particular needs. While follow-on work can be undertaken through more bureaucratic processes, coherent management remains the best insurance for successful development, close to original performance goals, schedules and cost. After the initial development stage is over it is less important to have the same individual continuously running successor projects, but there is no substitute for having someone with similar talents and powers in charge. It is no accident that the best follow-on projects are also associated with the guidance of individual managers.[56]

The need for clearly designated leaders also applies to sub-system development, often undertaken by laboratories or companies with autonomous research establishments of their own. In this way Ernst A. Steinhoff oversaw the large team of individuals and contractors involved in development of the guidance system for the V-2, and F. K. Mueller continued as his successor on the German rocket team for the US Army Redstone and Jupiter missiles. Most subsequent US ballistic missiles have relied on guidance systems developed under the leadership of Charles Stark Draper, the MIT professor who came to personify advanced guidance in the 1950s and 1960s.[57] In the Soviet Union, engine development was dominated by Valentin P. Glushko, Director of the Gas Dynamics Laboratory from the 1930s until his death in 1989. For much of that time Soviet guidance systems were associated with the leadership of Nikolai A. Pilyugin.[58] Similar patterns can be found in the development of fuels, control systems, actuating mechanisms, re-entry vehicles, test management, flight analysis, ground support equipment, and so on.

Engineers and design staff

A second personnel issue is the recruitment, training and support of a cadre of engineers to do the actual design work. The number of designers and engineers required tends to rise in direct proportion to the size of the rocket. While a small team of a few dozen engineers might be sufficient to complete an artillery

[55] Both countries obviously have policies prohibiting such revelations. There are valuable studies of French missile development, such as Villain (note 37), but these name no one directly connected with French rocket projects since the early 1950s.

[56] This paragraph is based on the work of Perry, R. L., *The Ballistic Missile Decisions*, P-3686 (Rand Corporation: Santa Monica, Calif., Oct. 1967); and Perry, R. L., *A Prototype Strategy for Aircraft Development*, R-5597 (Rand Corporation: Santa Monica, Calif., July 1972). A similar point is made by Dörfer, I., *Arms Deal: The Selling of the F-16* (Praeger: New York, 1983), p. 29.

[57] The dominance of Draper guidance systems is a theme of MacKenzie, D. A., *Inventing Accuracy: A Historical Sociology of Nuclear Missile Guidance* (MIT Press: Cambridge, Mass., 1990).

[58] Clark, P. S., 'Soviet rocket engine overview', *Spaceflight*, July 1990, pp. 240–43; and Glushko, V. P., *Rocket Engines*, GDL-OKB (Novosti Press Agency: Moscow, 1975). On Pilyugin, see Zaloga, S., 'The missiles of October: Soviet ballistic missiles forces during the Cuban missile crisis', *Journal of Soviet Military Studies*, June 1990, p. 322, fn. 19.

rocket with a maximum range of 90 km, a two-stage ballistic missile with a range of 1000 km will require the efforts of at least 200–300 engineers and technical experts.[59] For larger rockets the design and engineering team can easily run to more than 1000 men and women. There is no easy way to trim this requirement. Indeed, these numbers assume that the responsibilities of domestic designers are limited to a few basic items such as the rocket's airframe, propulsion system and re-entry vehicle, while other sub-systems are imported.

The number of designers a rocket requires is surprisingly large considering its conceptual simplicity, but the simple shape and flight trajectory conceal a multitude of design considerations, components and details that go into a system, all of which must work without any intervention. All these must be handled within very fine parameters. Changing a single item in the design is likely to require numerous compensating adjustments elsewhere. Von Braun reported that in the case of the relatively crude V-2, more than 60 000 design changes were made during the two years between the first flight-test and the first operational flight.[60] His experience in the 1950s with such rockets as the Hermes, Redstone and Jupiter showed him that these problems only multiply as projects become larger and more advanced.[61] Even if no new theoretical developments are involved, the amount of design work grows with the projects. As a programme advances, so must the number of its engineers and technical experts.[62]

A large rocket project can be started by just a few people, but successful projects grow quickly. In the mid-1970s, India assembled a team of 300 engineers to design its SLV-3 space rocket, a relatively small and simple vehicle which first flew in 1980. Some five years later, Argentina had a total staff of 350–400, mostly engineers, involved in the early stages of the Condor-2. For the initial design and development of France's much larger and complicated S-45 IRBM, a missile derived from a long series of highly successful previous designs, France relied on roughly 300 engineers and other experts for preliminary work alone.[63] Had these programmes been pursued to completion the engineering teams would have had to expand even more. At a comparable point in the development of the US Atlas ICBM in 1954, the prime contractor, Con-

[59] Balaschak, M. *et al.*, *Assessing the Comparability of Dual-Use Technologies for Ballistic Missile Development* (Center for International Studies, Massachusetts Institute of Technology: Cambridge, Mass., June 1981), pp. 14–19. A more conservative estimate of at least 300–600 engineers and manufacturing personnel is given in Harvey, J. *et al.*, *Assessing Ballistic Missile Proliferation and its Control* (Center for International Security and Arms Control, Stanford University: Stanford, Calif., 1991), p. 145.

[60] von Braun (note 11), p. 77.

[61] von Braun, W., 'Teamwork: key to success in guided missiles', *Missiles and Rockets*, Oct. 1956, p. 40.

[62] The need for personnel declines only as this team gains experience with one basic design and progressively modifies it for greater performance. Sequential development of rockets based on a single, proven basic approach makes most efficient use of previous experience. If, for any reason, a totally new design must be developed, the advantages of previous experience are all but wiped out and the design team must be expanded yet again.

[63] 'Fabrica Militar de Aviones (FMA)', *Military Technology*, Nov. 1984, pp. 112–13; and Isnard, J., 'France drops plans for new missile', *Guardian Weekly*, 28 Aug. 1991, p. 13.

vair, had a team of 300 designers working on the airframe alone. The number grew to 1500 design engineers at the height of the project in 1959.[64]

For regional actors, much of this expertise must be sought abroad. Many such countries have large numbers of aerodynamic engineers and other specialists and some countries are remarkably strong at the theoretical level, but few have the essential experience needed to work independently in this field. Nor are their universities capable of training graduate students to that level. Students must be trained abroad, and the best staff must be sent to foreign training programmes or seconded to foreign companies or laboratories to gain experience. To master a single liquid-fuel engine purchased from France, India sent a team of 50 engineers there on long-term assignment in the 1980s.[65] Most would-be proliferators will not be able to enter into comparable agreements and must compensate by hiring foreign experts to fill management positions.

All these measures are vulnerable to outside interference. Hiring foreign personnel creates the most serious vulnerabilities, especially to political pressures for their recall. Egypt's missile programme was weakened in 1963 when the West German Government demanded that the programme's German leaders cease their involvement; it stopped altogether in 1964 when West Germany demanded that the remaining German technicians return home. The Argentine and Iraqi Condor-2 missile programme was crippled in 1989–90 when several European governments compelled their citizens to end their participation.[66] In the most extreme example, Iraq's 2000-km range Superguns were designed entirely by Gerald Bull, his company in Brussels and European subcontractors. After Bull was assassinated in March 1990 and collaborators abandoned the project, Iraq was left with nothing but useless paper and parts.[67]

Those countries able to assemble a domestic design team may find it as much of a burden as a resource. Keeping the team intact and fully competent requires careful management. In an extreme case, capricious decision making can rapidly destroy an engineering team. In one of the most famous examples, Canada's Avro corporation built up one of the world's leading aeronautical design teams of the 1950s to develop an extraordinarily advanced tactical aircraft. When the project was cancelled, in a decision that even sympathetic observers regard as a fit of political pique by the government , the engineering team swiftly disintegrated. Within a few months Canada had lost the human resources to mount a comparable project.[68] Many of the most talented people

[64] Chapman, J. L., *Atlas: The Story of a Missile* (Harper: New York, 1960), pp. 61, 76.

[65] This was for the Vikas engine, a down-graded version of the Viking engine used on the European Ariane, which India uses for the second stage of its PSLV satellite launcher. 'Work progressing on PSLV stages', *The Hindu* (New Delhi), 20 Apr. 1990.

[66] Krosney, H., *Deadly Business* (Four Walls Eight Windows: New York, 1993), chapter 12.

[67] Adams, J., *Bull's Eye: The Assassination and Life of Supergun Inventor Gerald Bull* (Times Books: New York, 1992), chapter 17.

[68] Stewart, S., *Shutting Down the National Dream: A. V. Roe and the Tragedy of the Avro Arrow* (McGraw-Hill Ryerson: Toronto, 1988); Wilkinson, L. *et al.*, *Avro Arrow: The Story of the Avro Arrow from its Evolution to its Extinction*, revised edn (Boston Mills Press: Erin, Ontario, 1990).

went to NASA, where they played a prominent role in the US space programme.[69]

As a design cadre is built up, it must be kept productive with tasks of continuously greater sophistication, otherwise its talents will grow stale or even deteriorate. If the team is forced to linger unproductively between projects or is subject to raiding from other laboratories and projects, morale is likely to plummet. In such circumstances a design cadre can disintegrate in just a few months. Poor morale usually precipitates the team's utter collapse as members leave for more appealing assignments elsewhere.[70] This creates pressures to co-ordinate missile work not just with military requirements but also with the professional requirements of the designers themselves. In extreme cases, governments may feel compelled to develop technologies which military commanders find wasteful or useless in order to preserve the skills and integrity of the design team.[71]

Technicians and skilled workers

Finally, the rocket must be built by qualified technicians. A skilled work force is a resource to be developed in much the same way as the engineering team. Advances in numerically controlled machining and the automation of other manufacturing processes have not reduced the need for well-trained and experienced workers; rather, they have greatly increased the demands on their mathematical talents and mechanical skill, creating yet another potential stumbling-block.[72]

Many of the essential skills can be acquired from existing enterprises. Any country with a competent munitions industry can build artillery rockets. Most emerging powers have companies that are capable of co-producing foreign-designed fighter aircraft and these companies can also build short-range missiles. These are capabilities that are increasingly common in most regions of the world.[73] Building larger rockets, however, requires infrastructure and talents previously unheard of elsewhere in other civilian or military industries.

[69] Murray, C. and Cox, C. B., *Apollo* (Simon and Schuster: New York, 1989), pp. 33–36.

[70] Strong dictatorships are an exception to this problem, as they are able to force designers to keep working regardless of circumstances. Stalin had some of his best aeronautical engineers—Korolev and Tupolev are the best known examples—purged in the late 1930s. During World War II they continued their work in prison. Chinese engineers in the late 1950s and early 1960s could be motivated by a very real fear of starvation. Presidents Saddam Hussein and Kim Il Sung appear to have succeeded with more subtle coercion, but no maverick Iraqi or North Korean missile designer is free to move to California and write his memoirs.

[71] This problem is not restricted to the developing countries. It was one factor that led Germany to build the Tornado fighter aircraft even after its military leaders made their opposition known. Cowen, R., *Defense Procurement in the Federal Republic of Germany* (Westview Press: Boulder, Colo., 1986).

[72] Noble, D. F., 'Command performance: a perspective on military enterprise and technological change', ed. M. R. Smith, *Military Enterprise and Technological Change* (MIT Press: Cambridge, Mass., 1987), pp. 340–45.

[73] The best survey is that in Brzoska, M. and Ohlson, T. (eds), SIPRI, *Arms Production in the Third World* (Taylor & Francis: London, 1986).

A labour force proficient in the skills of fuel mixing, chemical milling, beryllium fabrication and the thousands of other exotic skills of missile making cannot be cobbled together merely by raiding existing companies or through advertising in newspapers. A labour force rather is a delicate resource that must be cultivated like any other. It requires years of deliberate planning and training to create, and careful coordination with other projects to ensure its survival and maintain its competence.

Hiring foreign technicians is a possible alternative to developing an indigenous labour force, but this creates new problems for security, cost and vulnerability to outside disruption. The weaknesses in security are not difficult to imagine; the single best source of information on Iraqi missile activity in the 1980s was disclosures by disgruntled former expatriate employees.[74] Excessive reliance on foreigners also tends to raise costs excessively, especially when hundreds or thousands of people are needed for only a few years and must be hired on contract instead of recruited as immigrants. Iraq was an extreme case, relying not only on foreign managers and engineers from Europe but also on thousands of foreign technical workers, mostly Egyptian.[75] Most emerging missile makers prefer to subcontract difficult jobs to foreign companies. This reduces the need for additional staff, but it creates new vulnerabilities to foreign export controls.

VI. Organizing for success

Organizational factors are not usually thought of as part of the technology of new weapons, but they are more important in some ways than bits of hardware like engines and warheads. While strong organizations can usually overcome problems with physical technology, even the best equipment cannot compensate for political weakness. Not only are goals, money and people essential to military innovation, but the way they are marshalled is crucial to success. Major technical innovations, as Stephen Peter Rosen has shown, take considerable time and are prone to interruption. In an atmosphere of uncertain threats and competing programmes, a major new technology cannot emerge by accident or luck. Organizational support is another essential requirement for success.[76]

Organization is the most purely domestic aspect of missile proliferation. Outside partners can help with designs, people, money and technology, but organizing agencies to guide overall programmes and specific projects is the one part of the process where would-be rocket makers are almost entirely on

---

[74] Friedman, A. (then of *The Financial Times*) and Windrem, R. (NBC News), Private communications with the author.

[75] The Egyptian Government withdrew most of its citizens following the deaths of over 100 in an explosion at the Iraqi rocket fuel facility at al Hillah on 17 Aug. 1989. This reportedly brought several Iraqi projects to a standstill. Pejman, P., 'Egyptians update Iraqi missiles', *Chicago Tribune*, 5 May 1988, p. 28; and Darwish, A., 'Iraqis recruited Britons for missile project', *The Independent*, 3 Mar. 1990, p. 10.

[76] Rosen, S. P., *Winning the Next War: Innovation and the Modern Military* (Cornell University Press: Ithaca, N.Y., 1991), pp. 76, 105.

Table 4.4. Decision-making processes for weapon development

Bottom–up The United States	Top–down The Soviet Union
1. Technocratic initiative Discovery of new technical possibilities; some scientists advocate military applications.	*1. Stifled initiative* Limited technical antecedents, discussion of possibilities, but innovation constrained by established priorities.
2. Consensus building Scientists and military associates generate interest in new technology within the military–technical community.	*2. Preparatory measures* Low-level efforts prepare broad technological background but continue to yield high-priority programmes.
3. Promotion Scientific, military and industrial 'entrepreneurs' promote new weapon proposals within the military services, Congress and Executive.	*3. High-level response* Directed response to foreign initiative, beginning of reassessment of priorities from the top.
4. Open windows External threats serve as windows of opportunity for the military to push a new weapon into production.	*4. Mobilization* Leadership endorses all-out effort to pursue innovation as nature of new priorities becomes evident; finds allies in military to implement new programme.
5. High-level endorsement Pentagon officials gain congressional support for mass production of a new weapon, justified with more specific reference to an external threat.	*5. Mass production* Mass production of new weapon coincides with implementation of new priorities, often publicly announced at high levels.

Source: Evangelista, M., *Innovation and the Arms Race* (Cornell University Press: Ithaca, N.Y., 1988), p. 52.

their own. Foreign companies and governments can offer advice and their own example, but little else. Consequently, the bureaucratic politics of regional rocketry are largely beyond the influence of outsiders, who can do little to strengthen or hinder the domestic division of responsibilities. Such factors are important to outside observers rather for a balanced appreciation of whether a country is likely to accomplish its rocketry goals in the foreseeable future, or whether its projects can be dismissed as so much dabbling.

In his study of the development of tactical nuclear weapons in the United States and the Soviet Union, Matthew Evangelista identified two approaches for managing major technological developments: a bottom–up process in which scientists advocate a new technology, gain institutional and financial support, and eventually win high-level endorsement (the US model); and a top–down process in which high-level officials initiate development by promulgating new national priorities (the Soviet model).[77] These approaches are outlined in table 4.4. Of the two, the top–down model is probably more productive for

[77] Evangelista (note 3), chapter 4.

emerging powers trying to initiate a major rocketry programme. No emerging power can hope to develop long-range rockets by tinkering with existing institutions and current budgets. For these countries, making a serious start in the missile business requires major adjustments in national priorities. This entails bureaucratic reorganization and financial reallocation which existing agencies cannot be expected to accomplish themselves.

For would-be missile proliferators, rocketry is not a matter of innovation but of emulation. The nature and capabilities of the technology are well known and do not have to be demonstrated or justified. Rather, what is needed is a high-level decision to commit resources to this particular priority. Otherwise the limited funds that can be obtained from current budgets will probably be squandered among small, rival organizations rather than integrated for greatest effect. Without a high-level initiative, the armed services and government laboratories may be able to develop some battlefield missiles, artillery and sounding rockets but almost certainly nothing larger. Long-range ballistic missiles can only be developed with intervention and direction from the top leadership.

Successful rocket development usually requires a single, integrated development organization. Contrary to an old cliché, rocketry is one field in which success cannot have many fathers. There can be only one agency of government responsible for the management of an individual rocket project. Ultimate authority for a country's overall rocketry programme can be shared among rival organizations, but not day-to-day decision-making responsibility.

The need for centralized management does not mean that other agencies of government must be excluded or constitutional oversight must be suspended. Nor does it forbid duplication. In the US case in the 1950s, success was not stymied by the lack of a single national rocketry programme. Broad government participation was healthy at the overall programme level, with strong participation by the President's Science Adviser, the Defense Department's Director of Research and Engineering, the three major armed services, NASA and the Congress. The same broad participation certainly would have been counterproductive or disastrous at the project level. Although the nation's rocketry programme seemingly embraced everyone, individual US rocket projects belonged to single government agencies, usually working with a single prime contractor.[78]

There is an understandable tendency for a project's advocates to broaden political support by allowing numerous agencies to become directly involved. With a technology as demanding as rocketry, however, this can invite endless squabbling unless carefully managed. Without an integrated chain of command, even an ideal rocket design may be impossible to build. When major decisions must be coordinated with every rocket enthusiast in town, nothing as complicated as a long-range rocket can be completed in a reasonable time. Dividing decision-making authority also encourages compromise decisions, undermining

[78] Beard, E., *Developing the ICBM: A Study in Bureaucratic Politics* (Columbia University Press: New York, 1976).

the integrity of the basic rocket design. With rivals competing to influence goals, performance specifications, choices over sub-systems, and so on, even the best design can be compromised into something unacceptable to all. Rather than broadening support, involving too many decision makers in an individual rocket project is likely to reduce support in the long run.

The ability of a newcomer to make rapid progress in rocketry depends largely on the ability of the state to make and implement policy in the field of advanced technology.[79] Creating an integrated organization for rocket development is easiest for 'strong states', those states with the ability to maintain order where it is needed. Strong states have centralized governments capable of developing policy on this issue with little interference from interest groups. A strong state is best able to establish an independent rocketry agency and protect its autonomy from the demands of other interested agencies, such as the armed services, scientific organizations and industry. As Evangelista has argued, top–down development strategies are usually feasible only in strong states, of which the Soviet Union was a classic example in the field of military technology.[80]

The different results of top–down and bottom–up development strategies are readily seen in regional rocketry programmes. The countries with the best performance have been strong states, such as Israel and North Korea where top–down strategies resulted in clear lines of authority and carefully integrated programmes. Neither country may be especially strong in an absolute sense—Israeli politics are notoriously factious and the long-term survival of North Korea is dubious—but when it comes to rocketry government power is unquestionably impressive. It is no surprise that they are (at the time of writing, in late 1994) the only regional countries to develop and deploy strategic ballistic missile forces of their own.

'Weak states', such as Brazil and India, relied on bottom–up strategies in which scientists and middle-level officials gradually built up support in the armed services, the ministries and parliament. These groups turned to the government for permission more than vigorous encouragement. But advocacy by scientists and engineers is not the same as systematic government planning. The results have been wasteful duplication and very slow progress. Somewhere in between is Iraq, a strong state from a Kuwaiti or Kurdish perspective but surprisingly weak on military industrial matters. President Saddam Hussein clearly sought ballistic missiles but allowed virtually every interested military agency to start its own projects. The result was a rocketry zoo unlike any seen anywhere before. Its most visible accomplishment was duplication, with at least a dozen rocket projects under way in 1990. Its only hope for success was extravagant funding and massive foreign help.

---

[79] The standard treatment of this theme is Skocpol, T., 'Bringing the state back in', eds P. B. Evan, D. Rueschemeyer and T. Skocpol, *Bringing the State Back In* (Cambridge University Press: Cambridge, UK, 1985), pp. 3–37.

[80] Evangelista, M., 'Issue area and foreign policy revisited', *International Organization*, vol. 43, no. 1 (winter 1989), pp. 147–71.

Weak states have been able to make impressive progress in technological–industrial fields so long as authority for the programme could be given to a single, powerful domestic agency. A large and well-funded bureaucracy can nurture an ambitious technological enterprise by itself if it is sufficiently powerful and independent—strong enough to insist on financial support from a weak central government and to parry the government's efforts at supervision. In some countries where the power of such agencies is actually greater than that of the central government, the agency also may have its own independent sources of funds.[81]

Two examples of this phenomenon are Egypt and Argentina in the 1980s. Egypt's General Staff ran its own rocketry projects under the direct authority of the Chief of Staff, General Abdel Halim Abu Ghazalla. It appears that he personally made decisions on cooperation with Argentina, Iraq and North Korea. The Condor-2 and improved Scud projects were entirely under his authority. Contracts with European firms and collaborating governments were signed by his office. He personally committed government funds. Only when the Condor project began to endanger Egyptian relations with the United States, and Ghazalla himself began to present a threat to President Hosni Mubarak, did the President get directly involved.[82] After Ghazalla was forced to resign, Egypt's rocketry programme came to a standstill.

In Argentina it was the Air Force, the strongest of the armed services, that conducted the Condor missile programme virtually without government oversight. Often the Alfonsín Government was not even informed about major programme decisions. The Air Force acted much like a sovereign state, securing private funding and arranged diplomatic cooperation with Egypt and Iraq. When the Menem Government finally recognized the need to restrain the project in 1990–91, asserting authority required massive and highly controversial changes in the way the country was run, stripping the armed forces of much of their autonomy.[83]

These are extreme cases, but all large rocket projects require some insulation from outside interference. The most successful rocket projects have enjoyed continuous leadership from one agency and often one individual manager. With continuity comes experience and skill, but also authority. The German V-2 programme was run by Walter Dornberger, who assumed command in 1932 and presided over it until 1945, rising in rank from Captain to Major-General. Wernher von Braun remained his Technical Director throughout this period.[84] One of the most successful US ballistic missile programmes, the Minuteman

[81] See the case studies of the Brazilian computer and Argentine nuclear industries in Adler, E., *The Power of Ideology: The Quest for Technological Autonomy in Argentina and Brazil* (University of California Press: Berkeley, Calif., 1987).

[82] Slavin, B., 'Defense chief's removal perplexes Cairo', *International Herald Tribune*, 7 Mar. 1989, p. 14; Ottaway, D. B., 'Egypt drops out of missile project', *Washington Post*, 20 Sep. 1989, p. 32.

[83] 'Secret missile project: it's Menem vs. Air Force', *International Herald Tribune*, 14 May 1991, p. 2; 'Argentine missile developments placed under civilian control', *International Defense Review*, Sep. 1991, pp. 908–9.

[84] Dornberger (note 10).

series, benefited from continuous leadership by a small coterie of Air Force officers, including Lieutenant-Generals Samuel Philips and John O'Neill, who in various capacities directed development of all three versions of the Minuteman from 1959 to 1972.[85]

The same appears to be true elsewhere; one only has to recall Korolev's role in the Soviet Union and Tsien's in China. In India, the only emerging power for which comparable information is available, a similar role has been played by Abdul Kalam but without comparable institutional support. Another reason for the weakness of India's rocketry programme was the excessive concentration of power in the hands of V. S. Arunachalam, the long-time Defence Ministry Science Adviser, at the expense of development specialists such as Abdul Kalam. Switched from project to project, Indian rocket specialists were unable fully to develop any of their major projects of the 1970s and 1980s. In July 1992 Arunachalam resigned and was replaced by Abdul Kalam, a change that promises greater insulation and probably greater accomplishments for Indian military rocketry.[86]

Because they are almost entirely outside the influence of foreign powers, organizational structures will be useful targets for missile control efforts only under curious circumstances. Their real value to outsiders is as a standard of measurement, a source of insight into a country's ability to prosecute a long-range rocket programme successfully.

VII. Finance

Large rockets are costly, but they are not beyond the budgets of almost any country seriously interested in acquiring them. A surprisingly large number of countries have all the money they need to afford large rockets of their own. Yet only a few are actively trying. It is not cost alone that keeps all the others at bay. Most regional actors, to put it simply, do not appear to be all that interested.

The growth and spread of wealth are the most important force behind the proliferation of military technology, opening options for countries previously at the margins of the global balance of power. While it may be lamented that the distribution of wealth is brutally uneven, its growth in the 1970s and 1980s was sufficient to make missile proliferation a truly global possibility. Dozens of countries can afford to develop ballistic missiles on their own without raising their current defence budgets at all. Most countries are already spending enough on defence to permit acquisition of some kind of ballistic missile. The financial resources are there; it is all a question of priorities.

---

[85] Greenwood, J. T., 'The air force ballistic missile and space program, 1954–1974', *Aerospace Historian*, Dec. 1974, p. 199.

[86] Updhya, R., 'Arunachalam quits DRDO', *Indian Express* (New Delhi), 1 Apr. 1992; and Victor, C., 'In DRDO an era ends', *The Patriot* (New Delhi), 10 July 1992.

Budgetary capabilities

At least 38 countries currently have annual defence budgets of $2.5 billion, enough to support a major rocket effort.[87] Their annual defence spending is roughly equal to the sum that must be spent over several years for domestic development and production of rockets with a range of 300–1000 km, rockets based on Scud-type technology but with even greater capability.

Finding the money might not be easy. For most of these countries, such an expenditure would require severe adjustments in military priorities. Outlays to the armed services and rival R&D projects would have to be cut enough to liberate a total of about $250 million annually over the 10-year life of the project. Rather than waste time debating who gets what, some countries might find it easier simply to raise military spending. For a hypothetical regional power spending $2.5 billion a year on defence out of a total GNP of $50 billion, adding an additional 10 per cent to the defence budget to finance a domestic ballistic missile programme would require raising defence spending from 5 per cent of GNP to 5.5 per cent.

An even larger number of countries, approximately 60–70 in all, have annual defence budgets of at least $800 million.[88] This is roughly equal to the amount needed to build ballistic missiles with a range of 250 km. By shifting out of current defence spending plans an average of about $80 million annually over 10 years, most of these countries could afford such a development project on their own without raising defence expenditures. If the list is expanded to include those countries able to generate an equivalent sum by raising defence spending no more than 25 per cent, the number of countries able to afford development of a Scud-type missile grows to about half of all the countries in the world, that is, in over 90 countries.

Sustained increases in military spending of 5–20 per cent annually may sound impressive, especially at a time when military budgets are declining in most countries, but they are hardly unusual. More extreme increases are not unknown. Countries faced with a new military threat often demonstrate the ability to reallocate resources almost overnight. Even very poor countries can raise military expenditures when sufficiently alarmed. For example India, after its brief 1962 border war with China, doubled its defence budget in less than four years, paying for the creation of 16 new Army divisions and the comprehensive modernization of its Air Force.[89] After neighbouring Libya fought a border war with Egypt in 1977, Tunisia raised its military spending fourfold in less than two years. In preparation for the war that toppled Ugandan President Idi Amin in 1979, Tanzania tripled its defence budget in two years.[90]

[87] *World Military Expenditures and Arms Transfers 1991–1992* (Arms Control and Disarmament Agency: Washington, DC, Mar. 1994), p. 36.

[88] See *World Military Expenditures and Arms Transfers 1991–1992* (note 87). The uncertainty here reflects the difficulty of assessing budgets in many ex-Soviet republics and Yugoslav states.

[89] Thomas, R. G. C., *The Defence of India* (Macmillan: New Delhi, 1978), pp. 45–53, 155–60, 184–91.

[90] *World Military Expenditures and Arms Transfers 1988* (Arms Control and Disarmament Agency: Washington, DC, June 1989), pp. 63, 64.

The cost figures used in the examples here assume starting from scratch with domestic development of a totally new rocket or reverse-engineering an old design. While the totals involved would be painful for most countries, they are feasible for almost all. The costs can be brought down tremendously if, instead of domestic development, a foreign supplier can be found to furnish missiles directly. Potentially, all countries can afford this option. When a Scud missile can be bought for no more than a few million dollars, the cost is all but irrelevant to limiting their spread.

Cost, then, is a minor barrier to ballistic missile proliferation. The record, and perhaps the limit, for what can be spent on large rockets was probably set by the United States after the shock of Sputnik on 4 October 1957. In a frenzy unlike any the world has seen before or since, the United States Air Force alone spent a total of $17 billion on long-range rockets during 1954–65 (roughly $55 billion in 1994 dollars). This paid for development and deployment of 800 ICBMs of three different types and 60 IRBMs of one type.[91] The $17 billion does not include the US Army's contemporary Jupiter, Sergeant or Pershing-1 missiles, the Navy's Polaris missile or several civilian space launchers paid for from NASA budgets. The United States's total investment in long-range rocketry during 1954–65 probably approached $30 billion (roughly $110 billion today). This was the cost of a superpower's panic and ambition. Had President Eisenhower succeeded in his effort to restrain 'missile gap' anxieties and won approval for a more leisurely and sequential development programme, the total cost could have been much less.[92] This was an extreme case, of course; no emerging power need spend anything remotely like this amount.

An emerging missile power, such as Iraq, can invest perhaps $10 billion in a 10-year rocketry programme, but this involves ambitious technical goals and a level of technology transfer, infrastructure investment and redundancy that only major powers found necessary in the past. The Iraqi outlays reflected more waste than sense; for its $10 billion the country acquired not one single domestically manufactured missile: all the missiles fired during the 1980–88 war with Iran and the 1991 war over Kuwait came from foreign suppliers. Iraq was able to modify its foreign-supplied missiles and assemble some artillery rockets from kits, an important feat, but far less than Saddam Hussein originally sought.[93] For a similar sum of money the United States completed the Atlas ICBM project in 1954–62, building over 300 and deploying 120 of these missiles, some of which are still ready for use as space launchers today.[94]

[91] Schwiebert, E. G., *A History of the U.S. Air Force Ballistic Missiles* (Praeger: New York, 1968), pp. 17, 37, 117.

[92] McDougall, W. A., . . . *the Heavens and the Earth: A Political History of the Space Age* (Basic Books: New York, 1985), especially pp. 211–30.

[93] Kaga, M., 'Iraq', eds W. C. Potter and H. W. Jencks, *International Missile Trade and Nonproliferation* (Westview Press: Boulder, Colo., 1994).

[94] Atlas budget of $3.826 billion in cumulative then-year dollars for 1954–62 (approximately $12.5 billion in 1994 dollars) from Greenwood (note 70), p. 194; and Neufeld, J., *Ballistic Missiles in the United States Air Force, 1945–1960* (Office of Air Force History, US Air Force: Washington, DC, 1990), p. 198.

Rocket costs

Precise comparison of rocket costs is an untidy business. Except for the United States and Britain, little systematic information on rocket costs is available. The limited data that are available tend to aggregate separate and unrelated projects or combine spending on development, infrastructure and procurement. Often the data are partial or unreliable. It is also difficult to compare individual projects, which vary dramatically depending on the role, sophistication and number of missiles involved.

As a general rule cost rises steeply with range and size. The cost of an individual rocket can be as high as $70–100 million for a large space launch vehicle or an ICBM such as the huge Soviet SS-18, or as low as a few thousand dollars for a small artillery rocket. The costs of producing a particular missile are often not known, but the following examples are illustrative.

1. *Brazil's* VLS space launch rocket is far from complete and a decade behind schedule, leading some observers to wonder if it may never be finished. According to a Rand Corporation study, fully developing the rocket and launching the first prototype would cost $283 million, plus a similar amount for launch facilities.[95]

2. *India's* first Agni IRBM, launched in 1989, cost a total of $157.2 million, including developments paid for indirectly through the civilian space launch programme.[96] In series production, unit costs would decline rapidly as R&D bills diminish and the production staff gain efficiency. A reasonable assumption is that costs will decline along a standard aerospace learning curve, yielding a 20 per cent decline in unit cost for each doubling of total production. If accomplished, this could lead to total production of 128 missiles—a deployed force of 64 missiles and a similar number for testing, training and rotation. The initial cost—without warheads, shelters, operations or maintenance—would be approximately $4.2 billion, or $33 million each, in 1988 US dollars (see figure 4.6).

3. For development and infrastructure related to the 1000-km range Condor-2, *Argentina, Egypt* and *Iraq* invested a combined total of approximately $4–5 billion from 1984 to 1991. Argentina spent roughly $800 million and Iraq most of the rest. Completing development would have required at least $1 billion more. Production would have required an additional $8 million or so per missile for a series of 200. The total value of the programme was at least $6.6 billion, giving a total price per missile of at least $33 million. Although considerably more sophisticated than the Agni, the Condor-2 had less than half

---

[95] Chow, B. G., *Emerging National Space Launch Program,* R-4179 (Rand Corporation: Santa Monica, Calif., 1993), pp. 21–23.

[96] 'IGMDP spin-offs sought', *Milavnews,* no. 358 (Aug. 1991), p. 13. The figure of $157.2 includes previous investments in the SLV-3 and ASLV space launchers, which formed the basis of the Agni first stage, and additional investments in the Prithvi, which served as the Agni's second stage.

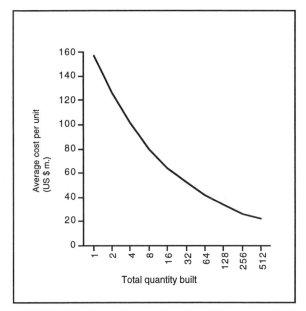

Figure 4.6. Approximate Agni IRBM production costs

the Indian missile's range but cost the same, making it rather expensive by comparison.[97]

4. For the Hadès, a nuclear-armed missile of 400-km range but generally comparable to the Condor-2 in sophistication, *France* was prepared to pay a total of $2.3 billion for development and production of 120 missiles (and their associated launchers and ground handling equipment) or $19 million each. This sum included 60 launchers. This relatively low price shows the savings that come from experience and a strong R&D base. It is not clear whether it also included the nuclear warheads. Hadès was stopped in 1991.[98]

5. For development in the mid-1980s of its Sakr-80, an unguided 80-km range artillery rocket, *Egypt* and the French company Société Nationale des Poudres et Explosifs (SNPE) invested a total of $100 million.[99] This does not include the cost of full-scale production, which apparently had not begun at the time of writing, in late 1994.

6. In the mid-1980s *Chile* set up a joint venture with Royal Ordnance of Britain for a 35-km range artillery rocket, the Rayo. The contract for rocket development and construction of a Chilean manufacturing plant was worth

[97] Frankel, G., 'Israel alleges Iraqi nuclear plan', *International Herald Tribune*, 1–2 Apr. 1989, p. 1; and Burns, J. and Friedman, A., 'US concern over Argentine missiles links to Baghdad', *Financial Times*, 9 Mar. 1992, p. 3.

[98] 'Hades plans move ahead', *Jane's Defence Weekly*, 10 Aug. 1991, p. 226.

[99] Turbe, G., 'Egyptian rockets and the French connection', *International Defence Review*, Feb. 1988, p. 202.

$16 million.[100] The cost of actually building the rockets and launchers would be considerably more.

These examples illustrate the importance of mass production. Although the cost of the first prototype of any kind of rocket is likely to be extremely high, series production gradually absorbs the high initial R&D investment and brings the cost of each successive unit down as well. The economics of this process reinforce the advantages of maintaining a skilled labour force, creating additional pressure to keep ballistic missiles in production long after the initial requirement has been satisfied.

Despite the advantages of building large quantities, in almost every case it is even cheaper simply to buy the desired rockets directly from a foreign supplier. A buyer need pay only a small share of the total R&D bill instead of the whole cost. If the supplier has already produced a large quantity, the development bill may have been amortized long ago while production experience has cut the price per rocket dramatically. A few clients, such as Israel and Afghanistan, received missiles as part of military aid packages and paid nothing while others, such as Iraq and Syria, purchased them on long-term, low interest loans. Again, the actual prices are known in only a few cases:

1. In the largest single missile deal to date involving regional powers, *Saudi Arabia* paid *China* a total of roughly $2.5–$3.5 billion for about 60 second-hand DF-3 IRBMs. This amounts to an initial purchase price of at least $40–60 million for each of the missiles, which were received in 1987–88.[101] Subsequent contracts for installation, maintenance and operation of these huge, 2500-km range rockets probably increased the total Saudi investment considerably.

2. *China* reportedly concluded an agreement with *Iran* and *Syria* in 1989 to supply a total of 140 M-9 missiles with a range of 600 km. The total contract was worth $170 million, or roughly $1.2 million per missile.[102] This was a bargain that China probably accepted only to attract an initial buyer for the previously unsold missile. The deal appears to have collapsed in the face of widespread international condemnation.

3. *North Korea* supplied *Iran* with some 100 Scud-Bs in 1987–88 for approximately $3 million each. The 330-km range missiles formed the largest part of a $500 million arms deal. Soon after delivery all but a few were fired at Iraqi targets during the spring 1988 War of the Cities.[103] According to Shahram Chubin, Iran was later able to buy additional North Korean Scuds for $2.4 million each.

[100] Foss, C. F., 'UK–Chile rocket test launched', *Jane's Defence Weekly*, 13 Oct. 1990, p. 695; and 'Chile/RO join up for Rayo', *Jane's Defence Weekly*, 7 Apr. 1990, p. 622.

[101] The lower estimate is from *World Military Expenditure and Arms Transfers 1991–1992* (US Arms Control and Disarmament Agency: Washington, DC, 1994), p. 133; the higher is from Kan, S., 'China arms sales', *China's Economic Dilemmas in the 1990s*, US Congress, Joint Economic Committee (US Government Printing Office: Washington, DC, 1991), p. 701.

[102] *Le Point* (Paris), 4 Dec. 1989, p. 118; and 'Libya trying to buy Chinese SSMs, say Israel', *Flight International*, 23–29 May 1990, p. 18.

[103] Bermudez, J. S., Jr, 'Ballistic missiles in the Third World—Iran's medium-range missiles', *Jane's Soviet Intelligence Review*, Apr. 1992, pp. 148–49; and Chubin, S., *Iran's National Security Policy* (Carnegie Endowment for International Peace: Washington, DC, 1994), p. 23.

4. The *Soviet Union*, having produced at least 5000 Scud-Bs since the 1960s, gave away almost 2000 to Afghanistan during its civil war in the late 1980s and early 1990s. Another 1500 or so were sold to customers such as Egypt, Iraq, Libya, Syria and Yemen for about $1 million each.[104]

5. Although it has less than half the range of the Scud-B, the *Russian* 120-km SS-21 Tochka is considerably more accurate and advanced. In 1992 it reportedly was offered to foreign buyers at $1.7 million for each missile and $3.3 million for each transport and launch vehicle, too costly to attract customers.[105]

Far more costly than acquiring large rockets is the acquisition of a complete strategic missile force. While many countries can afford a few missile battalions or squadrons, few have the economic resources to provide those missiles with nuclear warheads, to make them invulnerable to pre-emptive attack either with land-based silos or submarine basing, to train forces to the high level of professional expertise required to operate them, or to maintain them at a high level of readiness. For Britain, China and France, ballistic missiles were only part of the cost of creating independent strategic forces, the total cost of which amounted to about half of all their defence spending in the early years and has seldom sunk below 20 per cent of annual defence outlays since then.[106]

Although the cost of missiles, per se, may not be high enough to discourage many would-be buyers, the total system costs may be more decisive. Even if they can afford a few individual rockets, they may balk at the total investment required to keep them operational. For others, however, such comparisons may be irrelevant. Especially for governments motivated by the symbolism of missiles, mere possession of a rocket force may meet their requirements; everything else is unnecessary.

Financing

While a country may be able to afford a rocket programme, financing can still be a serious obstacle. The BNL scandal, centring on the Atlanta branch of the Italian Banca Nazionale del Lavoro, and the subsequent BCCI affair, centring on the Karachi-based Bank of Credit and Commerce International (BCCI), revealed how Iraq's advanced weapon programmes were hindered not by a lack of government revenue but by a lack of credit.[107] Iraq's missile programme,

---

[104] Zaloga, S., 'Ballistic missiles in the third world: Scud and beyond', *International Defense Review*, Nov. 1988, p. 1425.

[105] Zaloga, S., 'The Tochka tactical ballistic missile system', *Jane's Intelligence Review*, Jan. 1994, pp. 6–10.

[106] Häckel, E., 'Towards non-nuclear security: costs, benefits, requisites', ed. R. Cowen Karp, SIPRI, *Security Without Nuclear Weapons?* (Oxford University Press: Oxford, 1992), pp. 61–66.

[107] US House of Representatives, Committee on Banking, Finance and Urban Affairs, *The Banca Nazionale del Lavoro (BNL) Scandal and the Department of Agriculture's Commodity Credit Corporation (CCC) Program for Iraq*, Parts 1 and 2 (US Government Printing Office: Washington, DC, 1992); and *The BCCI Affair: A Report to the Senate Committee on Foreign Relations, US Senate, Subcommittee on Terrorism, Narcotics and International Operations* (US Government Printing Office: Washington, DC, 1992).

with redundant projects and numerous fall-back options, required immense quantities of foreign manufacturing technology. All of this had to be paid for in hard currency, more than even a major oil exporter could arrange so quickly. Letters of Credit guaranteeing the payment of billions of dollars for foreign purchases also had to be arranged through major international banks.

Saddam Hussein's greatest problem as he built up his military industries was finding not sources of technology but cooperative bankers. Most international banks respected the Western ban on dual-use exports to Iraq. Others thought that Saddam Hussein's military purchases were an excessive risk and that they might be left with the bills. By refusing to extend a routine service and provide Letters of Credit, the banking community was a bigger barrier to the acquisition of technology than some Western governments.

The hesitancy of the banking community was not uniform. Several banks, of which the BCCI and the Atlanta branch of the BNL were the most prominent, were willing to extend their services, making it possible for Iraq to make questionable foreign purchases worth several billion dollars.[108] The Iraqi example is undoubtedly extreme, but there is no reason to think it was unique. Other evidence from the BCCI scandal shows that Pakistan relied on the bank's help to finance illegal purchases of equipment for its nuclear weapon programme.[109]

Strict controls on banking could have a major effect in the short term. US Government documents show that BNL money funded Iraq's Condor-2 and Superguns. Foreign credit enabled Saddam Hussein to equip his military laboratories, buy manufacturing equipment and hire foreign design teams. Had the Reagan and Bush Administrations acted forthrightly to prevent BNL from extending $5 billion in questionable credits to Iraq between 1985 and 1989, and if the Bank of England or any other regulatory authority had likewise restrained BCCI, Saddam's missile programme would have been much smaller and slower.[110]

Substantial financial reforms have already been put in place to make illegal technology transfers and repetition of the BNL and BCCI affairs much more unlikely. These measures centre on more rigorous accounting and oversight of international banking and multilateral efforts to deal with money laundering. The most important reaction simply was greater international awareness of the problem; with many equally pressing problems on the international agenda, like the drug trade and massive tax evasion, eroding the credibility of national financial laws, national authorities in many states found that they had considerable authority to act more aggressively against illegal money. Formal collaboration, however, clearly was necessary as well.

International cooperation to restrain illegal financial transactions is the economic counterpart to export controls. As with export controls, national authori-

---

[108] Timmerman, K. R., *The Death Lobby: How the West Armed Iraq* (Fourth Estate: London, 1991), chapter 13.

[109] Coll, S., 'Global banking helped Pakistan pursue A-bomb', *International Herald Tribune*, 12 Aug. 1991, p. 1.

[110] Friedman, A., 'A paper trail of troubles', *Financial Times*, 6 Aug. 1992, p. 10; and Timmerman (note 93), chapters 13 and 16.

ties quickly realized that effective action required broad cooperation. The goal of these new controls is to make it more difficult for organized crime—including crime organized by rogue states—from finding the funds required to make their business possible or, if they do find the credit, to make it impossible to do anything with the money without getting caught. Aware that billions of dollars were being moved by organized crime with seeming ease, the Group of Seven (the G-7, bringing together the leaders of Britain, Canada, France, Germany, Italy, Japan and the United States) considered the issue at its Toronto summit meeting in June 1988. Laundering of drug profits was the immediate catalyst. Further impetus came in the wake of the BNL and BCCI affairs, which created grave concern throughout the international financial community and undermined the credibility of the entire system of financial oversight, and the issue became a key item at the 1989 and 1991 summit meetings.[111]

The most visible result of G-7 activity was the establishment of the Financial Action Task Force (FATF) to harmonize national laws on money laundering. This now includes central banking and police authorities in 26 countries, including financial centres like Singapore and Switzerland. It also includes formal cooperation with regional groups in the Caribbean and Persian Gulf and less formal cooperation with monetary authorities elsewhere.[112] The work of the FATF is buttressed by a new interest in regional law enforcement, seen in the creation of groups like Europol, the new European Union organization designed to combat organized crime. These changes clearly have made illegal international business much more difficult, even when going through previously complacent banking countries.[113]

No one should be so naive as to think that such reforms will stop the black market in missile technology, drugs or anything else; crime is a predictable human response to opportunities and temptation. According to the US Department of Justice, an estimated $7–20 billion in drug money was transferred out of the United States every year in the early 1990s. Several hundred million dollars in non-narcotics money, much of it for arms and technology, also crossed US borders annually.[114] So long as governments remain interested in illegally acquiring key technologies, criminal suppliers will dream up new schemes to profit from that demand. Reforms in banking and law enforcement will slow the process of proliferation, forcing would-be missile makers to adjust their goals and use less advanced technologies than they might prefer, but they cannot bring proliferation to a halt.

---

[111] MacDonald, S. B., 'The new 'bad guys': exploring the parameters of the violent new world order', in ed. M. G. Manwaring, *Gray Area Phenomena: Confronting the New World Disorder* (Westview: Boulder, Colo., 1993), pp. 50–52, 54–57.

[112] MacDonald (note 111); and Zagaris, B., 'Constructing a financial enforcement regime to reallocate assets from the 'bad guys' to the 'good guys'', in Manwaring (note 111), chapter 4.

[113] Interview with Europol Co-ordinator Juergen Storbeck, in 'Europol spans frontiers in war on crime', *Financial Times*, 19 May 1994, p. 2; and Rodger, I., 'Swiss clean up rules on dirty money', *Financial Times*, 23–24 Apr. 1994, p. 2.

[114] Green, E., 'Money laundering called threat to national security', *USIA Wireless File*, July 1994, pp. 9–10.

The anti-money-laundering regime makes it much more difficult for organized criminals—be they Colombian drug dealers or North Korean arms buyers—to move large sums of illegal money. Prospective sellers are less attracted to the idea of major technology transfer deals when the recipients cannot guarantee successful payment. The massive transactions that financed development of the Condor-2 missile by a European consortium in Argentina would be impossible today; the Argentine Air Force would not be able to borrow sufficient funds, and even if it could, the European consortium would not be able to deposit it. This does not mean that illegal technology transfers are themselves impossible, but they are much harder to organize and must proceed much more cautiously and slowly. Buyers and sellers must conceal their activities by breaking their transactions down into smaller components, a grave impediment when involved in a task as large and complicated as development of long-range rockets.

The problem may not, however, be so much a regulatory one as a fundamental policy issue. A substantial pool of evidence leads to the conclusion that the Reagan and Bush Administrations knew of, or even encouraged, the illicit lending to Iraq.[115] If true, this implies that the availability of cash for proliferators such as Iraq is the result of the shortcomings of policy and officials. The key to its control is in changing official attitudes.

Another approach to restraining finances is explicit conditionality. The World Bank and several governments led by Japan have urged that aid to regional countries be made conditional on reductions in military expenditures. If actively pursued, this policy could restrain missile proliferation, especially among uncommitted proliferators. Many of the countries of greatest missile proliferation concern, such as Egypt and Israel, are also major foreign aid recipients. Others, such as Argentina, Brazil, Pakistan and India, are heavily reliant on the support of the International Monetary Fund (IMF) to maintain national finances.[116]

There are limits to what can be achieved through conditionality. Such measures are unlikely to have any effect on governments deeply convinced that they require such weapons. In India, for example, advanced rocketry is an important source of national pride; any government seen to be abandoning projects like the Agni at the behest of outside interests would undermine its credibility and its chances of re-election.[117] Nor can they have much effect on countries that do not receive much aid from the West, such as Iran, North Korea, Libya and Syria. Some of these countries do receive donations and concessionary loans from other countries: Saudi Arabian support for Syria and Chinese aid for North Korea are prominent examples. Convincing all major aid donors to

---

[115] Friedman, A., *Spider's Web: Bush, Saddam, and Thatcher and the Decade of Deceit* (Faber & Faber: London, 1993).

[116] Ball, N., *Pressing for Peace: Can Aid Induce Reform?* ODC Policy Essay no. 6 (Overseas Development Council: Washington, DC, 1992).

[117] Gordon, S., 'Domestic foundations of India's security policy', eds R. Babbage and S. Gordon, *India's Strategic Future: Regional State or Global Power?* (Macmillan: London, 1992), p. 15.

subscribe to the same restrictive principles is a long-term goal, but one with enormous potential to inhibit proliferation.

VIII. Conclusions

Although it is easily overshadowed by the more concrete aspects of missile hardware, the soft technology is unquestionably more important. Without sound policy choices, good organization, skilled personnel and adequate financing, no amount of even the very best equipment can be sufficient to create long-range ballistic missiles. Good management can compensate for poor equipment, but by itself the best equipment is never enough. Among the examples noted above, North Korea had perhaps the worst technical endowments, yet its superior management enabled it to develop and deploy missile forces far superior to those achieved by many wealthier countries with much more generously supplied rocketry programmes.

The irony of soft technology is that its extreme importance creates only a few opportunities for outside control. After all, it is largely a matter of domestic politics, usually insulated from the influence of foreign powers. As such, soft technology is of greatest relevance to international non-proliferation efforts as an index of a country's proliferation potential, as evidence of the likelihood that a country will succeed in developing long-range rockets. Would-be proliferators pose the greatest threat of successful rocket development when they competently manage the gauntlet of soft factors that stand between success and unmitigated waste.

The regional missile programmes with greatest potential are not always those with easiest access to equipment but those best able to master the problems of designing and implementing a development programme. A nation's rocketry programme is more likely to lead to successful and timely deployment if it can meet the following five conditions.

1. The programme is conceived with *deliberate dual-use goals,* using the inherent relationship between military and civilian technology to maximize domestic support and strengthen international justifications for the programme.

2. It is implemented by a *strong state*, asserting top–down control over rocket development and concentrating resources into a single major programme, while insulating it from interruptions by domestic critics or international adversaries.

3. *Budgets* are set at reasonable levels early in the course of the programme while finances are concentrated on one overall programme and a single project at a time.

4. The programme utilizes an *incremental development strategy* to reduce technical risk and maximize the utility of accomplishments.

5. It has *strong and continuous leadership* by a small number of programme leaders and a large and well-trained support staff.

Although outside powers do not have a great deal of leverage over the soft side of a regional country's missile development, the foregoing analysis does point to the ways in which non-proliferation efforts can be more effective. A recurrent theme is the importance of early action. Stopping even a young project may not be easy, but if well run it will evolve into a full-scale programme that is even more difficult to deal with. As a programme matures and becomes more advanced and better institutionalized, it tends to lose its susceptibility to outside influence. A well-managed missile programme gains momentum as it advances, acquiring progressively more resources and support. Towards the end of the development process it may become so strongly insulated that only the most extreme combination of external and domestic pressure or political change can affect its progress.

Some aspects of soft technology are more dependent on the cooperation of foreign governments, making them more susceptible to control. The foreign education and training of engineering students and programme personnel depend entirely on the tacit approval of the host country. By inhibiting the staffing of a project, more aggressive restrictions on opportunities for students to study abroad could significantly slow proliferation efforts in most regional powers. Such measures will not stop rocket development in any but the least advanced countries; even technically weak countries like Indonesia, Iran or Libya have a small cadre of domestic engineers able to sustain rocketry projects at a gradual pace. Nor are proscriptions on access to foreign education and training likely to have a rapid effect. Restrictions on foreign training are more consequential in the long term, especially as a force against the acceleration or enlargement of a country's missile programme.

Another area where outside powers can influence the soft side of rocketry development is through control over financing. Much greater attention still needs to be paid to the reliance of emerging powers on commercial credit and foreign financial assistance. Initiatives like the FATF must be strengthened and oriented more explicitly to serve non-proliferation. An especially promising possibility for proliferation control is making foreign financial aid and assistance explicitly conditional on halting or restructuring rocketry programmes. If aggressively asserted, conditionality could have an almost instantaneous effect on rocketry development in many countries.

There are few other aspects of soft technology that promise facile influence over missile proliferation. An understanding of the role of soft technology is more important for appreciation of the general problems of missile development and the analysis of specific regional programmes. Outside control will have to rely more on the leverage of hard technology. The physical equipment, the hardware of rocketry and missile development, will remain the foundation of export controls and missile non-proliferation for years to come.

5. The hard technology: building ballistic missiles

I. Introduction

The creation of any large and complicated machine results from weaving together many different and often overlooked types of technology. The soft technologies—the political choices and organizational, economic and personal factors—form the general context for development, making large programmes possible and predisposing them to success or failure. They create the environment in which scientists and engineers apply their labours. The physical technology of rocketry naturally gets more attention. It is more impressive and tangible, but it is only part of the proliferation problem and not always the most important part.

Even if it is not the whole story of proliferation, the physical or hard technology is the basic target of non-proliferation efforts, if only because of its visibility and amenability to outside control. By examining a country's choices in its rocket hardware, the paths pursued and those not taken, outside analysts can begin to assess its missile potential. Even with relatively little information about specific projects it is possible to evaluate their potential performance and military implications. With more detailed information it is possible to identify the critical weaknesses of a project and the points where foreign controls are most likely to be effective.

This chapter gives an overview of the basic technical problems that would-be proliferators must overcome in order to build their own long-range ballistic missiles. The same technical problems have major implications for control. A fundamental conclusion is that the technologies required to build rockets with ranges of up to 120–150 km are so widely available that outside restraint of their spread will require immense effort and still achieve only partial success. The real battle for control will be fought over rockets of 150- to 1000-km range, within the *technological plateau*, where essential technologies are widely available but still require a great deal of foreign assistance to master. Beyond this plateau, proliferation control efforts are easier. Missiles which can carry a 500-kg payload beyond 1000 km depend on an immense variety of technology, much of it very different from that used in smaller rockets. The technical demands of such rockets create numerous opportunities for outside control.

The basic scientific and conceptual problems of rocket flight do not require elaboration here. Such considerations are not essential to an understanding of the technical aspects of proliferation, nor are they easily conveyed in normal language. Many authors have tried to convey advanced chemical, mathematical

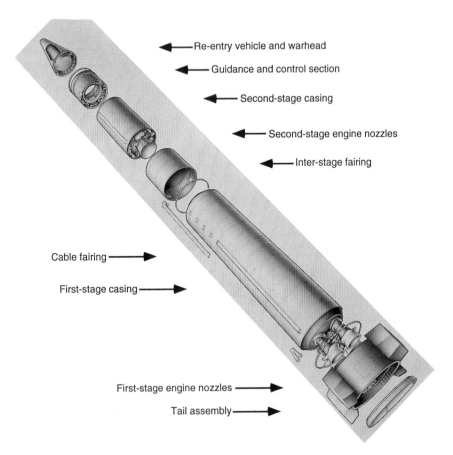

Re-entry vehicle and warhead

Guidance and control section

Second-stage casing

Second-stage engine nozzles

Inter-stage fairing

Cable fairing

First-stage casing

First-stage engine nozzles

Tail assembly

Figure 5.1. The major components of a long-range ballistic missile (Photograph courtesy of Aérospatiale)

and physical phenomena in everyday language, but few have succeeded. In practice, virtually all efforts to portray in normal language the theoretical side of a complicated technology like rocketry fall prey to the dilemma of being either banal or incomprehensible.[1]

Fortunately for policy makers and students of international security, the key to halting the spread of ballistic missiles does not lie in the arcane equations and impenetrable jargon of subjects like gas dynamics or delta-minimum inertial guidance. Rather, what matters most is an appreciation of the diversity and scale of the problems involved. The control of missile proliferation is, above all, a political problem of regulating technical activity. It does not require the

---

[1] A partial exception is the introduction to the theoretical problems of long-range ballistic missiles in Tsipis, K., *Arsenal: Understanding Weapons in the Nuclear Age* (Simon and Schuster: New York, 1983), chapter 5. A more mathematically derived review is given in Constant, J. N., *Fundamentals of Strategic Weapons: Offense and Defense Systems* (Martinus Nijhoff: The Hague, 1981).

work of rocket scientists, only the steady concern of technically alert public officials.

This chapter examines the physical characteristics of rocket development and production, stressing the most significant obstacles confronting countries trying to develop their first long-range missiles. These technical hurdles are divided into five basic categories and discussed in the approximate order in which a rocket maker must deal with them, starting at the tail and proceeding towards the nose, and finally to assembly of the entire package (see figure 5.1). The discussion starts with the major components—propulsion, guidance systems and re-entry vehicles—and finishes with the greatest problems of systems integration—stage separation and flight-testing. Chapters 6 and 7 deal with the final category of technology essential for a complete missile force: armament.

II. Propulsion

A century after large rockets were conceived they remain, despite their power and well-known capabilities, an amazingly inefficient way to move anything. About three-quarters of the weight of any rocket consists of its engine, propellants, containers and piping. A schematic drawing of a rocket basically shows a propulsion system, with other bits and pieces stuck here and there. The tremendous power of a large rocket is the product of controlled chemical burning, releasing explosive force but requiring a peculiarly delicate arrangement of parts and chemicals. Because of its innate inefficiency, designers have no choice but to accept risks to boost performance, risks that would be totally unacceptable in almost any other field. Even the most robust rocket is acutely sensitive to mishandling, liable either to explode at any time or to do nothing at the wrong moment.

All chemical rocket propulsion involves combining an oxidizer and a fuel for burning in a combustion chamber, releasing a stream of exhaust gases which moves the rocket. The basic requirement is for high power to carry useful payloads over long distances. The power that can be produced by typical propellant combinations is summarized in table 5.1. The usual measure of propulsive efficiency is specific impulse or I_{sp} (the kilograms of thrust released by burning 1 kg of propellant in one second).[2] The figures given in the table assume near-perfect combustion and gas flow. Actual performance tends to be lower owing to various inefficiencies and imperfect atmospheric conditions. In general, an actual I_{sp} of 190 or higher is potentially sufficient for large-rocket flight.

The propulsive efficiency of a propellant combination is only one aspect of its usefulness. Many of the theoretically most desirable propellants have huge disadvantages. The term 'rocket fuel' did not become a common metaphor by accident. Its high power often comes at the expense of numerous dangers and difficulties. Many of the most powerful oxidizers and fuels (e.g., liquid oxygen

---

[2] Sutton, G. P., *Rocket Propulsion Elements*, 3rd edn (John Wiley: New York, 1963), p. 19.

Table 5.1. Performance of major rocket propellants

Type	Oxidizer	Fuel	Storable?	T_c	I_{sp}
Liquid	Oxygen	Hydrogen	No	4 180	366
	Nitric acid (HNO_3NO_2)	Hydrazine	No	5 100	277
	Oxygen	UDMH ($(CH_3)NNH_2$)	Partially	5 450	276
	Oxygen	RP-1 (kerosene)	Partially	5 650	266
	Nitrogen tetroxide (N_2O_4)	Hydrazine	Partially	4 990	265
	Nitrogen tetroxide	UDMH	Yes	5 390	256
	Inhibited nitric acid	UDMH	Yes	4 900	250
Solid, double-based	Nitro-cellulose and nitro-glycerine		Yes	1 400	220
Solid composite	$KClO_4$	C_2H_4O	Yes	1 200	210
	NH_4NO_3	C_2H_4O	Yes	1 200	200
	$AP+KNO_3$	C_2H_4O	Yes	1 140	195

T_c = combustion temperature in degrees F.

I_{sp} = specific impulse in kilograms of thrust, per kilogram of propellant consumed per second, at sea level conditions.

Sources: Constant, J. N., *Fundamentals of Strategic Weapons*: Offense *and Defense Systems*, vol. 1 (Martinus Nijhoff: The Hague, 1981); and Sutton, G. P., *Rocket Propulsion Elements*, 6th edn (John Wiley: New York, 1992).

or hydrogen) must be stored at extremely low temperatures and will evaporate rapidly once pumped into a rocket. A few are virtually impossible to store for long: nitric acid, for example, will corrode its way out of almost any container. Others, such as nitrogen tetroxide, will not burn if the outside temperature rises or falls beyond narrow limits. Some fuels, such as hydrazine, are explosive when exposed to air or materials such as grease. Nitroglycerine is very intolerant of mishandling. Others, such as aniline, are highly poisonous when touched or breathed.

Liquid propellants

The first large rockets used liquid propellants because they produce more power than solids. This choice was an easy one at the time but could not obscure the greater dangers and disadvantages of liquid propellants. Not only are most liquid propellants themselves dangerous and volatile, but their use requires complicated tanks, high-speed pumps, fuel-injection systems, combustion-chamber cooling and high-pressure plumbing, regulators and ignition systems. Even in elegant designs, these can cause serious problems of excess weight, poor reliability and high maintenance requirements. Consequently, liquid propellants are usually regarded as poor choices for ballistic missiles.[3]

Some authorities dismiss the utility of liquid propellants for military applications altogether. A few—notably Indian officials—have gone so far as to argue that exports of liquid propulsion systems should be freed of controls because they are best suited for space launchers.[4] This argument overlooks important advantages of liquid propellants that make them well suited for ballistic missiles. Most can be produced by previously established chemical industries. They burn at lower pressures, permitting simpler construction of the rocket airframe and combustion chamber. They also permit the use of regenerative cooling of the combustion chamber.[5] Fuel flow can be regulated in flight or shut off altogether, making control of the rocket much easier. Above all, liquids can produce 15–40 per cent more thrust than solids—a vital consideration, especially when early and inefficient rocket designs are involved.[6]

Space launch vehicles undoubtedly are more tolerant of the peculiarities of liquid propellants; unlike ballistic missiles, SLVs do not need to be moved rapidly on the ground and they can be gently coaxed through countdown procedures lasting days or even weeks. In practice, space launchers can be designed around solid propellants almost as easily as liquids. Japan's first satellite, for example, was launched by a Lamba-series solid-fuel vehicle. All Indian space launch vehicles have solid-fuel main engines. Indeed, contrary to the assertions of some Indian spokesmen that solids are military and liquids civilian, in India liquid propellants play a bigger role in ballistic missiles than SLVs.

Some of the worst problems with liquid propellants have been tamed or solved over the years, making them much easier to handle. Most of this work, like most fuel research, originated in the United States and was subsequently transferred around the world. Techniques developed in the 1950s made it possible to store one of the best fuels for short-range missiles, nitric acid (Red Fuming Nitric Acid, or RFNA), by mixing it with other compounds.[7] Storable RFNA is used in the US Lance missile deployed widely in Europe in the 1970s and transferred to Israel in 1976, and also in the Soviet SS-21 Tochka, deployed in the early 1980s and sold to Syria and Yemen. Similarly, hydrazine was made storable and less explosive in the form of unsymmetrical dimethyl-hydrazine (UDMH) and a storable, reliable fuel was developed out of nitrogen tetroxide

[3] Balaschak, M. *et al.*, *Assessing the Comparability of Dual-Use Technologies for Ballistic Missile Development* (Center for International Studies, Massachusetts Institute of Technology: Cambridge, Mass., June 1981), pp. 45–46; and Manfredi, A. F., Jr *et al.*, *Ballistic Missile Proliferation in the Third World*, Report 86-29 (Congressional Research Service: Washington, DC, 24 Apr. 1986), pp. 7–8.

[4] 'India slams US for role in Russian rocket deal', *Journal of Commerce*, 27 Apr. 1992, p. 4.

[5] Regenerative cooling uses the flow of propellant coming out of the tanks, channelling it through ducting surrounding the combustion chamber, which it cools before it is injected into the engine. This permits lighter engine design and the use of relatively common materials. Although the method sounds complicated, it has been used since the early 1930s.

[6] Constant (note 1), pp. 101–3.

[7] The best version is known as Inhibited Red Fuming Nitric Acid (IRFNA), a mixture typically with 14% N_2O_4 and 2% H_2O, developed in the 1950s at the Jet Propulsion Laboratory, Pasadena, Calif.

(N_2O_4), usually by mixing it with kerosene.[8] The latter two were used together for the first time in the US Titan-2 ICBM, first deployed in 1964. These propellants were quickly applied to US space launchers, but their military origins are not in dispute.

For reasons that are not obvious, the results of this research were quickly declassified and are readily available today. The Soviet Union acquired these propellant concepts from the United States and, after experimentation and modification, applied them in almost all its liquid-fuel ballistic missiles introduced after 1964.[9] The first fully acceptable Soviet ICBM, sufficiently practical and reliable to justify extensive, long-term deployment, the SS-9, used a UDMH/N_2O_4 propellant combination very similar to that in the Titan-2. Soviet rocket designers continued to rely on this fuel combination in their new rockets until the early 1980s. China received these formulas from the Soviet Union in the late 1950s and also through the defection of Tsien Hsue-Shen, who brought propellant expertise from his work at the Jet Propulsion Laboratory, in Pasadena, California.[10]

Even engine technology for use with clumsy propellants like liquid oxygen or hydrogen may lead to military applications. Most early ballistic missiles—including the German V-2, the Soviet SS-6 and the US Atlas—were designed to use liquid oxygen. This choice was made largely because more easily storable propellants were still too experimental at the time. For a regional actor today, however, such a missile could be sufficient, especially if the principal motive is symbolic rather than purely strategic. Other countries may try to acquire such obsolescent technology with the intention of modifying it later to use more convenient storable fuels. This is how the Soviet Union was able to preserve the utility of some of its rockets originally developed for liquid oxygen propellant. Prominent examples include the SS-4 Sandal and SS-5 Skean IRBMs, designed in the 1950s to use liquid oxygen but converted in the early 1960s to use storable UDMH and N_2O_4 and kept in service for another 25 years. A similar propellant modification converted the Scud missile into a viable weapon.[11]

Smaller tactical missiles also can serve as a source for propulsion technology. Although they are designed for other roles, their sub-systems can be borrowed for ballistic applications. Liquid-propelled surface-to-air missiles have proved to be especially suitable. Virtually any tactical missile of sufficient size—an anti-ship or air-to-ground weapon, for example—can be adapted to ballistic missions. In the 1950s many larger surface-to-air (anti-aircraft) missile systems were designed with secondary ground-to-ground missions in mind. A classic example is Western Electric's Nike-Hercules, a large anti-aircraft missile

---

[8] Clark, J. D., *Ignition! An Informal History of Liquid Rocket Propellants* (Rutgers University Press: New Brunswick, 1972), pp. 43–46, 57–63.

[9] Clark (note 8), p. 118.

[10] Lewis, J. W. and Hua Di, 'China's ballistic missile programs: technologies, strategies, goals', *International Security*, autumn 1992, p. 13.

[11] The Scud-B uses SG-02 Tonka 250 (UDMH) and IRFNA. Zaloga, S., 'Thirty years of Scud development', *International Defense Review*, Nov. 1988, p. 1426.

weighing 4720 kg, almost as much as a Scud. It can be fired at ground targets as far as 180 km away.[12] In 1978 South Korea publicized its intentions to use its US-supplied Nike missiles in exactly this role, causing a diplomatic crisis.[13] More recently, Serbian forces in Bosnia used Soviet-supplied SA-2 Guideline (or V-75 Dvina) anti-aircraft missiles to attack cities controlled by Bosnian Muslims.[14] The Soviet counterpart to the Nike-Hercules, the SA-2, weighs 2450 kg and has a ground-to-ground range of up to 43 km.[15]

While many tactical missiles can be used in surface-to-surface roles, few have propulsion systems readily suitable for use in new ballistic missiles. Liquid-fuel engine missiles are most adaptable, but few tactical missiles introduced since the early 1960s have used liquid-fuel engines. Newer battlefield missiles also tend to be much smaller, having grown more efficient over time, making them even less suitable as a basis for ballistic missiles. Even though such systems provide a less than ideal starting-point, countries confronted by stiff export controls may try to work with tactical systems that were previously imported. Others may use tactical missiles as second or third stages to improve the range or accuracy of their ballistic missiles.

The liquid propulsion systems of older missiles like the SA-2 can be adapted for ballistic missiles, as seen in India's Prithvi. The propulsion system of the SA-2 main engine, using storable kerosene fuel and Inhibited Red Fuming Nitric Acid (IRFNA), is ideal for use in Scud-range ballistic missiles.[16] By clustering engines and increasing fuel capacity, ranges of up to several hundred kilometres can potentially be achieved. There are limits to this approach, however. The engines especially tend to be too small to be used in long-range ballistic missiles without massive re-development. While tactical missile engines may provide a would-be proliferator with a way to begin, other approaches must be found to propel rockets over 1000-km ranges.

While emerging powers can be expected to cope with the problems of most liquid fuels themselves, the mechanical and metallurgical demands of liquid-fuel engines raise more imposing barriers. Serious challenges come from the demands on high-performance pumps that inject huge volumes of propellant in precise quantities into the combustion chamber. Other difficulties come from the problems of cooling the combustion chamber and exhaust nozzle. So long as proliferators try to develop missiles with ranges of only up to about 300 km, equipment of the kind found in the Soviet Scud will usually be adequate. At longer ranges the burn time must be longer so that engine cooling becomes

[12] Gunston, B., *The Illustrated Encyclopedia of the World's Rockets and Missiles* (Crescent Books: New York, 1979), p. 171.

[13] Hayes, P., *International Missile Trade and the Two Koreas* (Program for Nonproliferation Studies, Monterey Institute of International Studies: Monterey, Calif., Mar. 1993), p. 8; and Nolan, J. E., *Trappings of Power: Ballistic Missiles in the Third World* (Brookings Institution: Washington, DC, 1991), p. 50.

[14] Cohen, R., 'Serbs attack Muslim town with anti-aircraft missiles', *New York Times*, 5 Nov. 1994, p. 5.

[15] Zaloga, S. J., *Soviet Air Defence Missiles: Design, Development and Tactics* (Jane's Information Group: Coulsdon, Surrey, 1989), p. 174.

[16] The characteristics of the SA-2 are examined at length in Zaloga (note 15), pp. 36–76.

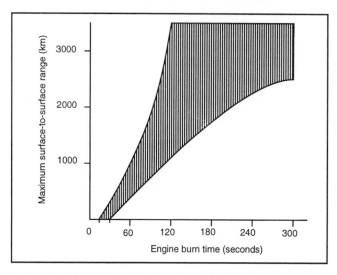

Figure 5.2. Typical engine burn times for single-stage rockets

progressively more difficult, pumps develop irregularities, and vibration inter-feres with the flow of propellants and control systems (see figure 5.2). Any of these problems can lead to catastrophic failure. At ranges beyond 800–1000 km, such a system tends to self-destruct in ways that cannot be minimized sufficiently through improvisation. Instead, entirely new engine materials, com-ponents and concepts are necessary.

The only reliable solution to these problems is foreign assistance. It was problems with such large rockets that led India to sign a contract with France in 1976 for the Viking liquid-fuel engine used in its PSLV space launcher. In 1989 Brazil tried unsuccessfully to acquire a version of the same engine for its VLS space rocket. In lieu of foreign help, a country has no choice but to scale up its existing engine technology and develop new methods and sub-systems when that fails. This is laborious and requires decades of maximum national effort. However, it is possible, as China showed by developing the engines it received from the USSR in 1957 (R-101s of 43 tonnes thrust) into the engines for its DF-4 ICBM of the 1980s (the YF-20, giving 284 tonnes thrust).[17]

Solid propellants

The elaborate machinery of liquid-fuel engines looks very messy and compli-cated, especially compared to the brutal simplicity of solid-fuel engines. Instead of tanks, pumps, pipes and numerous control systems, a solid-fuel entine needs no more than an igniter and a mass of fuel in a casing that ends with a nozzle. In practice, however, all the essential elements of liquid propulsion were

[17] Clark, P. S., 'Chinese launch vehicles—Chang Zheng 3', *Jane's Intelligence Review,* Aug. 1992, p. 373.

developed long ago in the days of Goddard and the V-2. Despite the intricacies, their technical demands are easier to deal with than some of the problems encountered in more advanced solid-fuel systems. The apparent elegance of large solid-propellant rockets can be very deceptive.

The choice between solid- and liquid-fuel engines is not as straightforward as is sometimes portrayed. Nevertheless, solid fuels are highly advantageous. Because they are much easier to handle and operate, solid propellants are typically assumed to be the best choice for ballistic missiles. Once deployed, most solid-fuel engines can be left for years with only minimal maintenance. The annual operating, maintenance and personnel costs of the USA's first solid-fuel ICBM, the Minuteman-1, were about 10 per cent of those of its liquid-fuel predecessors, the Atlas and Titan-1.[18] Unlike heavier and bulkier liquid-fuel systems, solid-fuel rockets are relatively easy to move, making them simpler to hide and shelter from pre-emptive attack. With few moving parts, they can usually be kept at a high state of readiness for extended periods, typically with several months between inspections and minor maintenance, and can be launched in minutes. As for longevity, NASA relies on Minuteman stages (especially the second-stage engine assembly) that are 30 years old for its largest contemporary sounding rockets. Retired Honest John, Terrier and Nike engines from the 1950s are still being recycled the same way.[19]

The operating advantages of solid propellants are offset by serious shortcomings and difficulties that newcomers to the field may find especially difficult to overcome. Above all, solid propellants produce lower thrust, pound for pound, than liquids. In practice this means that solid-fuel rockets will have shorter range and carry less payload. As a result there is a tendency to use solid propellants for short-range missiles and to rely on liquid systems for longer ranges. Although solids are easier to store and move, they are also sensitive to temperature changes, humidity and ageing as well as shocks and vibration. Without very careful treatment the propellant will decompose, often loosening from the sides of the rocket or cracking, which can lead to disaster in flight.

As with liquids, research on solid propellants of the 1940s and 1950s reduced some of their most serious disadvantages. Although the conceptual and quality control problems have changed little over time, fuel scientists had great success in reducing manufacturing problems and improving their useful thrust. The first fully successful solid propellants were the double-base solids, first developed in the Soviet Union in the 1930s for artillery rockets and other small tactical missiles. Still used in such systems today, these combined the standard artillery propellant, nitrocellulose, with nitroglycerine to achieve high thrust, of the order of 215 I_{sp} or greater.

Relatively simple to produce, double-base solids are within the reach of most ammunition companies experienced in large-calibre artillery shells. They have been mastered by several regional powers, including Brazil, India, Iran, Israel

---

[18] Greenwood, J. T., 'The Air Force ballistic missile and space program, 1954–1974', *Aerospace Historian*, Dec. 1974, p. 200.

[19] Discussion with NASA officials, Goddard Space Flight Center, Wallops Flight Facility, Nov. 1994.

and South Africa. The wide availability of double-base propellants is probably the most important factor in making the spread of smaller rockets and missiles virtually uncontrollable. Such rockets, after all, need little more than a double-base solid-fuel engine and a warhead. The only solace for control efforts lies in the fact that because of manufacturing and operating problems double-base solids are not appropriate for larger applications. Usually they must be extruded into shape (pressed through a form like a sausage) and cannot be cast for large-diameter engines without losing significant thrust. They also tend to burn too quickly and irregularly for large rockets.[20]

Solids for large rockets are based on a totally different approach. In the 1940s and 1950s scientists at the Jet Propulsion Laboratory developed the first composite solids, which mix an oxidizer—typically ammonium perchlorate (AP)—with a plastic, resinous fuel binder such as asphalt or rubber.[21] Although less powerful than earlier solids, with a typical I_{sp} of 180–210, composites can be cast in large diameters for use in larger rockets. One more innovation was necessary to raise thrust sufficiently for their use in rockets with ranges of 1000 km or greater. This was the single most important propellant development since the 1930s. By adding high-energy metal powder, such as 10 per cent of aluminium, to a solid-propellant mixture, thrust could be boosted by 10–15 I_{sp}.[22] Formulated by the US Thiokol Chemical Corporation in the mid-1950s, this seemingly small improvement created enormous possibilities. It led directly to the Polaris submarine-launched IRBM, the Scout space launcher and the Minuteman-1 ICBM, all deployed in the early 1960s.

For emerging missile manufacturers, however, serious obstacles still inhibit the development of solid-fuel rockets. By the early 1960s the theory and concepts of boosted composite solid propellants had been well publicized.[23] Nevertheless, many of the chemicals are not readily available and require special fabrication technologies. Countries such as Brazil and India were able to acquire production assistance in the 1970s and early 1980s, but foreign export controls have become a difficult hurdle since then. In 1989, for example, Iran was prevented from illegally importing 190 tonnes of ammonium perchlorate,

---

[20] The best introduction to double-base propellants is Warren, F. A., *Rocket Propellants* (Reinhold: New York, 1958), pp. 6–10 and chapter 3. The lack of progress since then is illustrated by Austruy, H., 'Double-based propellants', ed. A. Davenas, *Solid Rocket Propulsion Technology* (Pergamon: Oxford, 1993), pp. 369–414.

[21] Ley, W., *Rockets, Missiles and Space Travel*, revised edn (Chapman and Hall: London, 1957), pp. 190–96.

[22] A typical solid-propellant mixture for a long-range rocket might include 67.5% ammonium perchlorate, 22.5% fuel binder and 10% aluminium. Barräre, M. *et al.*, *Rocket Propulsion* (Elsevier: Amsterdam, 1960), pp. 215–21; and Davenas, A., 'The main families and use of solid propellants', in Davenas (note 20), pp. 329–68.

[23] See, e.g., Grove, A. and Conway, J. B., 'Combustion of metals in oxygen', *Industrial Engineering and Chemistry*, Apr. 1958; Yaffee, M., 'High energy solid fuels may be hybrids', *Aviation Week & Space Technology*, 23 June 1958; and Zaehringer, A. J., 'Polyurethane-polysulfide battle is raging', *Missiles and Rockets*, 12 Jan. 1959, pp. 16–17. Although no technical field can ever be considered completed, it is generally agreed that the chemistry of solid propellants is thoroughly understood and no substantially new fuels will be developed. Davenas, A., 'Conclusion', in Davenas (note 20), pp. 588–90.

enough oxidizer for about 300 rockets in the 90- to 140-km range class.[24] In 1993 Libya was prevented from completing a similar purchase.[25]

Not only is access to the necessary compounds restricted, but the manufacturing processes are still highly classified, albeit more for commercial than national security reasons. Casting an even, pure mixture is a serious test of manufacturing skill, as are the problems of carefully drying or curing and binding the propellant to the rocket airframe.[26] France overcame these problems only by swallowing its pride and turning to the US Government and Thiokol Chemical Corporation for help. Left to its own devices, China did not launch its first large solid-propellant rocket until 1982.[27] It appears that problems like these prevented the Soviet Union from deploying its first successful solid-propellant ballistic missile until 1976, when the SS-20 appeared. Not until deployment of the fifth-generation SS-24, initially deployed in 1987, did the USSR master solid propellants sufficiently to build a successful solid-fuel ICBM.[28]

Solid propulsion raises other technical problems in addition to those related to the characteristics of the propellant. Three deserve special attention. Among the most serious is the problem of engine cooling. Solid fuels burn at higher temperatures than most liquids, creating serious cooling problems. Unlike liquids, however, solid propellants cannot be circulated around the combustion chamber for cooling purposes. Instead, designers must rely on highly advanced materials and the use of complicated aerodynamic cooling techniques. Another problem is that solids are less powerful than liquids, even after the introduction of composites, making excess weight a more serious problem than with liquid propellants. One response has been to abandon metal in much of the airframe and to rely on fibreglass filament for external casings, creating yet another technical hurdle for newcomers. Finally, the propellant flow cannot be regulated or cut off, making control over the rocket's trajectory more difficult. Instead, designers must rely on a variety of aerodynamic braking systems for control.

These problems expose the irony of solid propulsion; although created to overcome the difficulties of relying on liquids to propel ballistic missiles, solids are in many respects more suitable for space launch applications. With space launchers, the problems with using solids can be addressed in advance. Satellite orbits, launch weights and rocket payload can be designed together, satellite

[24] Houston, P. and Kempster, N., 'U.S. trying to halt Iran rocket fuel', Los Angeles Times, 19 Mar. 1989, p. 1.
[25] Gordon, M. R., 'U.S. tries to stop Russia–Libya deal', International Herald Tribune, 24 June 1993, p. 3.
[26] Barräre et al. (note 22), pp. 221–31.
[27] Villain, J., La Force de Dissuasion: Genese et evolution [The deterrent force: creation and evolution] (Éditions Larivière: Paris, 1987), p. 61; and Lewis and Hua Di (note 10), pp. 26–31.
[28] Cochran, T. B. et al., Nuclear Weapons Databook, Vol. IV: Soviet Nuclear Weapons (Harper and Row: New York, 1989), pp. 124, 132, 210. The Soviet Union deployed limited numbers of an earlier solid fuel ICBM, the SS-13, in the early 1970s. Berman and Baker note that 'Serious technical problems associated with the SS-13's guidance system and solid-fuel motor apparently hampered its development'. Berman, R. P. and Baker, J. C., Soviet Strategic Forces (Brookings Institution: Washington, DC, 1982), p. 54.

launch trajectories are less demanding and allow cruder control, and engine cut-off can be designed in at the manufacturing stage. The cliché that solids are military and liquids are civilian may be useful at a general level, but it is almost meaningless in application.

Implications for control

Although rocket engine concepts, propellants and hardware were thoroughly developed by the mid-1960s, the technology remains difficult if not impossible for all but the largest and most advanced countries to master independently. Every country which has pursued rocket development since 1945 has begun by borrowing heavily from innovations elsewhere. Although most had performed important indigenous research, without exception they found their own capabilities insufficient and were compelled to rely on technology transferred from abroad. All evidence suggests that this need to start with the accomplishments of others has not been replaced over time.

None the less, the importance of technology transfer does not translate automatically into easy and effective export controls. With liquid propellant formulas already in the public domain, there is probably little that can be done to halt their spread. Better targets for control are the materials and manufacturing technology for critical items, such as rocket casings, fuel pumps, regulators, engine combustion chambers and igniters. None of these items relies on recent or highly abstruse technologies of the sort that is easiest to control. However, the expense and difficulty of mastering them on their own will be enough to discourage all but the most determined proliferators.

Large solid-fuel engines are even more amenable to outside control. Although many solid-propellant formulas are well known, the manufacturing equipment and skills for solid propellants impose technical demands, making them ideal for export control. Russia and China acquired solid-propellant formulas from the United States, but still needed decades of intense effort to apply them successfully. Their trials and tribulations leave no doubt that proper security and export controls can slow the spread of that technology. The fact that several regional powers were able to make faster progress with solids—especially Argentina, Brazil, India and Israel—is proof only of the enormous importance of foreign assistance, without which they would have achieved much less. For new proliferators, solid propellants may be technically appealing, but liquids will be easier to master, for both civil and military applications.

III. Guidance

Not all rockets require guidance systems. One of the many advantages of extremely short-range systems—artillery and sounding rockets—is that clean aerodynamics and high acceleration alone can provide acceptable accuracy at ranges of up to 90 km. With refinement and development, range might be extended to some 140 km. Beyond this distance drag, wind and drift conspire against the flight of even the best designed rocket, forcing designers to rely on active guidance to ensure acceptable accuracy. When accuracy is especially important, even short-range missiles such as the US Lance and the Russian SS-21 (maximum range of each typically 120 km) are designed with active guidance.

Rockets designed for longer maximum range are exposed to greater disruptive forces and require continuous compensation. Because of their physical mass, larger rockets accelerate more slowly than small ones. At the beginning of the engine burn they are subject to winds and innumerable engine irregularities. Without monitoring and correction during these first few seconds a large rocket will tend to corkscrew uselessly like a toy balloon suddenly released from one's fingers. During the longer period of acceleration, atmospheric conditions and the natural tendency to drift tend to push the rocket away from its intended course, and so additional correction is required. Finally, each stage must be terminated at a precise velocity to ensure a useful trajectory. The guidance system need not be perfect, but its role is essential.[29] No guidance system can eliminate inaccuracy; as range grows, inaccuracy becomes progressively more difficult to correct (see figure 5.3). The goal is rather to keep the missile sufficiently accurate to perform its mission at an acceptable cost.

Guidance is an ideal target for export control. Not only is it essential for large rockets, but it relies on highly advanced pieces of equipment, such as high-performance gyros, on-board computers and control mechanisms. Apart from Germany and the United States no country has managed to develop guidance systems for long-range missiles without large-scale foreign help. Even the United States built on a head start from its German inheritance. It is little wonder that guidance is seen as 'the Achilles heel of incipient missile development programs'.[30] A narrow technology available from few sources, it is the clearest point on which missile export controls can be focused.

Like all technical leads, this one is a diminishing asset. The degree of accuracy which a determined neophyte can achieve with minimal outside help is improving. There are relative limits to the accuracy which emerging missile powers can achieve on their own compared to the established powers, but their absolute abilities are undoubtedly improving over time. Their efforts are aided by the openness of Western engineering schools and major laboratories, where students from all but a few suspect countries can train. They also benefit from their ability to study and modify commercially available guidance systems for related applications, especially aircraft, artillery and tactical missiles. Above

---

[29] In the words of Frederick Winsor and Marian Perry:
    'Peter Pater, astrogator,
    lost his orbit calculator
    out among the asteroids.
    They rang the Lutine Bell at Lloyds.'
From Winsor, F. and Perry, M., *The Space Child's Mother Goose* (Simon and Schuster: New York, 1958).

[30] Nolan (note 13), p. 34.

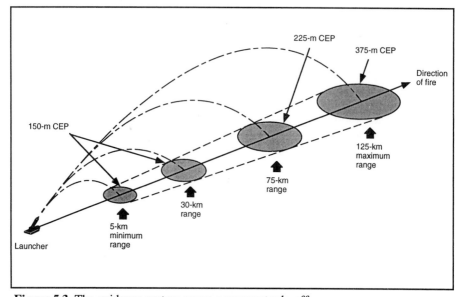

Figure 5.3. The guidance system range–accuracy trade-off

Illustrated by the US Lance missile, guided by strap-down gyros with radio correction.

all, they now enjoy the advantage of government support at home. In countries such as India, Israel, Taiwan and perhaps others, defence and science ministries have learned the same lesson as export controllers—that guidance matters.

The most important guidance options for the near future involve technologies that are relatively old and well understood, especially inertial guidance, strapdown systems and radio correction. In the long term other technologies that seem more exotic today may be even easier for emerging rocket makers to master. Some, such as laser gyros, are already in use but require more refinement for most applications. Others, such as optical and radar guidance for re-entry vehicles, are already well developed but are still too demanding for most countries. Some require major technical breakthroughs: one possibility is major refinements in filament technologies that would permit guidance signals to be sent along a wire connected to the rocket.

Although this chapter emphasizes the most mature and readily available guidance technology, one other possibility should be kept in mind in the not-so-distant future. The US Global Positioning System (GPS), a network of 24 navigational satellites, was developed with the needs of the US military in mind. The signals currently made available to commercial users can provide ground positions to within 100–150 metres. GPS is already used to guide commercial aircraft travelling at speeds below 850 km per hour and could be adapted to guide cruise missiles as well. The more accurate signals available to the US military are used for faster aircraft and Tomahawk cruise missiles.[31]

The commercially available GPS signals are too inaccurate and require too much computation time to be of much use for ballistic missiles. The closest application today is for missile ground crews, who can use GPS to help align a missile's guidance just before launch.[32] The more accurate and refined military GPS signals can be used by ballistic missiles, although a regional actor would have to provide huge computer facilities to make use of the same signals in a fast-moving rocket.[33] Such a system will have serious liabilities, because it depends on a foreign-controlled satellite system which can be turned off or altered. As commercially available GPS signals improve, however, the GPS option will become more important.

The most important form of active guidance available today for long-range applications, the inertial navigation system (INS), has long been the primary focus of missile technology controls. Export controls on guidance technologies have improved markedly since the days of lax controls in the late 1970s when the problem was first recognized. It is increasingly clear, however, that regional powers are acquiring the ability to manufacture INS on their own. Of greater importance, would-be missile proliferators are investing in simpler alternatives, especially strap-down and radio guidance, which promise to be fully suitable for their guidance requirements. Although export controls should continue to focus on guidance technology, it is clear that such controls are no substitute for across-the-board restraint. The effectiveness of controls on guidance will decline considerably in the next decade, with the result that guidance will lose its unique importance as a bottleneck in the process of missile proliferation. As it does, exporters will find it essential to compensate by strengthening the overall regime.

Inertial guidance systems

The advantages of a fully internal guidance system were obvious to the rocket pioneers of the 1930s. Goddard, von Braun's Rocket Team and to a lesser degree Soviet researchers all began developing gyroscope guidance systems for their initial rockets. They independently recognized the immense potential of gyros—then already used in shipboard, aircraft and artillery applications—for continuous monitoring of a rocket's motion without external assistance. By measuring the deviation of the rocket from the axis of a gyro, differences from

[31] Carus, W. S., *Cruise Missile Proliferation in the 1990s*, Washington Paper 159 (Praeger: New York, 1992), pp. 57–66; McMahon, K. S. and Gormley, D. M., *Controlling the Spread of Land-Attack Cruise Missiles,* AISC Paper no. 7 (American Institute for Strategic Cooperation: Marina del Rey, Jan. 1995), pp. 18–22, 26, 53; and 'GPS guides Tomahawk in flight test', *Flight International*, 6 Mar. 1991, p. 18.

[32] There were reports that Iraqi Scud crews tried to do this in 1991. Miller, B., 'GPS proves its worth in Operation Desert Storm', *Armed Forces Journal*, Apr. 1991, pp. 16–20.

[33] Another option is radio correction using GPS satellite guidance. In 1979 and 1980 the US Air Force tested Minuteman ICBMs with GPS receivers. Stares, P. B., *Space and National Security* (Brookings Institution: Washington, DC, 1987), p. 67.

Figure 5.4. The SG-66 inertial navigation system

A cut-away assembly of the SG-66, the first fully inertial navigation system. Developed in the closing stages of World War II for the V-2 rocket, it was not ready for use until the mid-1950s, when a more advanced version guided the US Army's Redstone rocket. Later versions were improved steadily through the addition of a second accelerometer to permit velocity measurement, use of air bearings to reduce drift, substitution of transistors and later microcircuitry to reduce size and improve reliability, and aggressive weight reduction. Later, the USA abandoned the SG-66 approach in favour of the more advanced and adaptable fluid-bearing design developed in subsequent years by Draper Laboratories. Conceptually similar sets still are in use, however, guiding Russian and Chinese missiles today. (Photograph: Smithsonian Institute)

the desired trajectory can be determined and compensating commands issued. For military applications the advantages were even greater: fully internal systems cannot be disrupted by an adversary.

The gap between mathematical theory and engineering reality is nowhere so broad as in INS. The physics and mathematics of inertial rocket navigation were completed by the Germans in the early 1940s.[34] It still took 20 years of intense work in Germany and the USA before hardware could begin to perform what theory specified with enough reliability and in a small enough package to be used in a long-range missile. Since then the science of missile guidance has matured and achieved previously undreamed of levels of accuracy.[35] Of greater relevance here is the middle stage in the operational development of INS, until the early 1960s, which saw the establishment of technical levels that regional powers can reasonably hope to emulate some day.

---

[34] A brilliantly concise review is Frye, W. E., 'On the accuracy of the long-range ballistic rocket', *Journal of Applied Physics*, May 1951, pp. 585–89. A less mathematical summary is Pitman, G. R., Jr, 'Historical notes', ed. G. R. Pitman, Jr, *Inertial Guidance* (John Wiley: New York, 1962), pp. 8–15.

[35] MacKenzie, D. A., *Inventing Accuracy: A Historical Sociology of Nuclear Missile Guidance* (MIT Press: Cambridge, Mass., 1990).

The V-2 missile was never tested with a fully independent INS. Although such a system was in an advanced stage of development when the war ended, it was years away from service. In its stead, operational V-2 missiles relied on less precise strap-down gyros and radio control, described below. The inadequacy of these systems was recognized even before they went into operation. For the future, the German rocket team expected to rely on a purely inertial system consisting of an independently stabilized platform housing three direction-sensing gyros. The gyros, supported by gimballed arms to preserve the independence of their motion, sensed changes in the missile's direction of travel. The system also included accelerometers (initially one, later two) which sensed changes in the velocity of the missiles.[36] Brought by veterans of the Peenemünde research station to the United States and the Soviet Union after World War II, the German inertial guidance project, the SG-66, became the father of all modern INS.[37]

Although elegant in concept, the reality of INS design and development quickly degenerates into innumerable small technical problems. Some devices require advanced materials, others highly advanced construction techniques. Most of these problems can be resolved only through inspired small-scale engineering and experience. The most serious problem is the tendency for gyros to 'drift' owing to friction on their mechanical bearings, losing their initial alignments and their ability to guide accurately. The first systems relied on jewelled bearings like a high-quality watch. When this proved inadequate, drift was reduced to acceptable proportions by mounting the gyros and accelerometers on a 'gas bearing', a microscopically thin layer of compressed air. Although conceived before 1945, it took years of effort to make this device work. Another team of guidance experts, under the leadership of Charles Stark Draper of MIT, achieved similar results by floating the gyros and accelerometers in a thin film of lubricating fluid. Both approaches reduced gyroscope drift from some 10 degrees *per hour* in the 1940s to less than 10 degrees *per month* by the early 1960s.

The other key to practical INS was weight reduction. The first missile to fly entirely on an active, purely inertial guidance system was a US Army Redstone fired in September 1955. Derived from the original German SG-66, the Redstone's ST-80 inertial guidance platform weighed 70 kg, or 110 kg including its external electronics and computational equipment. This was excessive, since the weight of the guidance package reduced the payload and range too much for

[36] As specified by Newton's Second Law of Motion, the velocity of a body cannot be sensed exclusively from within it. With the integration of 2 pendulous integrating accelerometers it became possible to detect changes in gravitational force equivalent to changes in velocity. See MacKenzie (note 35), pp. 66–74.

[37] MacKenzie (note 35), on whom the author otherwise relied in preparing this section, maintains (on p. 62) that the SG-66 was not a true INS because it had only one accelerometer. This misses the greater dimension of the German accomplishment. In the late 1940s, moreover, this fault in the SG-66 was rectified through the addition of a second 'Schuler tuned' accelerometer. Häusserman, W., 'Peenemünde to NASA', ed. R. H. Parvin, *Inertial Navigation* (D. Van Nostrand: Princeton, N.J., 1962), pp. 5–6; and Wrigley, W. 'The history of inertial navigation', *Journal of Navigation*, vol. 30, no. 1 (1977), pp. 61–68. Wrigley was largely responsible for this innovation, which perfected the INS concept.

the missile to complete its designed mission. Refined successively for the Jupiter and Pershing-1 IRBMs, system weight was further reduced and capabilities increased to include gyrocompassing. In the ST-120 version which guided the first Pershing missile in March 1960, weight was down to 25 kg for the guidance package, or 35 kg when including its transistorized electronics. There is no doubt that further refinement was possible. Politics, not technology, ended US work on gas-bearing missile guidance. The Pershing-1 was the last long-range ballistic missile developed by the US Army, which gave up long-range rockets to the Air Force. A relative newcomer to the rocketry business, the Air Force preferred all-American fluid-bearing gyros. Without a maker or a clientele, the gas-bearing approach became a dead-end.

Starting a few years after the German gas-bearing design was fully under development, the Draper fluid-bearing approach had to overcome even greater mechanical problems but soon surpassed the German accomplishments. Although the obstacles were difficult, the fluid-bearing approach clearly had greater potential for continuous improvement. In the US Air Force and Navy, Draper found ready converts to his alternative INS concepts. The first fully inertial Draper-designed guidance system, SPIRE, flew in a B-29 bomber in February 1953 but it was enormous—weighing several tonnes—and suitable only for large aircraft. A frenetic redesign effort packed a new Draper version into a Thor missile in 1955, but the system still weighed more than 300 kg, making it useless for any but the most generously designed missiles. Further improvement brought the weight down to a high but manageable 90 kg for the Polaris submarine-launched missiles in 1960. Inaccuracy was less of a priority while the weight battle was being fought and continued to plague Draper designs. Only after weight was brought down so that the system's bulk no longer crippled range and payload could the accuracy problem be tackled as well.[38]

Refinement of the fluid-bearing INS brought the era of rapid change and development in guidance systems to a close. Having trained what MacKenzie calls a 'guidance mafia' committed to fluid bearings, Draper has dominated US INS design ever since. This dominance narrowed the choices available to new rocket makers as well. All US ballistic missiles since Polaris and Minuteman-2 have been guided by Draper inertial systems. Further reductions in size and weight have come much more slowly, paced largely by advances in materials and microelectronics.[39] The advantages of fluid bearings did not escape other missile makers and they have gradually developed similar equipment. The Soviet Union switched to fluid designs in the ICBMs it introduced in the 1980s, and China seems likely to follow in the 2000s. Alternative INS technologies

---

[38] The gas-bearing Jupiter missile guidance permitted a CEP of 0.8 km, while the contemporary Draper fluid-bearing Thor never achieved a CEP better than 3.2 km at similar ranges. MacKenzie (note 35, pp. 131–32, 149) suggests this was due to doctrinal choice by the operating services. This makes a virtue of necessity; in those days Draper INS was just less mature.

[39] MacKenzie (note 35), pp. 118, 189.

have been developed, most notably the laser gyroscope perfected in the 1970s, but none can equal the performance of orthodox designs.[40]

With the maturation of guidance technology in the early 1960s, missile guidance reached an important juncture. Missile accuracy had reaped the greatest benefits of a technological revolution.[41] Designers could easily agree on the preferred ways to achieve desired accuracy. The equipment itself had reached a plateau; improvements would now come only slowly. Further, exponential advances in accuracy, weight, reliability and secondary features would come, but a point had been reached where progressively greater efforts would be needed to generate ever smaller improvements in performance. The leaps and jumps of revolutionary science gave way to the less exciting process of normal incremental engineering.[42]

For regional missile proliferators the INS revolution of the 1950s constitutes a plateau in performance; previous levels of performance are unacceptable, later levels are unachievable. Whether they try to buy guidance packages from abroad or to develop their own, they will almost certainly concentrate on accuracies, weights and standards of reliability comparable to those achieved by the United States in the late 1950s.

Any regional INS project will rely heavily on foreign technology. Technology transfer has been the basis for all major new inertial guidance projects since 1945. Every major missile guidance system can trace its roots from German wartime innovations, through the United States or the Soviet Union. The path of the diffusion of missile INS is outlined in figure 5.5. After starting with German gas-bearing designs, North American designers switched to fluid-bearing INS designs in the 1960s. These were passed directly to Britain and France, becoming the basis of the guidance systems used in all French long-range rockets today.[43] The Soviet Union, which relied on gas-bearing guidance systems, shared its designs and samples of early models in the late 1950s with China, where similar models remain in widespread use.[44] It is a process of diffusion that continues today, most visibly in transfers of Scud missile strap-down guidance.

The secrets of INS are closely guarded by all manufacturers, to preserve both military and commercial security. Even general performance specifications are difficult to obtain. This did not prevent the emergence of a large commercial market in the 1960s, mostly supplying INS for fighter aircraft and civilian airliners. By the mid-1980s more than 20 Western manufacturers in seven coun-

[40] The only ballistic missile known to use a laser gyroscope INS is the US ATACMS, a 135-km range weapon. It uses its internal guidance primarily to maintain stability, while relying on radio correction to guide it to the target. 'ATACMS', *World Missile Forecast* (Forecast Associates: Newtown, Conn., Jan. 1991).

[41] The concept of a technological revolution is developed by Constant, E., *The Turbojet Revolution* (Johns Hopkins University Press: Baltimore, Md., 1980).

[42] The distinction between revolutionary and normal science is from Kuhn, T. S., *The Structure of Scientific Revolutions*, 2nd edn (University of Chicago Press: Chicago, 1970), p. 10.

[43] Young, J. H., *The French Strategic Missile Programme*, Adelphi Papers no. 38 (International Institute for Strategic Studies: London, July 1967), p. 9.

[44] Hua Di, Private communication with the author, Feb. 1993.

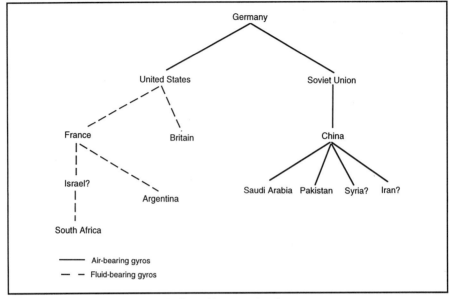

Figure 5.5. The diffusion of missile guidance technology

tries were building more than 100 different models of INS for aircraft.[45] One result is that sophisticated guidance systems are not as exotic as they once were. They are increasingly familiar to aeronautical engineers the world over, and there is a growing community of technicians who know how to work with the technology and a smaller community who know how to manufacture it.

A second and more immediate concern is the fear that, with hundreds and perhaps thousands of commercial INS being sold every year, a few could end up in the wrong hands all too easily. Complete systems could be removed from aircraft and fitted into missiles. One illicitly acquired system might even be enough to provide a basis for copying for local production. Another possibility is that commercial INS sets will be stripped and their individual gyros used as parts in a strap-down guidance system.

So far none of these possibilities has become reality, nor do any of them seem likely. The technical barriers were outlined in the first systematic study of the applicability of commercial missile guidance systems for ballistic missiles, which concluded that the demands on a missile guidance package could not be met by commercial aircraft systems.[46] Compared to missile guidance systems, aircraft INS lack accuracy, durability and reliability. Because an aircraft always has a pilot, often assisted by a navigator, its INS is required to do much less than a missile guidance system. An aircraft INS is usually recalibrated at the start of every flight, regularly updated and continuously checked. With aircraft

---

[45] *Military Avionic Equipment 1987/88*, vol. 1 (Interavia Publishing: Cointrin-Geneva, 1987), pp. 796–800. The same point is made with older data in Balaschak (note 3), pp. 39–44.
[46] Balaschak (note 3), pp. 24–30, 34–37, 64.

there is less need for extreme accuracy; if the guidance system fails the flight crew is usually exposed to little more than an inconvenience.[47] Instead of extreme accuracy, the design of aircraft INS places greater stress on low cost, easy use, easy maintenance and long-term reliability. Most commercial guidance systems also differ conceptually from those used in rockets in that they use only two gyros, which makes them useless in vertical flight.

Nor is diversion of aircraft INS easy or cost free. When sold abroad, INS systems are almost always transferred under safeguards, usually including agreements that permit servicing only by the original manufacturer or specified contractors. Removal of the guidance package from an advanced aircraft would be detected within a year or so when regular maintenance is scheduled at a foreign depot to certify flight-worthiness, probably provoking a diplomatic confrontation. With hundreds more commercial INS being built every year, however, it is probably only a matter of time before someone somewhere tries to transplant one.

A greater danger from the commercial market in guidance technologies is that manufacturers will use their skills to develop new systems for export to regional powers. With manufacturers in at least seven Western countries to choose from (as well as in China, Hungary, Russia and Ukraine), there is a danger that they will succumb to the prospect of a large order, be it illegal or merely unethical. Persistent reports indicate that the French guidance company SAGEM developed the guidance system for the Condor-2. According to the United Nations, an unknown German company developed a new guidance system for Iraq's enhanced Scud missiles.[48] The German space agency, the then DFVLR, helped Indian scientists with the computers and algorithms in the guidance systems for the SLV-3, Agni and Prithvi.[49] Although these cases involved the transfer of guidance technology, there is no evidence that any involved the transfer of an actual INS. The transfer of lesser technologies rather suggests how more advanced ones could follow.

The option of domestic development should not be overlooked. Forty years after the INS revolution took off in the early 1950s, many regional powers can make many key guidance components themselves. If a country has advanced electronics and precision tool manufacturing industries, as well as major engineering laboratories, domestic INS development is feasible. The key to success is foreign input. Even an indigenous INS project will rely extensively on foreign technology: concepts and designs, materials (such as beryllium), some

---

[47] This is not always the case. Trusting an aircraft's INS can be fatal. The navigational errors that led to the destruction of Korean Airlines flight 007 in 1983 may have been caused by the flight crew's failure to feed correct co-ordinates into their INS and regularly check its readings. Hersh, S. M., *The Target is Destroyed* (Random House: New York, 1986).

[48] See, e.g., Krosney, H., *Deadly Business: Legal Deals and Outlaw Weapons* (Four Walls Eight Windows: New York, 1993), p. 161; Timmerman, K. R., *The Death Lobby: How the West Armed Iraq* (Fourth Estate: London, 1992), pp. 251, 288; and Burrows, W. E. and Windrem, R., *Critical Mass* (Simon and Schuster: New York, 1994), p. 217.

[49] Rudert, R., Schichl, K. and Seeger, S., *Atomraketen als Entwicklungshilfe* [Ballistic missiles as development aid], Schriftenreihe Wissenschaft und Frieden 5 (Bund Demokratischer Wissenschafter: Marburg, 1985), pp. 94–103, 113–15.

parts and—most important of all—consultant advice. Also essential is generous official support and plenty of time; replicating US developments of the 1950s would be neither easy nor quick.

Regional development of INS will be paced by the same problems that slowed its emergence in the United States and the Soviet Union: low accuracy, high weight and poor mechanical reliability. As in other aspects of rocket technology, however, the efforts of regional powers will be eased by access to Western training and publications. They will also be aided by careful study of aircraft INS and previous experience with building less sophisticated gyros and accelerometers. Microelectronics, which were unavailable at the time of the 1950s INS revolution in the United States, now makes it much easier to shave vital weight off new designs and improve performance and reliability.

Rather than mounting a direct effort to conquer INS for missiles, some regional actors have taken an easier path, using foreign technology to develop key components and less demanding aircraft systems before graduating to more demanding missile systems. China started with a few sample Soviet guidance systems and designs. Work on INS development began with these in the late 1950s, but it was not until 1977 that China completed its first completely inertial guidance system for aircraft. Today China manufactures several different types of aircraft and missile INS, although of low performance by international standards.[50] Israel established its reputation in guidance technology as a manufacturer of INS for fighter aircraft, especially the 1970s Kfir and 1980s Lavi fighters. Although Israel apparently relied on non-inertial guidance for its early missiles, it may now be graduating to genuine INS for its latest versions. India and North Korea have demonstrated their competence with simpler strap-down gyros, indicating that they too have the potential to move on towards full-scale inertial systems.

Strap-down guidance

Commonly disparaged by Western designers, strap-down guidance offers regional powers a cheap and accessible alternative to INS. Instead of having all its individual gyros and accelerometers housed in a stabilized platform, strap-downs are directly attached (strapped down) to the missile's airframe. Unlike a true inertial system which measures motion from its own independent frame of reference, a strap-down gyro can only detect a change in the motion of the rocket itself, which is then compared to a pre-set trajectory stored in a mechanical cam or on a computer. Although this arrangement is inferior to an inertial system, it may be adequate for emerging missile makers.

Strap-down guidance systems earned much of their bad reputation from experience with the V-2 missile. Although they carried the most advanced strap-downs of their day, the V-2 missiles fired against London in 1944 were

---

[50] Duan Zijun (ed.), *China Today: Aviation Industry* (China Aviation Industry Press: Beijing, 1989), pp. 253–54.

Figure 5.6. A Prithvi missile

India's Prithvi, shown here being prepared for a test shot into the Bay of Bengal in the early 1990s. It is the first entirely original ballistic missile developed by a regional power other than Israel. The missile testifies to both India's technical potential and its liabilities. It relies on foreign technologies—especially for its propulsion and guidance systems—but its configuration and development are entirely Indian. Because ideal technology is not available, several key systems were improvised. Instead of a preferred INS, its guidance system relies on strap-down equipment, possibly backed by radio correction. Unable to control direction by steering the engine nozzles, it uses large and inefficient aerodynamic surfaces. The great size of the system—suggested here by the inspection ladder at the bottom of the launch platform—indicates more fundamental inefficiencies. In essence, India has re-invented the Scud. (Photograph: Jane's Information Group)

notoriously unreliable, achieving an accuracy (CEP) of about 8 km after a flight, from occupied France and the Low Countries, averaging 220 km. The same average error would translate into a CEP of about 35 km at 1000 km range. At that range, such a missile would need luck to hit even a city the size of New York or Paris. Against military targets, it would be completely useless, even if armed with nuclear weapons.

The V-2 had been prematurely rushed into service in the last days of the Third Reich. Its poor accuracy reflected many problems in its design, above all with its guidance system, the LEV-3. This combined two gyros and an accelerometer mounted to the missile's airframe.[51] The LEV-3 could not sense mistakes in the original alignment of the missile or detect the effects of shifting winds after the launch since it had no independence from the rocket itself. Its accuracy was further reduced by the friction on its mechanical bearings. The virtues of the system were that it was cheap (costing probably only a few thousand dollars) and could be produced by semi-skilled labour.

By the mid-1960s strap-down systems had reached levels of accuracy far beyond that of the LEV-3. Because of their small size and low cost, strap-down systems are especially well suited for use in tactical weapons, such as surface-to-air and anti-ship missiles. The same refinements make them more suitable for use in ballistic missiles with ranges of up to 300 km. The strap-down system which went into operation in the Soviet Scud-B missile in 1965 achieved a CEP of 950 metres at a range of 280 km. This was an enormous improvement over the V-2, but it has not been easy to improve further. Strap-down accuracy did not improve in early versions of the Soviet SS-21 (or OTR-21 Tochka), which was deployed in 1976 with a strap-down system giving it a CEP of around 300 metres at its maximum range of 120 km. (A special, terminally guided version of the SS-21 reportedly has a CEP of 30 metres, and there is great concern that this system may enter the international market.)[52]

For missile proliferators, strap-down guidance is a natural choice, virtually ideal for their initial needs. It is far more affordable, costing tens of thousands of dollars instead of hundreds of thousands or millions of dollars. Apart from its low cost, it is within their technical reach and it can be reverse-engineered from models found in missiles they already have, such as the Scud-B and other tactical missiles. Strap-downs are the only guidance systems that have been confirmed in regional actors' ballistic missiles. India's 240-km range Prithvi, first tested in February 1988, uses a strap-down system, probably derived from the Soviet SA-2 surface-to-air missile (the Prithvi's engines are adapted from those of the SA-2). The principal Indian innovation appears to be the on-board computer that issues control commands. Official Indian press releases insist that the Prithvi 'is extremely accurate' and that its CEP 'is lower than most missiles in its class'.[53] Such statements should be regarded as nothing more than a nationalist bromide. More credible are reports giving it a CEP of 300 metres at 150-km range, or 500 metres at 250-km range.[54] Strap-downs guide all Scud missiles, including those modified for increased range by Iraq and the improved versions manufactured by North Korea. They have also been used in large sounding rockets, such as Brazil's Sonda-4, a 1980s German-designed sounding rocket with a potential surface-to-surface range of 600 km.[55]

[51] Mueller, F. K., *A History of Inertial Guidance* (Army Ballistic Missile Agency: Huntsville, Ala., n.d., 1960?), pp. 7–15.

[52] Cochran (note 28), pp. 220–24; and Lennox, D., 'The SS-21 "Scarab"—an update', *Jane's Intelligence Review*, July 1992, pp. 295–96.

[53] Banerjie, I., 'Aiming for the sky', *Sunday* (Calcutta) 22 Oct. 1989.

[54] 'More on missiles', *Milavnews*, no. 354 (Apr. 1991), p. 15; and 'Prithvi', *World Missiles Briefing* (Teal Group: Fairfax, Va., Dec. 1994), pp. 1–3.

[55] Rudert, Schichl and Seeger (note 49), pp. 48–52.

Beyond a range of 300 km strap-downs begin to lose their advantages. Their inaccuracies are exaggerated by greater range, making it difficult to hit any but the largest targets. In extending the range of their Scud missiles and versions of the Scud, both Iraq and North Korea apparently tried to compensate by improving their electronics. Iraq went so far as to enlist a German company to develop an entirely new guidance system. Such efforts are necessary but can only accomplish so much, as the pathetic accuracy of Iraq's missiles in the 1991 Gulf War showed. At ranges beyond 900 km strap-downs are all but useless by themselves. Their effectiveness is nibbled to nothing by the cumulative effect of small errors. Any effectiveness that remains is undermined by the lack of sufficiently sensitive accelerometers to cut off engine thrust at precisely the right moment.

Attempts have been made to guide long-range missiles with strap-downs. This decision has usually reflected dire necessity. For almost 20 years China relied exclusively on strap-down guidance in its ballistic missiles, including very large ones such as the DF-4 ICBM. After developing its first INS in the late 1970s, however, China immediately abandoned its previous guidance methods, except in smaller missiles. The first Chinese missile with fully inertial guidance appears to have been the DF-5 (CSS-4) ICBM, which became operational in 1981.[56] No details of Chinese missile accuracy have been released.

Efforts by other countries to use strap-downs in longer-range rockets may be sensible as experiments, but the results are not encouraging. India's Agni IRBM 'technology demonstrator' uses the same basic guidance package as the Prithvi. This may be one reason why Indian officials seem hesitant to consider deploying it.[57] In the late 1980s China returned to strap-down guidance for its export-oriented ballistic missiles. The largest of these, the 600-km range M-9, was developed with a minimum of trouble. Curiously, adapting the same strap-down system for its smaller cousin, the 300-km range M-11, has been more difficult.[58] Rather than rely on strap-downs alone, emerging missile powers will almost certainly try to enhance their performance, probably through radio guidance.

Radio guidance

For countries lacking ready access to inertial navigation systems, one other alternative remains. Radio guidance was invented by the V-2 Rocket Team in a last-ditch attempt to improve the weapon's operational performance. There are several radio command techniques, but all use strap-down gyros within the rocket to detect changes in trajectory and acceleration. Ground-based radars and transmitters then issue guidance instructions or commands to terminate the engine burn. Developed too late for the attack on London in the autumn of

[56] Lewis and Hua Di (note 10), pp. 9–11.

[57] Joshi, M., 'Agni: importance and implication', *Frontline* (Madras), 16 Apr. 1992, p. 7; and Joshi, M., 'Waiting for Agni: will it fly, or won't it?', *Frontline* (Madras), 8 May 1992.

[58] Hua Di, 'Ballistic missile exports will continue', *Asia–Pacific Defence Reporter*, Sep. 1991, p. 14.

1944, radio correction supplemented the LEV-3 strap-down system in the German attacks on Antwerp in the following months and greatly improved the effect of V-2 attacks. While London more or less shrugged off its V-2 bombardment, the port of Antwerp was all but closed to the Allies for two critical months.[59]

Radio correction was used later to supplement strap-downs and early inertial platforms. The first US Atlas and Titan-1 missiles, for example, used strap-down gyros to save weight, supplemented by radio links from General Electric and ground-based computers from Borroughs.[60] The first Soviet ICBMs, the SS-6, SS-7 and SS-8, all used comparable equipment. Early US and Soviet radio correction was sufficient to guide ICBMs through a 9000-km flight to accuracies of CEPs of 3 km or better.[61] Despite this effectiveness, neither superpower was happy with this arrangement. It was viewed as a temporary improvisation awaiting the refinement of INS. Although radio guidance was more accurate than early INS, it was suspect since its signals are vulnerable to interception and jamming by an adversary.

As regional powers develop long-range missiles, radio guidance seems likely to be the method that they, too, will rely on. In his study of missile guidance, Donald MacKenzie argues that radio correction remains a viable alternative even for established nuclear forces.[62] For emerging powers its appeal is even greater, especially because of its low cost and ease of development. The theory is well known and the equipment is available in radar and high-performance radios already in the hands of regional powers. With most of the equipment on the ground, radio correction saves weight in the missile, which can be used instead for greater range or payload. It is also more accurate than any INS a regional actor is likely to develop itself. The most serious disadvantage is security, and this can be improved through directional beams and frequency hopping.

An example of a radio-corrected missile in current use is the US-made Lance, first deployed in 1972 and transferred to several NATO countries and Israel. The Lance uses a very small strap-down system with radio correction to achieve a CEP of 375 metres at its maximum range of 120 km. For a modern rocket such accuracy is unimpressive. What is impressive is the guidance system's tiny size, contributing to the Lance's weight of only 1527 kg at launch, making it one of the most efficient designs ever.[63] The comparable French Pluton, deployed in the mid-1970s, appears to use a similar guidance system.

As for regional projects, some reports indicate that the Indian Prithvi will be deployed with radio correction. A system has been designed for Prithvi using Flycatcher anti-aircraft radars supplied by the Netherlands (built in India under

[59] Frye (note 34), p. 588–89.

[60] Chapman, J. L., *Atlas: The Story of a Missile* (Harper and Brothers: New York, 1960), p. 82; and MacKenzie (note 35), pp. 121–23.

[61] MacKenzie (note 35), pp. 310–13, 428–29.

[62] MacKenzie (note 35), pp. 117–23, 361.

[63] The complete Lance guidance package, including simplified inertial components, radio telemetry, computer and controls, weighs 16.4 kg. 'MGM-52 Lance', *World Missile Forecast* (note 40).

licence) and ground-based computers to augment the missile's on-board strap-downs.[64] Another likely example is the Jericho-1, Israel's first ballistic missile, which has a maximum range of 500 km and needs more than simple strap-down guidance. When the Jericho-1 was deployed in the early 1970s, however, Israeli industry did not have the expertise to develop its own INS. Nor was a foreign system available: even France, the likely source of the Jericho-1 design, could not have supplied an INS because its only appropriate models were based on US licences and subject to US Government control. Radio correction is the most likely alternative that Israel could add by itself or with minimal foreign assistance.

Implications for control

Guidance will remain the most vulnerable part of regional rocketry and an obvious point on which to concentrate export controls for many years to come. In the past, regional weakness in guidance technology made control over this key technology an almost certain barrier to the proliferation of long-range ballistic missiles. Broader consideration of guidance issues, however, leads to the conclusion that this advantage is subject to the same erosion that has been seen with other rocket technologies.

Several would-be proliferators are acquiring sufficient competence in related fields to develop guidance systems effective for missiles with ranges of up to about 500 km and probably adequate up to 1000 km. An appropriate INS might make their missiles especially deadly, but it is not essential for the missions for which they are likely to plan. Almost all these countries have unfettered access to strap-down gyros and radio correction techniques that are adequate for most of the missiles they are trying to develop today. Some countries, such as Iran, Libya and Pakistan, will need foreign assistance to make these technologies work, but this is the kind of help that is easiest to buy from the world's ever growing community of high-technology consultants.

At missile ranges beyond 1000 km even the most impoverished regional missile programmes would prefer inertial guidance. Without it they can try to make the most of available technology by developing radio-correction techniques. In the long term there is reason to think that dedicated proliferators with advanced electronics industries will be able to develop their own inertial guidance systems. If they choose that path, they will probably not pursue highly accurate INS of the calibre developed for the superpowers' ICBMs of the 1980s. Rather, their efforts will concentrate on systems similar to the first acceptable missile INS of the early 1960s. Maintaining effective export controls on INS will require regular expansion of technology control lists to cover more and more fundamental technologies.

---

[64] 'Fourth Prithvi test', *Milavnews*, no. 358 (Aug. 1991), p. 13.

Rather than continue to think of guidance systems as the key bottleneck in the process of missile proliferation, it is more sensible to view it as one among many important areas for control, all of which must be controlled together.

IV. Re-entry vehicles

One of the most serious technical problems in ballistic missile technology is the development of the re-entry vehicle, the nose-cone that protects the missile's armament during re-entry through the atmosphere. As a general rule, the farther a missile travels, the faster the speed at which its re-entry vehicle returns to earth and the greater the heat it generates. At short ranges the speed and concomitant heat are not serious problems, but at longer ranges these problems are all but overwhelming. Re-entry may be the most difficult single technical problem for emerging rocket powers, making it extremely difficult for them to create effective ballistic missiles with ranges greater than 1500 km or so.

At greater ranges, solution of re-entry problems requires highly advanced and costly materials and elaborate testing. For a typical ICBM travelling a distance of 10 000 km and reaching a peak altitude of 1500 km, the temperatures at the front of the re-entry vehicle can reach 6600° C (12 000° F). This is some 1100 degrees Celsius higher than that of the surface of the sun. Some regional actors may be able to build rockets capable of flying such distances, but it will be very difficult for them to bring their payloads down safely.

For missiles travelling less than 600 km, the demands on re-entry vehicle performance need not be as great, especially if high accuracy is not important. The re-entry vehicle on a German V-2 or a Scud-B missile (both with maximum ranges of about 300 km) consisted of little more than a cone-shaped piece of insulated steel sheet.[65] One of the simplest parts of either missile (except for its sophisticated fuse), it could be built in any well-equipped machine shop. It may look crude, but it serves its purpose even in modified Scuds such as the 500- to 600-km Iraqi al Hussein and the North Korean Scud-C. At these distances re-entry heating is usually not great enough to endanger the warhead. Even at these lower velocities, however, it is no easy matter to ensure sufficient accuracy of the re-entry vehicle.

The designers of the Scud missile, working in the 1950s under the authority of the famed Chief Designer Sergei P. Korolev, tried to give their creation sufficient accuracy simply by designing the re-entry vehicle with a clean aerodynamic shape, although this required extensive development work.[66] To aid accuracy further, the warhead separates from the rocket body in its final descent. Separating the re-entry vehicle like a final, unpowered stage frees it from the drag and unpredictable tumbling of the spent rocket. This modest re-entry vehicle matched the capabilities of the missile's strap-down guidance

---

[65] The V-2 warhead is described in Kooy, J. M. J. and Uytenbogaart, J. W., *Ballistics of the Future* (Technical Publishing Company H. Stam: Haarlem, the Netherlands, 1946).

[66] Berman and Baker (note 28), pp. 96–98; and Lennox, D., 'Inside the R-17 'Scud-B' missile', *Jane's Intelligence Review*, July 1991, pp. 302–5.

package. The most common version, the Scud-B, can deliver a nuclear warhead with a CEP of just under 1 km at its maximum range of 280 km.[67] This was sufficient when used with a nuclear warhead but inadequate with conventional high explosives, as demonstrated by the weapon's poor performance in Afghanistan and Operation Desert Storm. The results of such a lash-up may not be outstanding, but they are likely to be sufficient to meet the initial requirements of an emerging missile power.

At ranges beyond 600 km, however, re-entry problems become far more serious. Unless carefully designed and built, a re-entry vehicle is likely to tumble unpredictably and turn into a harmless piece of junk as it overheats or even explodes prematurely. For every country developing ballistic missiles with a range of 1000 km or more, re-entry has been an extremely demanding problem. In the three programmes on which information is readily available—those of Britain, France and the United States—it was the most serious single technical problem that had to be overcome in the early years of missile development. Newcomers inevitably will have an easier time in this field as in others—this is one area where access to sophisticated computers appears to be especially helpful—but unlike most other aspects of rocketry, the critical details of re-entry technology remain highly classified everywhere.[68] More so than in other areas, in re-entry technology missile proliferators are virtually on their own, able to glean little more than general ideas from published reports and compelled to repeat much of the R&D previously completed by the major powers.

Alternative approaches to re-entry vehicle design

The two principal techniques for protecting the interior of a rocket's nose-cone as it re-enters the earth's atmosphere are *heat sink* and *ablation*. Of the two, heat sink is by far the easiest to master, relying on a wide, rounded metal surface lining the bottom of the nose-cone. The blunt bottom re-enters first, dissipating some of the heat of re-entry through shock waves and absorbing much of the rest. By presenting a large surface area in the direction of travel, the blunt shape creates enormous drag, further reducing heating by slowing the re-entry vehicle down to subsonic speed.

Heat sinks were employed in the first US ballistic missiles, including the Jupiter, Thor, Atlas, Titan and the early versions of the submarine-launched

---

[67] Collins, J. M. and Victory, B. C., *U.S./Soviet Military Balance: Statistical Trends, 1980–1987* (Congressional Research Service: Washington, DC, 15 Apr. 1988), p. 40.

[68] According to McFate, P. A. and Graybeal, S. N., 'A new proliferation threat from space?', eds W. T. Wander and E. H. Arnett, *The Proliferation of Advanced Weaponry* (American Association for the Advancement of Science: Washington, DC, 1992), p. 94, 'Soviet heat shield and RV design technology is available in the open'. A careful search found no substance to this assertion. The most thorough public review is Yevsikov, V., *Re-entry Technology and the Soviet Space Program* (Delphic Associates: Falls Church, Dec. 1982). This insightful study shows that the Soviet Union continued to rely on round re-entry shapes—a variation on the blunt body concept—even in its most advanced work of the early 1970s. The most relevant chapter of Yevsikov's book (chapter III, 'Coating materials, methods and technologies') is devoted to the problem of developing high-performance coatings to ensure the safe return of spacecraft. This suggests that similar problems continued to plague missile re-entry vehicles as late as 1982.

Polaris, and in the first generation of French ballistic missiles, the S-2 and M-2 IRBMs.[69] In the public mind the heat sink is more familiar since the heat shield used to protect all US manned space craft from Mercury to the Apollo command module. The Soviet Union relied on a spherical version of the same concept until the mid-1970s; China still does. The approach owes its appeal to its relative simplicity, but even if it is less demanding than other re-entry approaches, a heat sink is far from easy to master. As the best unclassified treatment of the subject observes, 'Of the myriad puzzles involved in designing, building, and flying the Atlas, the first American ICBM, the most difficult and expensive to solve was re-entry heating'.[70]

A serious disadvantage for missiles is that this backwards, upside-down looking shape exposes the re-entry vehicle to considerable drag and makes the warhead vulnerable to winds, greatly reducing accuracy. Another disadvantage is its construction, usually based on a heavy metal such as copper, tungsten or beryllium, which forces designers to trim either the weight of the armament or the rocket's range.[71] Use of these metals, along with the complicated coatings they require, also introduces severe manufacturing problems.

In the United States, the invention and development of the heat sink were made possible only by prior innovations in high-speed wind tunnels. Subsonic wind tunnels have been a mainstay of aeronautics research since the days of the Wright brothers, but getting air to flow evenly through ducting in a laboratory at supersonic speeds is extremely difficult. To perfect the shape of the V-2, German aerodynamicists from the University of Göttingen developed a wind tunnel capable of speeds up to Mach-4.4. Remembered as one of the greatest technical accomplishments of the V-2 programme, this was a machine the size of a large industrial building, capable of sending a single burst of high-speed air through a duct 40 cm square—half the size of a postcard.[72] The US Air Force and civilian laboratories spent much of the 1950s developing wind tunnels capable of generating a continuous stream of air at speeds of between Mach-8 and Mach-20 to imitate the velocities encountered by longer-range missiles. Equally difficult was the problem of creating temperatures of at least 4400° C (8000° F), comparable to the surface temperature of a re-entry vehicle entering the atmosphere at Mach-10. The development of suitable wind tunnels was one of the greatest but least acknowledged accomplishments of the US rocketry programme.[73]

The other approach to high-speed re-entry, the ablation re-entry vehicle, is conceptually much simpler but even more difficult to develop. These are the

[69] Detailed descriptions of the latter are not available in non-classified literature, but pictures of the protective capsules clearly reveal the conical shape of a heat sink nose-cone.

[70] Swenson, L. S., Jr, Grimwood, J. M. and Alexander, C. C., *This New Ocean: A History of Project Mercury* (National Aeronautics and Space Administration: Washington, DC, 1966), p. 59.

[71] The best unclassified description remains Swenson, Grimwood and Alexander (note 70), pp. 58–65.

[72] Kurzweg, H. H., 'The aerodynamic development of the V-2', eds T. Benecke and A. W. Quick, *History of German Guided Missile Development*, AGARDograph no. 20 (E. Appelmans and Co.: Brunswick, Germany, 1957), pp. 50–69.

[73] Baals, D. D. and Corliss, W. R., *Wind Tunnels of NASA* (National Aeronautics and Space Administration: Washington, DC, 1981), pp. 51–85.

familiar pointed nose-cones of all the US nuclear warheads introduced since the mid-1960s. They are extremely low-drag designs, narrow cone shapes, which re-enter pointed-end first and at much higher speeds and temperatures. Heat is dissipated by allowing the thin outer layer of the vehicle to burn away or ablate very slowly, while allowing virtually none of the heat to spread inside. In order to ensure that this occurs at an even and predictable rate, highly advanced materials and manufacturing standards are essential.

The speeds and heat encountered by such shapes surpass the ability of any wind tunnel simulation. Instead, missile programmes in the United States, Britain and France all relied on large, specially designed experimental test rockets to launch test versions and drive them back to earth at extreme velocity. In the United States this was the purpose of the multi-stage Jupiter-C and Lockheed X-17 test rockets of the 1950s. Britain relied on its specially designed Black Knight research rocket launched in Australia in the 1960s, and France used a series of test rockets during the 1960s, including the Bérénice, Topaze and Saphir.[74]

How important is foreign assistance?

Despite considerable efforts, emerging missile powers may be unable to develop fully acceptable re-entry vehicles by themselves. Although no emerging power will require a test establishment comparable to that created by the United States to create a reliable long-range ballistic missile, it will need to replicate much of the test results produced by this programme. Some of the data can be reproduced through less costly test facilities, such as those used by the US aerodynamicist H. Julian Allen to develop re-entry vehicle concepts in the early 1950s.[75] Larger facilities are still necessary for testing an original design, as are rocket tests. The only substitutes are large-scale espionage or guesswork and faith.

Even the Soviet Union, with all the resources and expertise at its command, made uneven progress in re-entry technology. Initial development of heat sinks was straightforward, as demonstrated by the early success of its manned space programme. The same spherical shape was used for both manned space flight and first- and second-generation ballistic missiles.[76] The problem of developing more accurate ablation re-entry vehicles was far more vexing. According to MacKenzie, initial Soviet efforts to deploy ablative re-entry systems on third-

[74] Miller, J., *The X-Planes* (Aerofax: Arlington, Tex., 1988), pp. 133–37; Becklake, J., 'The British Black Knight rocket', *Journal of the British Interplanetary Society*, vol. 43, no. 4 (July 1990), pp. 283–90; and Villain (note 27), pp. 88–100.

[75] For conceptual development of the heat sink, Allen simulated high speeds by improvising. He used a surplus artillery piece to fire test shapes into a small Mach-3 wind tunnel, simulating speeds of Mach-5 to -6. This rig cost only $20 000 in the early 1950s. While it was adequate for proving theoretical concepts, it was not suitable for more refined development purposes. Ambitious regional countries can be expected to experiment with comparable improvisations. Baals and Corliss (note 73), p. 75. See also Swenson, Grimwood and Alexander (note 70), pp. 59–60.

[76] Zaloga, S. J., *Target America: The Soviet Union and the Strategic Arms Race, 1945–1964* (Presidio: Novato, Calif., 1993), p. 257.

generation ICBMs in the early 1970s failed and had to be abandoned.[77] Not until the late 1970s was it possible to deploy fourth-generation missiles (the SS-18 Satan and SS-19 Stiletto) with ablative re-entry vehicles comparable to those perfected in the United States 15 years earlier.[78]

It is highly suggestive that even a country as technically advanced and independently minded as France, with its own large and costly programme, turned to the United States for assistance when it was developing its first heat sink re-entry vehicles in the 1960s. Later, in the mid-1970s, when its ablative re-entry programme was foundering, French officials again turned to US colleagues for clues, an apparent violation of French policy and US law.[79] It should be noted that they were not thwarted by the extreme range and accuracy requirements of ICBMs. In the 1960s and 1970s the French *Force de frappe* emphasized intermediate-range missiles with typical ranges of 3000 km and guidance and warheads designed to hit only city-size targets.[80] It is impossible to determine, at the time of writing, in late 1994, whether French engineers sought outside help out of absolute necessity or merely to accelerate their work. If France resorted to outside help to solve its re-entry problems, it is difficult to imagine regional powers like Brazil or Israel developing similar equipment completely on their own.

China relied on foreign concepts in re-entry vehicle development, starting with the nose-cones on missiles transferred from the Soviet Union, themselves patterned on the V-2. More advanced re-entry vehicles introduced in the late 1960s were based on ideas gleaned from the Western press, although China had to make a large investment to reproduce actual R&D experience.[81] For long-range missiles Chinese designers developed round re-entry vehicles with an improvised ablation technique. Such rockets as the DF-2, introduced in the late 1960s, used filament winding and chemical coatings for protection.[82] In the 1970s carbon composite materials were bought from Japan. Chinese designers never emphasized high accuracy in re-entry vehicle design. Given the lack of precise guidance methods, there was little sense in creating sophisticated re-entry systems. Nor was it thought necessary. 'When targeting Moscow, a city 36 km in diameter, it doesn't matter what your CEP is: 3 km, 6 km, it's all the same.'[83]

---

[77] MacKenzie (note 35), p. 328.

[78] Smith, R. J., 'An upheaval in U.S. strategic thought', *Science*, 2 Apr. 1982, pp. 30–34.

[79] Ullman, R. H., 'The covert French connection', *Foreign Policy*, no. 75 (summer 1989), pp. 8–13.

[80] On French nuclear strategy and weapons requirements, see Young (note 43).

[81] This paragraph is based on discussions with the former Chinese rocket engineer Hua Di, who was careful to note that his expertise is in propulsion, not re-entry.

[82] Details of filament winding, a technique developed in the USA for solid-engine casings, were also available in the open literature. See, e.g., *Filament Winding Conference, March 28–30, 1961* (Society of Aerospace Materials and Process Engineers: Azusa, Calif., n.d., approx. 1962).

[83] Hua Di, Private communication with the author, 10 Feb. 1993.

Controlling re-entry vehicle technology

Tight controls on high-speed wind tunnels can slow the development of re-entry vehicles, as can restrictions on relevant materials. The appeal of ablation techniques will make this regional method the natural choice for long-range missiles and a key item for control efforts to focus on. The best documented case, the Condor-2, was designed with an ablation re-entry vehicle. A major problem in the programme was acquiring suitable materials. The engineer Abdelkader Helmy was convicted in California in 1989 of espionage for his part in an Egyptian conspiracy to illegally export carbon–carbon materials suitable for this application.[84] The fact that espionage occurs does not prove that technology controls are sufficient, but it does suggest that they are necessary.

The importance of skilled designers and plentiful test data make re-entry vehicle development one area in which foreign scientists can be instrumental.[85] Ballistic missile development is too demanding for a handful of foreign engineers—even the very best—to transform an embarrassing project into a certain success. Even most sub-systems typically involve too many technologies for success to arise from inspired design alone. Re-entry vehicle development appears to be somewhat different, relying largely on conceptual progress. It is one area of rocket technology where, for example, a few top Russian or Ukrainian experts could contribute dramatically to the missile capabilities of an emerging power.

So far the market for re-entry technology is a small, almost inconsequential aspect of the international missile trade. This could change, especially as regional actors become more ambitious and competent. Such countries as Russia and Ukraine may soon be tempted to move into this emerging market.

For missile proliferators foreign help will matter even more than it did for a country like France. Without foreign technical assistance—be it officially sanctioned, the result of espionage or the work of expatriates—it will be extremely difficult and perhaps impossible for proliferators to develop ballistic missile re-entry vehicles comparable to those France needed for its IRBMs. Unless newcomers can find a new technique for circumventing re-entry problems, or can receive plentiful assistance from an established missile power, their largest ballistic missiles may be unable to reliably hit a meaningful target. Proliferators may proceed anyway and build missiles capable of travelling 2000 km, 3000 km or even farther, but without suitable re-entry vehicles they cannot be relied upon for anything but show.

---

[84] Government's Sentencing Memorandum, United States of America versus Abdelkader Helmy *et al.*, United States District Court for the Eastern District of California, 27 Nov. 1989.

[85] McFate and Graybeal (note 68), p. 94.

V. Stage separation

After the essential component technologies have been fully developed, a country trying to produce long-range rockets still faces the problems of integrating them into a single system. Because a rocket is an integrated mechanism, its performance depends not only on the reliability of individual components but also on their ability to work together. The problem of integration shows up continuously through the design and development process, but nowhere is it more explicit than in the problem of stage separation.

Most long-range rockets are built in two to four individual stages, each with its own engines and propellants. By allowing the rocket to discard excess weight and drag as it ascends, multiple staging can improve overall performance by as much as 50 per cent—in range or payload—over single-stage designs of the same dimensions. This advantage is not cost free. With the improved performance comes a tremendous increase in mechanical complexity, in opportunities for something to go wrong. While the silky smoothness of a fully developed rocket executing its many operations in flight makes stage separation look easy, for emerging rocket makers this is a tremendous technical hurdle. After the basic problems of acquiring foreign equipment, stage separation is more likely to delay a programme than any other technical problem.

Although it is not a particular piece of equipment like a guidance package or warhead, stage separation is an especially troublesome technology. It involves a series of carefully timed mechanical processes, with virtually no tolerance for error. In a typical first-stage separation the following major events occur, although the exact sequence varies:

1. The guidance system must determine that the rocket has reached a predetermined velocity and point in its trajectory.
2. A command shuts down the main engines of the first stage.
3. The first-stage vernier engines are cut off.[86]
4. Guidance and command signals are re-routed to the second-stage engines.
5. The protective fairing over the second-stage engines is released and cable connections between the stages are broken.
6. Pins release to disconnect the two stages.
7. The second-stage vernier engines ignite.
8. The second-stage main engines ignite.

In a large rocket with several stages this sequence might be followed three or four times, culminating in the release of the warhead. Each stage introduces numerous opportunities for something to go wrong.

The problem is sufficiently daunting to discourage most new rocket makers from using multiple staging, despite its great advantages. The first US and Soviet long-range rockets of the 1950s, such as the SS-4, SS-5, Jupiter and

---

[86] Vernier engines are small rocket engines mounted on the sides of the rocket fuselage to aid stability and control. They are not essential, but are commonly used on large ballistic missiles and space launchers.

Thor, were single-stage IRBMs. Despite the inefficiency of such designs and the huge penalties they put on performance, decision makers were unwilling to risk multiple-stage designs. These were followed by the SS-6 and Atlas ICBMs, both of which used stage-and-a-half designs to balance performance requirements and the burden of technical risk. Basically these were single-stage rockets surrounded by strap-on engines attached to the sides of the rocket. The latter were discarded early in the flight while the main engines continued to burn. An early US effort to improve the range of the Atlas by adding a genuine second stage (the Atlas-E/F) found that the problems of stage separation were 'extremely vexing and came close to causing the cancellation of the programme'.[87]

Only with the introduction of second-generation ICBMs such as the Titan and SS-8 did the superpowers begin to rely entirely on multiple staging. China faced equally serious barriers to multiple staging and relied initially on single-stage designs. Its first successful multiple-stage rocket, the two-stage DF-4, was tested in 1970, but serious development problems (compounded by the political turmoil of the Cultural Revolution) delayed its deployment until 1980.

Most missile proliferators of the 1980s managed their way around such problems by building single-stage designs, such as the extended-range Scuds developed by Iraq and North Korea. There are limits, however, to what can be accomplished with a single-stage design unless a country is willing to countenance an enormous rocket similar in size to an Atlas or SS-6. As range and payload requirements rise, multiple staging becomes necessary to keep the cost and size of a missile within acceptable proportions. Regional projects for larger weapons—such as the 1000-km Condor-2, the 1450-km Jericho-2 and the 2500-km Agni—all use two-stage designs. The largest regional space launch projects—Brazil's VLS and India's PSLV and GSLV—are based on three to four stages. As other countries try to develop rockets capable of ranges beyond 1000 km, they will feel compelled to develop multiple-stage designs as well. For this there is no substitute for experience and lengthy test programmes.

Contemporary regional difficulties

A review of missile test flights in regional powers in the 1980s and early 1990s shows continuous problems with stage separation, problems revealed only through flight-testing. Indian rocketry has been plagued by such problems. An SLV-3 launcher lifted the country's first satellite into orbit in 1980, but all other SLV-3 flights failed because of stage separation problems. Its replacement, the ASLV, was first launched in 1988 but crashed prematurely into the Bay of Bengal when its second stage failed to ignite.[88] The first two test flights of the Agni also fell short, the first when its second stage failed to ignite. Several modifications simplified stage separation in the next ASLVs and Agnis,

---

[87] Hujsak, E. J., 'The bird that did not want to fly', *SpaceFlight*, vol. 34 (Mar. 1992), pp. 102–4.

[88] 'ASLV fails at first stage', *The Hindu* (Madras), 14 July 1988; and Lawler, A., 'India succeeds with third ASLV launch attempt', *Space News*, 25 May 1992, p. 6.

but in the next Agni flight the second stage failed again, this time igniting prematurely. None of India's multi-stage rockets is immune. The first launch of the ambitious PSLV rocket on 20 September 1993 ended in failure when the third stage failed to fire properly.[89]

The chief sponsor of the Agni, then Director of Defence Research and Development V. S. Arunachalam, dismissed the stage separation failures as 'minor problems' capable of being overcome.[90] It is not clear, however, whether the Indian development and test programme can do this without a much more intense effort than has been made so far. Among Indian rockets, only the short-range, single-stage Prithvi has been free from similar problems, successfully completing 85 per cent of its test flights.[91] Of all the ballistic missiles and space launchers India had under development in the mid-1990s, only the modest Prithvi seems likely to be deployed.

Although India's problems have been unusually well publicized, they probably do not reflect unique Indian technical weaknesses. Iraq's most complicated rocket, the three-stage al Abed—a cluster of six or seven Scud missiles—lifted off impressively on 4 December 1989. The film released by the Iraqi news agency stops short, near the point at which Western intelligence indicates that the first stage burned out and the upper stages coasted uselessly into the upper atmosphere before crashing to earth.[92]

Even Israel has not been immune to staging problems. Unlike most regional missile programmes, many details of the Arrow anti-tactical ballistic missile (ATBM) being developed by Israeli Aircraft Industries have been made public, probably because the United States supplies most of its funding. With the Arrow, a fast accelerating, solid-fuel missile, Israel apparently reached beyond its capabilities. The first three tests were failures, experiencing stage separation and telemetry problems. There is nothing remarkable about failures early in a missile's test programme: the main reason for testing is to uncover technical problems. With funds short, however, an otherwise commonplace series of test failures endangered the entire project. With the Arrow's test schedule already compressed because of funding limitations, Israeli officials were forced to turn to the United States for additional technical aid in an effort to save the project.[93] Other countries, unable to call on emergency help, may find their most advanced rocket projects brought to a halt at this point.

[89] 'India's remote sensing . . .', *Aviation Week & Space Technology*, 23 Sep. 1993, p. 19; and Government of India, *Department of Space Annual Report, 1993–94* (Indian Space Research Organization: Bangalore, 1994), pp. 40–42.

[90] Beri, R., 'Ballistic missile proliferation', ed. J. Singh, *Asian Strategic Review 1991–92* (Institute for Defence Studies and Analyses: New Delhi, 1992), pp. 191–98.

[91] Joshi, M., 'A partial success: Agni's second firing', *Frontline* (Madras), 19 June 1992.

[92] Gordon, M. R., 'U.S. confirms Iraq has launched rocket that can carry satellites', *New York Times*, 9 Dec. 1989, p. 7.

[93] 'Arrow astray', *Jane's Defence Weekly*, 16 Nov. 1991, p. 935; Clarke, D. L., 'The Arrow missile: the United States, Israel and strategic cooperation', *Middle East Journal*, vol. 48, no. 3 (summer 1994), pp. 475–91; and Opall, B., 'Arrow test buoys U.S., Israeli officials', *Defense News*, 28 Sep. 1992, p. 18.

Clustering: a non-starter

The problems of stage separation help to explain one of the most glaring mysteries of missile proliferation. Ever since first identifying the problem of missile proliferation in the late 1970s, analysts have expected that emerging powers would try to maximize the capabilities of their rockets by clustering rocket sections and adding stages. An influential report from the period predicted that long-range ballistic missiles could be fashioned by mating the sections of various rockets already in wide use and transforming them into two- or three-stage missiles with ranges of 2000 km, 3000 km or even more.[94] The theme has been reiterated more recently in a report sponsored by a prominent North American defence contractor. This report noted that by successfully clustering some 13 Scud missiles—nine in the first stage, three in the second and one in the final stage—a regional power could use relatively primitive technology to create an ICBM with a range of 7000 km. The report went on to envision combinations of other available rocket boosters, potentially creating enormous systems with ranges of 14 000 km or more, enough to hit targets anywhere in the world.[95]

Clustering and staging can potentially be used by any country with access to enough rocket sections to create an impressive looking system. The technique was used in 1958–61 by NASA to create the Saturn-1 and -1B vehicles, based on a cluster of eight enlarged Redstone boosters. Clustering also was used in subsequent Saturn-5s.[96] The possibility is sufficiently intriguing for at least two countries to have tried it: Libya in its Otrag rockets of the early 1980s and Iraq in its al Abed of 1989. More recently it has been suggested that North Korea is trying the same approach in provisional designs revealed in the Western press in 1994. What is conceptually obvious may all too often be impossibly demanding in practice. Indeed, it is revealing that none of the established missile powers took the approach seriously, even in the desperate days of the nuclear arms race.

Clustering and staging of identical rocket sections do not build on simple principles. Instead, the effect is to compound difficulties. The problems in each individual booster—such as unreliability and inaccuracy—are compounded. The problems of making Saturn rocket clusters work properly were among the most severe encountered in the US moon programme, leading even von Braun to quip about 'cluster's last stand'.[97] With the addition of enough sections, the individual uncertainties accumulate and rapidly reach a point at which it is virtually certain that the entire system will fail. A Scud missile, for example, has an individual reliability of 85 per cent; in other words, there is an 85 per cent chance that any Scud operated properly will work correctly and deliver its warhead within an area of reasonable expectation. However, for a system

[94] Balaschak *et al.* (note 3).

[95] Howe, J. R., *Emerging Long Range Threat to CONUS* (Rockwell International, Space Systems Division: Washington, DC, Dec. 1992).

[96] Bilstein, R. E., *Stages to Saturn: A Technological History of the Apollo/Saturn Launch Vehicles* (National Aeronautics and Space Administration: Washington, DC, 1980), pp. 176–83, 323–45.

[97] Bilstein (note 96), p. 80.

combining five Scuds into an individual airframe, the odds are less than 38 per cent that it will function properly. Even this low standard assumes ideal performance. Once one adds the uncertainties of how the clustered sections interact and the problems of staging, the likelihood that the system will perform properly is minimal.

In the early 1980s German engineers in Libya tried to use this approach in developing the Otrag rocket, which would have clustered and staged dozens or even hundreds of thin booster sections to create rockets capable of placing satellites in orbit. The failures of Otrag are well known; the design team was unable to perfect the basic booster. Clustering and staging were never tested, but the primitive and erratic technology of the individual boosters doomed the approach to almost certain failure.[98]

Efforts with proven boosters are not ensured any more success, as Iraq discovered with its al Abed. The three-stage rocket integrated a total of six or seven Scuds—four in the first stage, two in the second and one unidentified rocket (most likely another Scud or a modified Soviet surface-to-air missile) as the third stage. The failure of its one and only test flight need not have ended the project: some successful US and Soviet rockets started with even more catastrophic first flights, but the al Abed clearly had immense obstacles to overcome. The Iraqis apparently understood the implications and discontinued most work on the project.[99]

North Korea appears to have a comparable project. In February 1994 it was revealed that North Korea was developing similar weapons, the largest of which is the Taepo Dong-2, thought to have a maximum range of roughly 3500 km. Since North Korea's rocketry is based entirely on Scud technology, the most likely way that a missile of such capabilities could be assembled is through clustering and staging Scud sections. Some observers argued that this effort presages an eventual North Korean ICBM. While this may be Pyongyang's goal, the odds against the success of an endeavour based on existing technology are overwhelming.[100]

The inherent problems of technology and the laws of probability all but ensure that large rockets created through clustering and multiple staging of Scud-type sections cannot be militarily effective weapons. Unable to carry out any military mission and too costly to be deployed in large numbers, they have no role on a battlefield. Their performance is so uncertain that even a nuclear warhead cannot ensure that they will work. This is not to say that they can be

[98] *Aviation Week & Space Technology*, 23 Mar. 1981, p. 25; and Miller, J., 'U.S. uneasy over military potential of commercially produced rockets', *New York Times*, 12 Sep. 1981, p. 4. The fullest account is given by Barth, K. G., 'Gahdafis geheime Raketen-Oase' [Gaddafi's secret rocket oasis], *Der Stern*, no. 22 (1987), pp. 20–26.

[99] Navias, M. S., *Going Ballistic: The Build-Up of Missiles in the Middle East* (Brassey's: London, 1993), pp. 101–11.

[100] R. James Woolsey quoted in, 'C.I.A. warns of new North Korean missiles', *New York Times*, 18 Mar. 1994, p. A12; and Wright, D. and Kadyshev, T., 'The North Korean missile program: how advanced is it?', *Arms Control Today*, Apr. 1994, pp. 9–12. Not all authorities are convinced of the weaknesses of the North Korea development plans. See, e.g., Bodansky, Y., *Crisis in Korea* (SPI Books: New York, 1994), chapter 12.

ignored. While they may be all but useless when aimed at an adversary's cities and bases, they can work perfectly as symbols of a country's intent. Their effect on perceptions may be sufficient to force outsiders to take such weapons seriously regardless of their scanty technical merits. Just as the mere rumour of nuclear weapons can sober the ambitions of a potential adversary, there are times when any missile, even a bad one, may be sufficient to intimidate or provoke.

Any ambitious rocket power can use clustering and staging to create an impressive looking missile, but very few can make such a contraption work. The only countries capable of overcoming the problems of ignition sequencing, stage separation and unpredictable interactions are those with considerable experience with large rockets. Those countries, however, are sufficiently advanced and technologically endowed to skip the clustering and staging approach altogether. They can proceed directly to development of their own long-range rockets based on a much more advanced design. In other words, those countries able to use clustering and staging successfully are unlikely to find it appealing; those countries that take the method seriously cannot make it work without immense outside help.

VI. Flight-testing

Before a large rocket can enter service, it must be fully developed. Each component must be put through its own independent test programme to ensure that it can perform its tasks under the extreme conditions of rocket flight. It must be able to operate under serious vibration, low or non-existent atmospheric pressure, accelerations as high as 20 times the force of gravity and extreme heat. Each series of tests must be repeated as components are assembled into sub-systems. This process culminates in flight-tests of the completed rocket. The number of flight-tests is critical to determining the utility of a rocket. The need to test also helps determine the total number of rockets which must be built since additional rockets must be built for testing, not just for deployment.

First flights are dramatic occasions, often attended by national leaders and commemorated for years afterwards. Because of the great prestige of large rockets, the first test flight is commonly viewed as proof that the country has a new capability, that it has arrived on the world stage or joined an exclusive club. The reality is that a first flight only demonstrates its potential. Just as the launch of a new ship comes months or years before the vessel is fitted out and ready to go to sea, so it is with a rocket's first flight.

At the first flight, the rocket typically is a stripped-down model for testing only a handful of key sub-systems over a short flight. Before a rocket can be declared operational it must usually go through at least 20 test flights, each introducing progressively greater realism and complexity.[101] Each flight is necessary to identify and correct design faults and establish actual performance

[101] Kaplan, F., *The Wizards of Armageddon* (Simon and Schuster: New York, 1983), p. 164.

capabilities. In the case of a country's first large rocket or a highly experimental model, 40 or more test-firings may be necessary to establish confidence in the system.[102]

Testing not only reveals flaws in physical technology. It also clarifies problems in programme conception, in the soft technology of design and organization. Poor design choices and organizational and personnel problems tend to become visible through testing. As testing starts, it becomes impossible to escape the effects of excessive ambition or duplication. A healthy rocket project goes through a comprehensive series of test flights over a period of about 5 years in a major power or no more than 10 years for a regional actor. A poorly managed project, in contrast, leads to test programmes that are very slow, with perhaps only one test-firing per year, sometimes less often. In the case of the Indian ASLV space launcher, the first and second tests were separated by more than four years, and test flights of its military cousin, the Agni IRBM, were three years apart.[103] At that rate neither is likely ever to be deployed.

Development testing

The number of test flights required before a missile can be declared operational varies. Data on the number of test flights in missile development are scarce, especially for emerging missile powers. Although the data in table 5.2 are not comprehensive enough to establish just how much testing is necessary, they do show that the number of missiles expended in development is so great that sometimes it even exceeds the number actually deployed. Not included are the additional missiles that must be expended later in operational or reliability testing, to train crews and to determine how a missile is ageing.

The number of development test shots will be determined in part by the maturity of a nation's programme and the degree of reliability that its leaders are willing to accept. The large number of test flights the United States required in the late 1950s (typically 30–50 before a missile was declared operational) was partially a result of inexperience, but high standards played a role as well. The Strategic Air Command, still sceptical of ballistic missiles, insisted that early ballistic missiles achieve the highest feasible reliability. Even after initial development testing using 30–70 missiles, the reliability of early US long-range missiles was very disappointing, typically less than 50 per cent.[104]

Through a carefully planned and executed incremental development process, the number of developmental test flights can be reduced. As shown by the French example examined in chapter 4, by gradually adding new capabilities and recycling proven technology the risks for each new rocket are minimized.

---

[102] The record for a US ballistic missile probably belongs to the Lance. A total of 156 were launched from its first flight in 1965 until it was declared operational in 1972. See *World Missile Forecast* (note 40).

[103] Joshi (note 91).

[104] Neufeld, J., *Ballistic Missiles in the United States Air Force, 1945–1960* (Office of Air Force History, US Air Force: Washington, DC, 1990), pp. 215–19.

Table 5.2. Number of select US, Soviet and French ballistic missiles tested and deployed

Country	Type	First flight	Maximum range[a] (km)	No. tested before deployment	Highest no. deployed	Total no. built
USA	Redstone	1953	500	37	..	..
	Atlas	1957	8 000	45	132	(300)
	Titan-1	1960	11 000	47	54	163
	Pershing-1	1960	740	69	216[b]	827[b]
	Titan-2	1962	11 000	33	54	..
	Lance	1965	125	156	..	2 391[b]
	Pershing-2	1982	1 800	26	108	336
	MX	1983	10 000	20	50	117
USSR	SS-13	1965	..	44	60	..
	SS-17	1972	..	30	150	..
	SS-18	1972	..	35	308	..
	SS-19	1973	..	27	360	..
	SS-20	1974	..	(40)	405	(740)
	SS-23	1976	..	(40)	310[b]	(420)[b]
France	S-2	1965	2 700	27[c]	18	55[c]
	S-3	1977	3 000	21	18	52
	Pluton	1968	120	36	44	106

Data in parentheses are author's estimates.

[a] Maximum range with normal payload.

[b] Includes missiles transferred to other countries.

[c] Includes special development versions, the S-112 and S-01.

Sources: Taylor, J. W. R. (ed.), *Jane's All the World's Aircraft, 1964–65* (London: Sampson Low, Marston, 1964); *World Missile Forecast* (Forecast Associates: Newtown, Conn., 1990); Blake, B. (ed.), *Jane's Weapon Systems, 1988–89* (Jane's: Coulsdon, Surrey, 1988); Cochran, T. B. *et al., Nuclear Weapons Databook: Vol. IV, Soviet Nuclear Weapons* (Ballinger: New York, 1989); Neufeld, J., *Ballistic Missiles in the United States Air Force, 1945–1960* (Office of Air Force History, US Air Force: Washington, DC, 1990); and Burrows, W. E. and Windrem, R., *Critical Mass: The Dangerous Race for Superpower Weapons in a Fragmented World* (Simon and Schuster: New York, 1994), pp. 454–55.

By following such a development strategy, France was able to deploy its 2750-km range S-2 missile in 1971 after only 12 test launches. However, this figure conceals the many specialized development rockets that came before (61 in all before the S-2 itself), in which individual sub-systems and concepts were proven.[105] Consequently, incremental development may reduce the risks of missile engineering, making the overall process more elegant and efficient, but it seems unlikely to ensure great financial savings.

---

[105] Villain (note 27), pp. 72–73, 78, 82, 100, 123.

Deployment without testing?

The minimum number of test launches required to deploy a large rocket is not determined by any concrete rules. It varies depending on the novelty of the technology, its cost and designers' expectations. This leads to a curious point: Can long-range rockets be deployed with little or no flight-testing? The evidence here is ambivalent. The only major rocket ever deployed without flight-testing was unique in every way. Emerging powers clearly must test, but depending upon their goals for the rocket, they may be able to suffice with surprisingly little testing.

The only major rocket ever deployed without flight-testing, the Saturn-5 moon rocket, was unique. NASA never conducted a proper test flight of a complete Saturn-5: although the upper stages were test fired extensively, the massive first stage flew for the first time as part of the Apollo-4 mission, when the rocket was launched 'all-up' on 8 November 1967.[106] This extraordinary risk was made necessary in part by the enormous cost of the rocket, but more by the political pressure to meet the goal of sending a man to the moon before the end of the decade. The Saturn-5 owed its technical feasibility to the unparalleled resources of the German-led design team at the Marshall Space Flight Center—with experience stretching back 35 years through the V-2 and many more advanced rockets. Further security came from an extensive ground testing programme. After all the precautions, launching a Saturn-5 still required a countdown lasting four days. Even so, the 'all-up' decision was regarded by the NASA leadership as the greatest risk of the entire Apollo programme; it worked only because of circumstances that probably cannot be repeated ever again.[107]

The Soviet Union developed its own enormous moon rocket, the N-1, in a compromise fashion. Unwilling to gamble on the same lucky streak but unable to afford a complete test sequence, the Soviet Union condensed its testing programme. Instead of testing individual stages one by one, the process was started with four complete test rockets. Although this was less of a leap than the United States took with the Saturn-5 rocket, it actually was far riskier: because the Soviet Union had stretched its limited technical resources much further, the N-1 rocket actually needed more testing. Although the risk was justified by the immense political pressure to match the United States, the reduced test programme cut one corner too many. The first rocket blew up in 1969 as did the other three. This was the end of the Soviet manned moon programme.[108]

No regional power can develop a large rocket under similar circumstances, certainly not a ballistic missile which must stand ready for months, waiting to

---

[106] There were limits to the risks NASA decision makers would accept; the first 2 Saturn-5 missions, Apollo-4 and Apollo-6, were unmanned.

[107] Bilstein (note 96)), pp. 349–51; and Murray, C. and Bly Cox, C., *Apollo: The Race to the Moon* (Simon and Schuster: New York, 1989), pp. 159–62.

[108] Covault, C., 'Soviet Union reveals moon rocket design', *Aviation Week & Space Technology*, 18 Feb. 1991, pp. 58–59; Covault, C., 'Russian reveal secrets of Mir, Buran, lunar landing craft', *Aviation Week & Space Technology*, 10 Feb. 1992, pp. 38–39; and Zaloga (note 76), p. 310.

Table 5.3. Testing of the Israeli Jericho-2 missile and related rockets

Event	Date	Range (km)
Initial deployment reported	1985	–
1st reported test launch	1986	465
2nd reported test launch	May 1987	820
3rd reported test launch	Sep. 1988	–
Ofeq-1 satellite launch	19 Sep. 1988	–
South African test launch	5 July 1989	1 450
4th reported test launch	14 Sep. 1989	1 300
5th reported test launch	Jan. 1990	–
Ofeq-2 satellite launch	3 Apr. 1990	–
South African test launch	19 Nov. 1990	–
6th reported test launch	Dec. 1990	–
7th reported test launch	Mar. 1992	–

Sources: 'Israel said to deploy Jericho missile', *Aerospace Daily*, 1 May 1985; 'Israel's Jericho IRBM completes long range test', *International Defense Review*, July 1987, p. 857; Lopez, R., 'Israel in second secret test of Jericho IRBM', *Jane's Defence Weekly*, 19 Nov. 1988, p. 1258; Banks, T., 'Soviet claim Israel has launched ballistic missile', *Jane's Defence Weekly*, 23 Sep. 1989, p. 549; Gordon, M. R., 'U.S. says data suggest Israel aids South Africa on missile', *New York Times*, 27 Oct. 1989, p. A1; 'Israel orbits Ofeq-2 spacecraft', *Aviation Week and Space Technology*, 9 Apr. 1990, p. 20; and Burrows, W. E. and Windrem, R., *Critical Mass: The Dangerous Race for Superpower Weapons in a Fragmented World* (Simon and Schuster: New York, 1994), pp. 454–55.

be launched in minutes or seconds. Smaller compromises in development testing may still be tempting, however. Emerging missile powers willing to deploy less reliable forces may be satisfied with less thorough testing. Instead of dozens of developmental tests, they may be willing to deploy a new missile after as few as six or eight successful tests. India will probably deploy its 240-km range Prithvi after 12–15 tests.[109] Israel's far more demanding 1450-km Jericho-2 appears to have been deployed after even fewer test flights (see table 5.3).

This abbreviated testing is not enough to establish a missile's statistical reliability, but it could be sufficient to confirm mechanical integrity: circumscribed testing cannot prove that a missile *will* work, but may show that it *can*. Given the high cost of developmental test flights, the temptation to reduce the number will be strongest in programmes for large and complicated ballistic missiles, especially multiple-stage rockets designed for ranges beyond 1000 km. It is one of the ironies of ballistic missile proliferation that the rockets that need extensive testing most are least likely to get it.

[109] 'India', *Milavnews*, Sep. 1991, p. 15.

Operational testing

A second major need is for operational or life-cycle testing to maintain readiness and reliability. Soon after a missile is deployed to active military units, and as long as it remains in service, regular test firing is necessary to ascertain how the system is ageing, to train crews and commanders, and to certify modifications.[110] The scale of this testing will almost always surpass that of developmental testing and contribute greatly to the total cost of the programme. To verify performance and reliability an operational ballistic missile must usually be test fired at least twice a year throughout the 20 years or more that it stays in service. For a missile force that must be maintained at a high state of readiness and reliability, monthly operational testing is desirable.[111]

The number of operational tests can be staggering. To take an extreme example, the United States launched more than 52 Minuteman missiles in a single year, 1964, some for development of more advanced versions but most to train crews and improve the reliability of its rapidly expanding ICBM force.[112] If a missile is deployed in relatively small numbers—such as the 50 US MX/Peacekeeper ICBMs or the 44 French short-range Plutons—the number required for reliability testing can easily exceed the number actually deployed in the field. In one of the best documented examples of a programme that matured through a complete life cycle, the United States built a total of 827 Pershing-1 missiles in the 1960s. When the last of these were destroyed under the 1987 INF Treaty, only 169 remained. All the rest had been used in development and operational testing.[113]

Planning for testing

Testing requirements can seriously strain a missile force unless they are planned early in the life of the project. If too few missiles are built, a regional power may soon have to choose between not testing and watching reliability decline or testing and watching its inventory disappear. To avoid this dilemma, an emerging missile power can be expected to build far more missiles than it actually expects to deploy. Testing needs can also be expected to create tension with outside observers who count not just deployed missiles but all the missiles in a country's inventory.

To give a hypothetical example, a country trying to deploy a force of 60 ballistic missiles of a single type will have to build many more, typically at least 160, to get the missile into operation and keep it there. As a rule of thumb, one

[110] The different categories of missile tests are discussed in Wilkes, O., van Frank, M. and Hayes, P., *Chasing Gravity's Rainbow: Kwajalein and US Ballistic Missile Testing*, Canberra Paper 81 (Strategic and Defence Studies Centre, Australian National University: Canberra, 1991), pp. 75–80.

[111] Neufeld (note 104), pp. 231–32.

[112] Wilkes, van Frank and Hayes (note 110), p. 55.

[113] All these remaining missiles had been modified into Pershing-1a versions. Griffiths, S. I., 'The implementation of the INF Treaty', *SIPRI Yearbook 1990: World Armaments and Disarmament* (Oxford University Press: Oxford, 1990), p. 448.

would expect to see 20 missiles fired in development tests, 60 for initial deployment, an equal number for rotation while deployed missiles undergo maintenance and at least 20 more for operational testing. The cost of the additional missiles is not beyond the means of most would-be missile proliferators, but it must be planned for in the budget. In reality many proliferators do not plan so systematically or test so thoroughly. A likely reason for the painfully slow progress of many missile projects in the developing world is a failure to plan enough rockets for essential testing.

There is no way for a country to avoid testing large numbers of its first ballistic missile without undermining trust in the weapon. The only successful strategy for reducing testing requirements stresses continuity in subsequent designs. Rather than developing entirely new missiles for each new requirement, a luxury only the Soviet Union and the United States could afford, smaller powers can improve existing designs for greater performance incrementally. By gradually increasing engine thrust, enlarging fuel tanks or adding additional stages, the proven capabilities of old technology can be preserved. Some testing will be necessary for new or altered components and to integrate the system, but much less than for an entirely new missile.

Despite its great importance, testing is not as easily controlled as physical technology. But because it is so dramatic and because of the difficulties of concealing it, it is not immune to outside influence either. The need for periodic test flights throughout the life-cycle of a missile creates special opportunities for arms control. A ballistic missile test ban would make the introduction of new missile types extremely difficult if not impossible. It would reduce a nation's ability to rely on its existing missile force within months and render the entire force untrustworthy in a few years.

VII. Conclusions

The hard technology of ballistic missiles is the most visible aspect of the proliferation problem. For all its obviousness it is no less deceptive than the more subtle problems of soft technology. Despite decades of experience, would-be missile powers and controllers still find the technical requirements of rocketry development difficult to apprehend. When Libya began to invest in domestic rocketry in the late 1970s, to return to a well-worn example, there was no serious appreciation of the quantity, cost and complexity of hardware which had to be acquired and mastered. In Europe, several prominent governments displayed equally serious misunderstandings of the nature of basic rocket technologies when they permitted critical exports during the 1980s.

Much of the confusion arises from the assumption that hard technology dictates particular paths of development. While certain technologies are obviously preferable, there are usually alternatives. Hard technology is better appreciated as a spectrum of opportunities for would-be proliferators and control advocates alike. For proliferators there is the 'catalogue problem', the long list of mechanical, chemical and electronic technologies which must be acquired and integrated into a long-range rocket. For controllers there is the mirror image of the catalogue problem in the control lists of items that form the basis for export controls and offer numerous chances to hinder or stop a dangerous programme.

The problem of developing policies to cope with the hard technology is further complicated by the 'fungibility problem'. Some technologies are more easily substituted than others, and they are not equally amenable to outside control. In some areas, rocket technologies are easily substituted. While the most appealing technical options may be very vulnerable to outside control, would-be missile makers can turn to other hardware options if the ideal ones are too difficult to secure. Other technologies are unique and essential, offering few or no chances for bypassing, but these tend to be poorly suited to outside control.

For most proliferators the goal of missile policy is no different from the rocketry goals that fuelled the ambitions of the established powers: to develop the most advanced and best-performing weapons possible. The realities of hard technology rarely make this feasible. Instead, emerging missile powers must choose either to emphasize high-performance technologies while risking heavy reliance on potentially fickle foreign suppliers or to pursue less impressive but still effective technology which can be acquired even in the face of international opposition.

Until the mid-1980s most emerging missile powers chose to emphasize performance over secure supply. Countries as diverse as Argentina, Brazil, South Africa and Taiwan took the technological high road. This exposed them to considerable risk. It is no coincidence that their programmes were among the most vulnerable to the Missile Technology Control Regime (MTCR). The only emerging powers still devoting their rocketry to top-end capabilities are those such as India and Israel, which were able to acquire most of the technology they needed before export controls became serious. The only other countries still making progress since the imposition of the MTCR are those such as Iran and North Korea, which choose to rely on less appealing but still adequate technologies, those which are most difficult to control.

Rather than emphasize the most impressive technical options, the missile proliferators of the future are more likely to pursue less demanding technologies. Instead of sophistication, they will tend to choose adequacy and fungibility. This will lead them back to technologies of the late 1950s and early 1960s, technologies long ago discarded by the major powers but perfectly suitable for less demanding military planners. Some hard technologies offer considerable scope for such substitution, others do not.

1. The propulsion choices are several but not without consequences. Solid fuels naturally are more appealing to military planners. Double-based solid fuels suitable for large artillery rockets are especially hard to control, but more advanced composite fuels are considerably more difficult to master without foreign assistance. Consequently, regional rocket makers are likely to return to liquid propulsion, especially storable liquids, for their long-range systems.

2. Guidance systems are an inviting target for control, but the ideal INS can usually be replaced with systems using a combination of strap-down gyros and radio correction without sacrificing too much accuracy.

4. Re-entry vehicle design offers fewer options. While easily mastered for rockets up to 1000 km in range, at longer ranges it imposes problems which can only be overcome through extensive development and testing.

5. Stage separation, the most visible aspect of systems integration, is especially important for rockets of over 1000 km range. It, too, forces development along a narrow path which can be mastered only through focused effort.

6. Flight-testing can be trimmed, but only at the cost of reduced reliability, undermining the credibility of the system. Although it is easy to plan for the large numbers of rockets needed for testing, few regional powers appear to do so—probably for budgetary reasons.

Virtually any regional power can build small artillery rockets and many can seriously consider building short-range ballistic missiles, especially systems with top ranges of 120–150 km. If a country is serious in its efforts to develop these small rockets, there is little that outsiders can do to stop it. Much short-range rocket technology is also too easily available for any but the most draconian control system to have much effect. The hard technology of larger rockets creates serious impediments to the grander dreams and aspirations of national leaders. It may be easy to establish a programme to develop long-range ballistic missiles, but only a few countries have the technical resources and ability to pursue it to success.

As has been seen with many different technologies, the most serious battle over the control of rocket hardware takes place on the technological plateau. The hard technologies for missiles of less than 150-km range are too widely available for export controls to be uniformly effective, while those for systems with ranges above 1000 km are too demanding for all but a handful of regional powers to master. The most serious battles over the control of rocket technology are fought between these extremes. Here most regional actors depend on foreign assistance, leaving them sensitive to foreign influence. Their vulnerability is offset by the advantage of several alternative paths towards missile development, making it possible to circumvent outside controls. This problem turns the struggle for technical mastery on the technological plateau into a game of geopolitical cat and mouse.

Export controls will retain their greatest potential against rockets designed for ranges of 1000 km and beyond. These require considerably more sophisticated technologies than their smaller relations. Not only must they have substantially different propulsion systems, engine designs and re-entry vehicle concepts, but they also require mastery of multiple-staging. Many of the short-cuts that are acceptable in shorter-range rockets—such as double-based fuels and strap-down or radio guidance—are not suitable at such ranges. These differences make such projects far more vulnerable than earlier, more modest ones. Even so, for export controls to be most effective against a proliferator's long-range potential they must still be imposed early, when a country is developing only short-range rockets. Although they probably will not stop work on short-range rockets, if applied early enough controls will prevent most proliferators from acquiring the capacity to build larger ones.

Technical hurdles are far from insurmountable, however, and the penalties for short-term thinking are harsh. Over the next few decades, as global resources grow and technological problems recede, more and more countries will be able to master the concepts and hardware of long-range ballistic missiles. If they choose to develop rockets using the incremental design strategy discussed above, their programmes may appear modest and benign at first. It is one more irony of missile proliferation that, when regional missile programmes are most vulnerable to export controls and political pressure, they seem least threatening and are least likely to be correctly evaluated and challenged. Later, when the threat they represent to regional peace and security becomes obvious, they will be much more difficult to stop.

6. The deadly technology I: conventional and CBW armaments

I. Introduction

Armament is more than just another aspect of the hard technology of ballistic missile development. To be sure, armament does not present completely different technical problems: all evidence suggests that its acquisition and control are regulated by processes that are very similar to those noted in previous chapters of this volume. Nor is it more important than other major rocket technologies; a rocket is an integrated package in which all components must perform adequately or the entire system will fail. Armament is distinguished rather by its overwhelming effect on a rocket's military capabilities and its political salience.

The first ballistic missiles of World War II carried only conventional high explosives, as has every ballistic missile fired in anger ever since. There is no evidence that the Peenemünde station rocket team ever seriously considered adapting the V-2 rocket to carry anything else. Not only did work on the German atomic bomb fail to make rapid progress, but it was also apparent that any early nuclear weapon would be far too large for rockets to carry. In retrospect, the armament of the V-2 was an historic anomaly: there would be other conventionally armed ballistic missiles, but never again would designers or strategists assume that rockets would carry conventional warheads exclusively. Soon after the news of the bomb dropped on Hiroshima, the association between the rocket and the atomic bomb was complete, not only in the public mind but in the thinking of defence professionals as well.

The relationship between the two most spectacular weapons of World War II is natural and probably unavoidable. Nevertheless, it is essential for anyone concerned with the spread of ballistic missiles to recall that their significance has never depended exclusively on the armament they carry or their precise military effects. As largely psychological weapons, they matter because of the fears they elicit—fears that arise almost independent of their particular armament.

No doubt ballistic missiles will always be thought of as nuclear-armed missiles, especially the large missiles designed to travel thousands of kilometres. Yet any of several other armament options are far more likely to be chosen to fill the nose-cones of a regional actor's ballistic missiles. With sufficient improvements in accuracy, these alternatives—even if less deadly—may be militarily effective.

II. Conventional high explosives

It is no accident that every ballistic missile fired in anger has carried a high-explosive warhead, from the first V-2 launched against London on 8 September 1944 to the Serbian missiles fired in Bosnia in the 1990s. While conventional explosives may not be the most efficient weapon for long-range rockets, they are the easiest armaments to fabricate for missile delivery. Conventional explosives are familiar to weapon designers and military commanders. Their effects are thoroughly understood.

The only thing easier than fabricating a high-explosive warhead is to leave a missile with no warhead at all; even an unarmed ballistic missile can cause great destruction on impact. The kinetic energy of an unarmed missile such as a V-2 or Scud is sufficient to dig a crater the size of a building—typically 10 metres deep and 20 metres across—and spread destruction across an area of a city block.[1] To be a credible weapon, however, an unarmed ballistic missile would require almost unimaginable accuracy. Even then it would be useful only in very specific war-fighting situations.

Yet this is exactly what has been suggested as a future option for the most advanced US missiles, such as the Trident II.[2] Even for the United States such a weapon would be useful only in the most peculiar and exceptional situations. It requires no magical insight to conclude that regional ballistic missile forces will rely, at a bare minimum, on the destructive power of conventional explosives. Although it might not seem like much, for short-range missiles in particular this may be enough to make them fully credible weapons.

The advantages of conventionally armed short-range missiles

As a rule, the efficiency of conventionally armed missiles is inversely proportional to their range; as range increases, their potential effectiveness declines. The larger the rocket, the higher its cost and the less armament it can carry as a share of total take-off weight. While larger rockets usually carry more in absolute terms, they must burn much more fuel per kilogram of payload. In theory, they can be very deadly with ordinary explosives; in reality, they are just too costly. Only if missiles are cheap enough to allow them to be used in large numbers can they promise to be effective when armed with conventional explosives alone. The individual payloads of short-range rockets may be less than those of larger missiles, but their low cost facilitates procurement of large numbers of them. Consequently, short-range missiles tend to be much more

---

[1] Klee, E. and Merk, O., *The Birth of the Missile*, trans. T. Schoeters (Harrap: London, 1965), p. 54; Carus, W. S., *Ballistic Missiles in Modern Conflict* (Praeger and the Center for Strategic International Studies: New York, 1991), p. 35; and Roche, J., 'Proliferation of tactical aircraft and ballistic and cruise missiles in the development world', eds W. T. Wander, E. H. Arnett and P. Bracken, *The Diffusion of Advanced Weaponry* (American Association for the Advancement of Science: Washington, DC, 1994), p. 75.

[2] Hacket, J., 'KE penetrator would make its point', *Defense News*, 29 Mar. 1993, p. 25.

Table 6.1. Large artillery rockets available in 1994

Source	Designation	Launch weight (kg)	Payload (kg)	Length (m)	Maximum range (km)
Brazil	Astros SS-60	576	(150)	5.4	68
	X-40	654	150	4.9	66
China	Type 83	484	(90)	4.7	40
Egypt	Sakr-80	660	200	10.3	80
Iran	Nazeat	950	150	5.9	90
	Oghab	360	70	4.8	40
Iraq[a]	Laith, based on the FROG-7	(2 500)	(300)	(9)	90
Israel	MAR-350	850	300	5.8	80
Russia	FROG-7	2 400	450	9.5	70
	BM-30	800	300	(5.0)	70

Data in parentheses are author's estimates.

[a] The status of Iraqi programmes is unknown.

Sources: Foss, C. F. (ed.), *Jane's Armour and Artillery 1994–95* (Jane's: Coulsdon, Surrey, 1994); and *Missile Monitor*, spring 1992, pp. 2–3.

efficient, permitting the creation of forces with much greater total capability, able to bombard a target with a greater total weight of explosives than an equally expensive force of larger rockets.

The relative advantage of short-range missiles with conventional armament is illustrated by the very smallest surface-to-surface rockets—artillery rockets such as the Soviet Katyushka. A typical version is the Soviet-designed BM-21, a 122-mm calibre rocket weighing 77 kg and with a maximum range of 20 km. Such short-range artillery rockets are ideal for the task of bombarding targets on or near the battlefield. A normal battalion of 18 BM-21 launchers can fire 720 rockets in 20 seconds, enough to obliterate a target the size of a small military base (approximately 1000 x 500 metres).[3] For almost half the world's countries, artillery rockets were an introduction to ground-to-ground rocketry, a starting-point on a path which may lead to interest in long-range ballistic missiles.

Larger artillery rockets are increasingly popular with the world's armies. Previously available only to select clients of the Soviet Union, these weapons became the subject of widespread interest in the 1970s. Today, large artillery rockets can be purchased from a growing number of suppliers (see table 6.1). They are gaining in popularity largely because they represent the technology for the largest rockets that emerging scientific establishments can develop with

[3] Lee, R. G., *Introduction to Battlefield Weapons Systems and Technology* (Brassey's: London, 1981), pp. 46–47; and Zaloga, S. J. and Loop, J. W., *Soviet Tanks and Combat Vehicles 1946 to the Present* (Arms and Armour Press: Poole, UK, 1987), pp. 126–27.

Table 6.2. Payload and payload proportion of selected ballistic missiles

Category/range	Type	First flight	Maximum range[a] (km)	Launch weight (kg)	Normal payload weight (kg)	Payload as proportion of total weight (%)
ICBMs	Atlas-D	1957	14 500	117 930	(3 000)	*(.03)*
9 500 +	Minuteman-1	1961	10 000	29 400	(1 000)	*(.03)*
	DF-5	1971	13 000	183 000	3 200	*.02*
	SS-18	1972	11 000	220 000	7 600	*.03*
	MX	1983	9 600	88 450	7 200	*.08*
IRBMs	Thor	1956	3 180	47 630	(3 000)	*(.06)*
2 500–3 200	S-2	1965	2 750	31 900	(1 000)	*(.03)*
	DF-3	1966	2 650	64 000	2 150	*.03*
	Agni	1989	2 500	14 200	250[b]	*.02*
500–750	Pershing-1	1960	740	4 600	320	*.07*
	SS-23	(1976)	500	4 690	700	*.15*
	al Hussein	1987	600	(7 000)	190	*(0.3)*
	M-9	(1990)	600	6 200	500	*.08*
Short-range	V-2	1942	320	12 870	910	*.07*
250–320	Scud-B	1957	280	6 370	985	*.15*
	Prithvi-250	1988	250	(4 200)	250[b]	*(.06)*
	M-11	1988	300	(5 000)	500	*(.10)*
Shortest-range	Sergeant	1958	140	4 536	(500)	*(.11)*
120–150	Lance	1965	125	1 527	455	*.30*
	Pluton	(1970)	120	2 423	(400)	*(.17)*
	SS-21	(1976)	120	2 000	482	*.24*
	Prithvi-150	1988	150	(4 200)	1 000	*(.24)*

[a] Maximum range with normal payload.

[b] Sources disagree on the payload of the Agni and Prithvi at maximum range. Although a payload of 250 kg is used here, many Indian sources maintain that it is 500 kg, which would raise the payload proportion in the Agni at maximum range to 4% and the Prithvi-250 to 12%.

Sources: Taylor, J. W. R. (ed.), *Jane's All the World's Aircraft, 1964–65* (Sampson Low, Marston: London, 1964); Blake, B. (ed.), *Jane's Weapon Systems, 1988–89* (Jane's: Coulsdon, Surrey, 1988); Carus, W. S. and Bermundes, J. S., Jr, 'Iraq's al-Husayn missile programme', *Jane's Soviet Intelligence Review*, May 1990; Lennox, D., 'The SS-21 Scarab—an update', *Jane's Intelligence Review*, July 1992; Banerjie, I., 'Aiming for the sky', *Sunday* (Calcutta), 22 Oct. 1989; and Zaloga, S., 'Ballistic missiles in the Third World: Scud and beyond', *International Defense Review*, Nov. 1988.

little outside help and which their armed forces can operate with relative ease. Large artillery rockets are, in effect, low-technology ballistic missiles, lacking active guidance systems but endowed with considerable range and payload capability.

Although they cost far more than smaller versions, even large artillery rockets are still cheap enough to be bought by the dozens or hundreds, sometimes even many thousands. In 1992, for example, the Brazilian company Avibras sold 50 328 artillery rockets, including the largest models, to Saudi Arabia.[4] Fired individually, like the Palestinian rockets occasionally directed at Israel in the 1970s and 1980s, they are not very dangerous. Used in the thousands, however, as was seen in the Afghan capital of Kabul in 1989–92, their effects can be horrific.

Despite their rising popularity, the utility of the largest artillery rockets is very questionable. At longer ranges, the accuracy of an unguided rocket drops rapidly, undermining the ability to engage targets. Their advantages diminish both in comparative terms against other delivery systems (especially manned aircraft) and in absolute terms of effectiveness—the simple ability to destroy a target. As weapons, their effectiveness declines rapidly at ranges much greater than 40 km. Beyond this range, conventionally armed artillery rockets are too costly to be used in the large numbers needed to knock out a target. Instead they are most useful for interfering with enemy operations through harassment and interdiction, suppressing an enemy's reactions rather than destroying his capabilities. The technology of unguided weapons imposes an absolute ceiling for military effectiveness somewhere within the range of 70–140 km, beyond which they cannot even be expected to hit even large military bases and cities.

Ballistic missiles—with active guidance—are even less efficient than artillery rockets with conventional armament. As a general rule, the larger the rocket, the lower its efficiency. As a rocket's range increases, the proportion of its mass left for its payload declines. This is illustrated in table 6.2, which shows the efficiency of different ballistic missiles in terms of weight and payload.

The largest ICBMs typically deliver only 2–4 per cent of their total weight as payload: the rest is devoted to the rocket's structure, sub-systems and propellants. For short-range ballistic missiles, such as the Scud, the payload proportion rises to some 15 per cent. Some of the shortest-range ballistic missiles, such as the Russian SS-21 and the Indian Prithvi-150, can carry as much as almost 25 per cent of their total weight in their warhead. Only one ballistic missile shown here can lift 30 per cent of its weight as payload, the 120-km range Lance.

Clearly, the shortest-range ballistic missiles are the ones to be feared most on a conventional battlefield. Given their accuracy, in adequate numbers they can be highly effective for particular tactical circumstances, such as suppressing large military targets or bombarding cities.

---

[4] *United National Register of Conventional Arms*, A/4B/344 (UN: New York, 11 Oct. 1993), p. 16; see also Laurance, E. J., Wezeman, S. T. and Wulf, H., SIPRI, *Arms Watch: SIPRI Report on the First Year of the UN Register of Conventional Arms,* SIPRI Research Report no. 6 (Oxford University Press: Oxford, 1993).

The limits of conventional destructiveness

Although there is little doubt about the comparative inefficiency of the largest ballistic missiles, table 6.2 also shows that the absolute efficiency of ballistic missiles in each class has been increasing over time. The development of better technology, the accumulation of experience and the refinement of design skill have led to consistent improvements in missile performance. Not all missile makers advance at the same rate; newcomers typically have to learn and improve on their own. But the direction of their progress is clear. In any range category, a country's second- and third-generation missiles can be 200–250 per cent more efficient than its first-generation weapons, carrying more payload as a proportion of total launch weight. As a result they can carry more of a punch, even when armed only with high explosives. This process still has a long way to go, however, before long-range missiles are truly efficient when conventionally armed.

This is made clearest through strategic assessments of the kind noted in chapter 3. Although the effectiveness of conventionally armed missiles against political targets such as cities depends on too many circumstances to be predicted reliably, against military targets the problem can be reduced to an arithmetic calculation of payloads and accuracies. In an illuminating study, Benoit Morel and Theodore Postal stress the importance of accuracy as the crucial variable affecting the destructive capability of conventionally armed short-range missiles. They calculate that, if such missiles have extreme accuracy (a CEP of 30 metres), at least 15–30 missiles would be necessary to put a single air base out of action for up to a few days, the exact number depending on missile capabilities and tactical circumstances. As accuracy decreases, much greater numbers of missiles are necessary to accomplish the same result.

At moderate levels of accuracy (CEPs of 250–300 metres, roughly the accuracy of the US Lance or Russian SS-21), even the largest imaginable force could not destroy a major military base outright. A more feasible goal would be to close a facility like an air base, making it temporarily unable to operate. Even so, a total force of 200–300 conventionally armed missiles would be needed to close a single air base. Using relatively inaccurate missiles, such as the Scud (with a CEP of 950 metres), the task of closing an air base of a determined adversary could be virtually impossible, regardless of numbers.[5] A more recent study by the Rand Corporation concludes that fewer missiles may be enough; just 12 missiles like the Lance or SS-21 would have a 50 per cent chance of closing a small air base. The study also notes, however, that rudimentary measures, such as building extra taxi-ways and dispersing aircraft, would greatly increase the number of missiles necessary.[6]

---

[5] Morel, B. and Postal, T. A., *A Technical Assessment of Potential Threats to NATO from Non-Nuclear Soviet Tactical Ballistic Missiles* (Center for International Security and Arms Control, Stanford University: Stanford, Calif., 1 Feb. 1987).

[6] Rubenson, D. and Slomdvic, A., *The Impact of Missile Proliferation on U.S. Power and Projection Capabilities*, N-2985 (Rand Corporation: Santa Monica, Calif., June 1990), pp. 17–18.

Some analysts carry this logic a step further to argue that 'conventionally armed missiles cannot be decisive militarily'.[7] This view arises from the conviction that tactical aircraft are more deadly than missiles. Not only are manned aircraft reusable but they can also almost always carry larger payloads to greater distances and deliver them with much better accuracy. The relative advantages of manned aircraft diminish only against a very well-defended opponent capable of destroying a large proportion of the attacking force. Fetter argues that 'missiles are cost-effective for very short ranges or if aircraft attrition rates are very high. For example, at a range of 500 km, a single-stage missile is cost-effective only if aircraft attrition rates are greater than 35 per cent per sortie'.[8] None but the very best air defences are as deadly as this. Outside Europe and North America, only Israeli, South Korean and Taiwanese defences have any chance of destroying so large a share of an attacking aircraft force.

This perspective is undoubtedly correct, confirming the limited destructiveness of conventionally armed ballistic missiles. As an assessment, however, it is misleadingly lopsided for the reasons outlined in chapter 3. First, it idealizes aircraft performance while emphasizing the weakness of ballistic missiles. As demonstrated in Operation Desert Storm, even under favourable conditions, manned aircraft are rarely as deadly as their technical capabilities might suggest. Second, and of equal importance, it ignores the less visible ways in which even modest air defences force an attacker to tailor aircraft missions carefully and shepherd their attacking forces from harm with vast fleets of support aircraft.[9] Third, it misses the point that an attack need not destroy a military base; it may be enough to make it temporarily unusable or just to slow its operations. Finally, it ignores the great psychological effects of ballistic missiles.

Making a virtue of necessity

The destructive weakness of conventional warheads has been obvious since the V-2 rocket failed to disrupt the Allied war effort. Since then conventional explosives have been pursued mainly as a fall-back option in case other armaments—especially nuclear armaments—are not available. One of the primary reasons why the US Department of Defense refused to finance a major ballistic missile programme in the years just after World War II was the lack of a suitable nuclear warhead. An exception was the Redstone rocket, which first flew in 1953—the largest US ballistic missile for which a high-explosive warhead was developed. This was an enormous warhead weighing 2700 kg (6000 lb), taking up one-third of the total length of the rocket and bringing its maximum range down from 800 km, as originally intended, to only 300 km—although the

---

[7] Fetter, S., 'Ballistic missiles and weapons of mass destruction: What is the threat? What should be done?', *International Security*, vol. 16, no. 1 (summer 1991), p. 13. Similar views are expressed in Harvey, J. *et al.*, *Assessing Ballistic Missile Proliferation and its Control* (Center for International Security and Arms Control, Stanford University: Stanford, Calif., 1991), chapter 2.

[8] Fetter (note 7), p. 9.

[9] See the discussion on aircraft ambiguities in chapter 3, section II.

missile was deployed exclusively with nuclear warheads.[10] After refinements in nuclear warhead design and huge increases in the production of fissile materials in the mid-1950s led to an abundance of appropriate nuclear devices, the United States all but forgot about conventional warheads for long-range ballistic missiles for the rest of the cold war.[11]

Not all countries have been persuaded that large ballistic missiles must be nuclear armed. Soviet military doctrine apparently left commanders with some latitude over what kind of ballistic missiles to use, leading to the stockpiling of conventional and chemical as well as nuclear warheads. In 1980 the Red Army deployed the SS-23, a 500-km range missile which was designed with both nuclear and conventional warheads. Conventional warheads were stockpiled and conventionally armed versions were sold to Bulgaria, Czechoslovakia and the German Democratic Republic. The Red Army also had some conventional warheads for the SS-12B Scaleboard (also known as the SS-22) 900-km range rocket, although the logic in this is unfathomable.[12]

Emerging missile powers have been steered into reliance on conventional armaments by simple necessity; most lack the ability to manufacture any other kind of warhead and no foreign supplier has volunteered to supply one. Although the Scud-B was designed to carry a 70-kt nuclear weapon, there is no evidence that the USSR seriously considered furnishing its clients with such a warhead. The story that a Soviet freighter delivered nuclear warheads for Egyptian Scud missiles during the final days of the 1973 Middle East War appears to be a tall tale, although it is possible that the warheads were loaded on a Soviet vessel but never dispatched.[13] Missile deliveries to countries within the sphere of US influence have been conditional on assurances that the rockets will be armed exclusively with conventional warheads. A prominent example is the roughly 160 Lance missiles sold to Israel in 1976. Similarly, when Saudi Arabia began to take delivery of physically huge DF-3 missiles from China in 1987–88, the White House successfully pressed the Saudi king to sign the Non-Proliferation Treaty and also to declare that the missiles would not carry chemical weapons. Even a country as contemptuous of international norms as North Korea appears to respect this rule when selling missiles, all of which appear to have been delivered conventionally armed (although there is no evidence that North Korea cares how its clients arm their missiles after they are delivered).

---

[10] Willinski, M. I. (formerly an engineer on the Redstone and Navaho missile projects), Private communication with the author, Feb. 1990. The US Army's unhappiness with Redstone's performance, crippled by its huge warhead, is described in Wulforest, H., *The Rocketmakers* (Orion Books: New York, 1990), p. 235.

[11] With the probable continuing improvements in guidance which would permit near-perfect guidance after the year 2000, the US Air Force began to reinvestigate conventional warheads for its ICBMs. Hitchens, T., 'AF re-considers non-nuclear ICBM', *Defense News*, 28 Nov. 1994, p. 24.

[12] Loasby, G., 'The Soviet INF ballistic missiles', *Jane's Soviet Intelligence Review*, Apr. 1989, pp. 156–60.

[13] Although the evidence consists exclusively of rumour and repetition, journalists seem to find this story irresistible. See, for example, Howe, W. R., *Weapons: The International Game of Arms, Money and Diplomacy* (Doubleday: Garden City, N.Y., 1980), p. xix; and Hersh, S. M., *The Sampson Option: Israel, America and the Bomb* (Faber and Faber: London, 1991), p. 234.

Other missile proliferators may wish to build nuclear warheads at a later date or at least to keep that option open, but in the short term they have only been able to develop conventional warheads. Had the Condor-2 project been completed, the missiles would have been delivered exclusively with conventional warheads, although the partners clearly sought broader options for the future. India's Prithvi has also been portrayed in the press exclusively as a conventionally armed missile.[14] Public statements on these and other missiles may represent crafted subterfuge, but Israel's Jericho missiles remain the only regional missiles assumed to carry non-conventional warheads. For other countries, chemical and biological weapon options, discussed below, may be opening faster.

Maximizing conventional effectiveness

The inherent limits of high explosives ensure that the effects of conventionally armed missile will never be confused with a weapon of mass destruction. Even so, there are several things regional countries can do to improve the effectiveness of conventional warheads.

Instead of a single mass of high explosive, the warhead can be packed with as many as several thousand cluster munitions. Instead of concentrating destruction at a single point, this spreads it around a wide area. Dispersed at an appropriate altitude, cluster munitions spread destruction over a greater area, although at the cost of reducing the maximum blast at any one point. This was the path followed in designing the conventionally armed versions of the Honest John (50-km range) and Lance (120-km range) missiles. The former can be equipped with a warhead carrying 860 anti-personnel bomblets weighing 450 g each. A similar warhead equipped the Lance missiles sold to Israel in 1976.[15] Cluster munitions have been developed by Israel and Brazil for their largest artillery rockets and for India's 240-km range Prithvi.

Another approach is to maximize the impact of a conventional warhead by equipping the missile with guidance and control mechanisms enabling it to manœuvre and achieve much greater accuracy. This approach was developed for the US Army Tactical Missile System (ATACMS), a 135-km range weapon used for the first time with partial success in the 1991 Gulf War. It relies on a comparatively inaccurate but cheap laser–inertial guidance platform supplemented by radio commands and optical target location to steer it to a target. The result is a system with a potential for remarkable accuracy. The manœuvring surface-to-surface missile has been described as 'the wave of the future' in missile design, although its technical problems have been difficult to solve. Despite

[14] Josji, M., 'Vehicles of war: the Prithvi, the MBT, the ALH', *Frontline*, 25 Sep. 1992.
[15] Lumsden, M., SIPRI, *Anti-Personnel Weapons* (Taylor & Francis: London, 1978), p. 143.

its goal of extreme accuracy, ATACMS still relies on an armament of 950 anti-personnel bomblets to improve its destructiveness.[16]

With a unit cost of $423 000, the US ATACMS is not cheap, but it is also not prohibitively expensive.[17] The low costs have led some analysts to conclude that the weapon may be the longest-range missile that is 'just as cost-effective as manned aircraft'.[18] Several regional actors have indicated their interest in buying ATACMS, although so far the USA has refused to consider exports to customers other than European NATO allies.[19] In the absence of a foreign supplier, the key question for proliferators is whether or not they can develop comparable technology themselves. Cost may be a serious barrier to domestic development of comparable weapons. For the ATACMS, costs were reduced by borrowing concepts and components from other projects. Guidance is based on ideas borrowed from the Pershing-2 missile and an off-the-shelf laser gyroscope. The manufacturer also economized by building the missile on a previously established production line.[20] For regional actors, unable to borrow technology from related projects and lacking experienced firms to rely on, the costs will undoubtedly be much higher.

Even when they cannot destroy military targets efficiently or reliably, conventionally armed ballistic missiles can still be effective weapons. Of the 22 regional powers with large artillery rockets or ballistic missiles in their forces, only Israel has probably fitted nuclear warheads. All the rest appear to rely on conventional explosive warheads, although some may have developed chemical options as well. Theirs is a waste of effort in terms of strategic logic, a logic which would lead them to deactivate their missiles and spend the money on more efficient delivery platforms such as aircraft. Yet most of these countries have maintained their missiles in active service for 15–25 years. This seemingly irrational loyalty offers tacit testimony that their rockets are prized for other, less tangible criteria.

The political and symbolic importance of ballistic missiles also explains the otherwise inexplicable willingness of some countries to *reduce* their conventional destructiveness. Rather than uniformly try to maximize the amount of high explosives their missiles can carry, some regional powers have elected to reduce missile payloads in order to extend their range, even when this cripples their battlefield potential. The best known examples are probably the modified Scud-Bs fired by Iraq in 1988 and 1991. In the most successful version, the al Hussein, the size of the warhead was reduced from 985 kg in the original Scud down to 290 kg or 125 kg (reports vary), with the effect of doubling the

[16] Carus, W. S., quoted in 'Future missiles will outpace Scuds', *Defense News*, 4 Feb. 1991, p. 38. Command and control difficulties undermined ATACMS effectiveness in the 1991 Gulf War. Munro, N., 'Poor communications slows ATACMS in Gulf', *Defense News*, 11 Feb. 1991, p. 4.

[17] Calculated from 'ATACMS contract', *Jane's Defence Weekly*, 21 Dec. 1991, p. 1195.

[18] Carus (note 1), pp. 10, 38.

[19] 'Turkey seeks ATACMS', *Defense News*, 21 Oct. 1991, p. 2.

[20] 'MGM-140 ATACMS', *World Missile Forecast* (Forecast Associates: Newtown, Conn., Jan. 1995); and 'MGM-140 ATACMS', *World Missiles Briefing* (Teal Group: Fairfax, Va., Sep 1994).

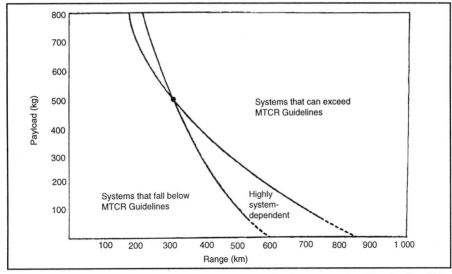

Figure 6.1. Range–payload trade-offs for a typical single-stage rocket like the Scud-B

missile's range.[21] The trade-off between Scud-B range and payload is illustrated in figure 6.1. The main problem with this approach is that extreme cuts in payload are necessary to achieve significant improvements in range. India's Prithvi, which carries an impressive 1000-kg payload to a range of 150 km, reportedly can only carry 250 kg in its 250-km range version.[22] It is evidence of the symbolic importance of ballistic missiles that countries are willing to sacrifice virtually all of a missile's serious military capability in order to extend its range.

Even a militarily ineffective, conventionally armed missile can be effective politically, affecting regional perceptions of a country's power and its willingness to use it. The symbolic power of a ballistic missile can easily surpass its actual military destructiveness. When dealing with a democracy, where public opinion is decisive, the appearance of strength may be as important as its reality. Authoritarian governments, too, almost inevitably drawn to symbols of power, find ballistic missiles politically useful. This explains why countries such as Algeria, Cuba, Kuwait (before the 1990 Iraqi invasion) and Yemen keep their small missile forces—not because their conventionally armed missiles give them greater physical power, but because they affect perceptions of their power.[23]

---

[21] An authoritative source places the al Hussein's payload at 190 kg. Carus, W. S. and Bermudez, J. S., Jr, 'Iraq's al-Husayn missile programme', *Jane's Soviet Intelligence Review*, May 1990, p. 205.

[22] Earlier reports erroneously stated that the Prithvi SS-250 (as the 240-km version is formally called) carried a 500-kg payload. Bedi, R., 'Successful launch for Prithvi missile', *Jane's Defence Weekly*, 23 May 1992, p. 880; and 'Latest trial for Prithvi', *Jane's Defence Weekly*, 13 Feb. 1993, p. 5.

[23] For their owners, missiles are an *index* of capability which can be manipulated to exaggerate their actual destructiveness and the owner's actual capabilities. Jervis, R., *The Logic of Images in International Relations* (Princeton University Press: Princeton, N.J., 1970), pp. 38–61.

In addition to their military and symbolic power, conventionally armed missiles also have *potential* power. They indicate an ability to carry other armaments. Conventional warheads often appear to be temporary measures, a way of filling the space in the rocket's nose-cone while waiting for more potent things to come along. Acquisition of ballistic missiles is typically perceived as evidence that a country is also interested in acquiring weapons of mass destruction. When evaluating an adversary's conventionally armed missiles, other countries must consider not only their proven capabilities but also their potential. Is there a reasonable chance that these missiles could be armed with chemical or nuclear weapons? The threat of nuclear armament does not have to be overwhelming to be convincing; any serious risk may be sufficient to compel other countries to treat the missiles as if they were nuclear armed.

III. Fuel–air explosives: mini-nukes?

The shortcomings of conventional weapons have encouraged intense efforts to develop alternatives—armaments that are more destructive than high explosives but free of the political and ethical complications of chemical and nuclear weapons. In recent years considerable attention has focused on fuel–air explosives (FAEs). These rely on the detonation of a combustible material mixed with air (hence the name) to create large blast effects. Using the right fuels under the right conditions, the blast can be several times more destructive than that of an equal amount of ordinary high explosive. Several regional powers have shown interest in fuel–air explosives, especially for use with their ballistic missiles. The press has been quick to popularize fuel–air explosives as 'miniature nuclear weapons'.

Research on fuel–air explosives can be traced back to the Allied and Axis search for wonder weapons in the early 1940s. The concept was investigated most aggressively in Germany, as well as in the United States and Britain, but the difficulties of developing a practical weapon led investigators seemingly everywhere to abandon the idea. Regular research did not begin again until 1960 under the sponsorship of the US Navy. Researchers at the Naval Weapons Center at China Lake, California, showed that detonating a cloud of volatile hydrocarbon mixed with air created a blast wave several times as powerful as that produced by TNT. With ethylene oxide, one of the easiest and most practical substances to be used, the detonation produces a blast wave equivalent to that produced by 2.7 to 5 times as much TNT. Unlike ordinary high explosives, which concentrate their effects at the point of detonation, fuel–air explosives produce their blast evenly over the entire area of their aerosol cloud. For a 227-kg (500 lb) bomb, the blast radius at peak over-pressures for a typical FAE mixture is almost three times as great as with TNT, extending across an area 60 metres in diameter. This gives fuel–air explosives much greater effectiveness in many situations, especially against soft targets such as personnel, radars, parked aircraft or even ships at anchor.[24]

Development of fuel–air explosives into a practical weapon was slowed by the difficult problems of rapidly dispersing and igniting an aerosol cloud under battlefield conditions. The US Navy's research programme cost only $5 million, but this low figure conceals the severity of the conceptual problems that had to be solved.[25] The first practical FAE weapon, the Navy's 227-kg CBU-55 bomb, was tested in 1971 and quickly released for service in Viet Nam, where its large blast effects were especially effective for clearing mine-fields and for clearing jungle for helicopter landing zones. Within two years the US Air Force, Army and Marine Corps were also operating comparable weapons, often as anti-personnel weapons, against both Viet Cong and North Vietnamese forces.[26]

Although their effectiveness has been proven in operation, fuel–air explosives remain a singularly cranky weapon. The most serious impediment to their further development is the problem of controlled release and dispersal of the liquid fuel for detonation. Unless laid down properly on the target and allowed to mix with the right proportion of air, it is liable to fizzle ineffectively, if it detonates at all. Fuel–air explosives are very sensitive to wind over the target, which can also interfere with detonation. These riddles limited early employment of fuel–air explosives to delivery by slower vehicles such as helicopters and propeller aircraft. A version capable of being carried at speeds of up to 800 km/h was developed for use with high-performance aircraft, but this still has to be released at much slower speeds and its fall has to be retarded (through drag fins or a drogue parachute) to even slower speeds for effective detonation.

These are practical problems which may be solvable. In theory, fuel–air explosives can be operated under diverse conditions, including missile delivery. In 1973 it was reported that the US Air Force investigated the possibilities of using high-altitude detonation for interception of ballistic missiles. The US Army initiated a project in 1976 to develop an FAE warhead for its Lance missile.[27] In the late 1970s one researcher uncovered at least 15 different US Government-sponsored FAE R&D projects, several involving missile applications.[28] Few if any of these projects to create more advanced fuel–air explosives appear to have gone beyond the experimental stage. Despite the excitement generated by the initial declassification of US military FAE programmes in 1972, it does not appear that their development continued to be a high priority. Indeed, there is no evidence that any of the second- or third-generation FAE

[24] The best general treatments in the open literature are Johannsohn, G., 'Fuel air explosives revolutionise conventional warfare', *International Defense Review*, June 1976, pp. 992–96; and Lavoie, L., 'Fuel–air explosives, weapons and effects', *Military Technology*, Sep. 1989, pp. 64–70.

[25] Biass, E. H. (ed.), *Aircraft Armament 86* (Interavia Publishing Group: Geneva, 1986), p. USA 561.

[26] Robinson, C. A., Jr, 'Services ready joint deployment plan', *Aviation Week & Space Technology*, 19 Feb. 1973, pp. 42–46.

[27] 'Fuel air explosive work placed under joint service program', *Aviation Week & Space Technology*, 23 Aug. 1973, p. 28; and 'Latest US Army equipment on show', *International Defense Review*, Feb. 1977, pp. 101–8.

[28] Gervasi, T., *Arsenal of Democracy II* (Grove Press: New York, 1981), p. 206.

weapon ideas mooted in the Pentagon in the 1970s resulted in operational weapons. Reviewing these frustrations, one analyst concluded that 'while FAE warheads almost certainly continue to be investigated, high explosives will almost certainly continue to be used for the next LRCM [long-range conventional missile] unitary payload'.[29]

By the mid-1980s the US armed services had accepted first-generation fuel–air explosives as an orthodox element in their inventory of conventional munitions. A degree of disillusionment was also evident. While fuel–air explosives can be more effective than conventional high explosives under the right circumstances, the comparison with nuclear weapons is more a literary metaphor than a scientific statement. Responding to fears expressed in the press, the US Chairman of the Joint Chiefs of Staff cautioned that they 'are nowhere near the horror weapons that some have tried to portray [them] as being'.[30] They resemble nuclear weapons by relying mostly on blast effects for destruction, unlike conventional high explosives which usually do most of their damage by spewing deadly fragments. While the reach of their blast wave is greater than that of high explosives, it is much less than that of even an absurdly small nuclear device. As one scientist notes, 'the quantity of FAE fuel needed to substitute for a tactical nuclear weapon of even fractional kiloton yield does not suggest a very practical device. An FAE weapon with a yield equivalent to a 0.1-kiloton nuclear weapon would weigh 45,000 kilograms'.[31] Fuel–air explosives are 'miniature nuclear weapons' only in the sense that, at some abstract level, a hand grenade also is.

Nevertheless, there was wide international interest in the FAE idea in the 1970s, with tests conducted in several Western countries including France and Sweden. The Soviet Union apparently pursued this work most diligently. By the mid-1980s there were reports from Afghanistan that Soviet forces were using weapons with characteristics resembling those of fuel–air explosives. Around this time Western intelligence sources also revealed Soviet experiments with FAE warheads for ballistic missiles as part of a doctrinal shift aimed at developing alternatives to nuclear weapons for a European war.[32] Stories of Soviet interest have not been confirmed, however; nor is it known if any experiments led to operational deployments.

The United States remains the leader in FAE technology and the natural source of assistance for interested foreign governments. US policy has been to maintain strict controls on the dissemination of FAE technology in most cases. FAE bombs were transferred to the Government in Saigon during the final stages of the Viet Nam War, but later in the 1970s proposed sales to Canada

---

[29] Harschberger, E. R., *Long Range Conventional Missiles: Issues for Near-Term Development*, N-3328-RGSD (Rand Corporation: Santa Monica, Calif., 1991), p. 111.

[30] Powell, C., 'Fuel air explosives understood by U.S.', *USIA Wireless File*, 11 Oct. 1990, p. 10.

[31] Lavoie (note 24), p. 68.

[32] Robinson, C. A., Jr, 'Soviets begin fuel air explosive tests', *Aviation Week & Space Technology*, 22 Oct. 1973, p. 24; Bellamy, C., *Red God of War: Soviet Artillery and Rocket Forces* (Brassey's: London, 1986), p. 120; and Hines, K. L., 'Soviet short-range ballistic missiles: now a conventional deep-strike mission', *International Defense Review*, Dec. 1985, pp. 1909–14.

and Israel were denied.[33] Other exceptions have been made: in another case the German firm Messerschmitt-Bolkow-Blohm received data on fuel–air explosives as part of an SDI contract with the Pentagon.[34] Over the years, other countries have clearly begun FAE programmes. Nothing in the open literature indicates that any of them have solved the remaining technical problems of fuel–air explosives or successfully adapted them for missile delivery.

In the late 1980s there was a new surge of interest in fuel–air explosives, this time from regional missile programmes. There is no evidence that any newcomers were able to develop fuel–air explosives on their own or to solve the problems of high-speed delivery. Instead they rely on foreign assistance. In one of the most egregious cases, in 1984 technical experts with Honeywell of Minneapolis prepared a report on the feasibility of FAE armament of ballistic missiles for a Swiss company, IFAT, known to be working for the Egyptian Government. Completed in early 1985, the report was entitled *A Preliminary Study for the Development of an FAE Warhead for Application to a Ballistic Missile*. It envisaged a cylindrically shaped weapon weighing 400 kg, obviously intended for the warhead of a Condor-2. The report apparently described only the feasibility of various options and contained little hard engineering data. Even so, it caused great misgivings on the part of Honeywell management, which recognized the volatility of the issue and subsequently withdrew the firm from further cooperation.[35]

Even after this rebuff, the Condor-2 managers remained interested in FAE armaments. With no firm possibility of acquiring nuclear warheads—Condor's Western designers apparently knew little about Iraq's nuclear programme—an improved conventional warhead was of great importance. Fuel–air explosives not only seemed technically promising but were not forbidden by any treaty. Further searching led them to a subsidiary of Messerschmitt-Bolkow-Blohm. According to the German firm, its involvement began with development of fuel–air explosives for Egypt, which passed the relevant data on to Iraq. This project advanced to the point of actual weapon tests, although there was still far to go when West Germany ended all its work on Iraqi weapons in 1988–89. Although the project's goal was an FAE warhead for Iraq's ballistic missiles, it reportedly got no further than experimenting with a bomb for manned aircraft.[36]

The publicity surrounding the Condor-2 apparently aroused the interest of other would-be suppliers. Ever ready to adapt to new export opportunities,

---

[33] Perry Robinson, J. P., 'Qualitative trends in conventional munitions', eds M. Kaldor and A. Eide, *The World Military Order* (Macmillan: London, 1979), p. 99.

[34] Timmerman, K. R., 'Fuel–air explosives from MBB', *Mednews*, 1 Oct. 1990, p. 1.

[35] George, A., 'A bigger blast', *The Middle East*, Jan. 1991, pp. 15–16; and 'Erhielt Irak Benzinbombe aus Waffenschmiede in USA?' [Did Iraq receive petrol bomb from the US weapons-smithy?], *Frankfurter Rundschau*, 3 Dec. 1990, p. 4. The role of Honeywell has been examined most thoroughly in Burrows, W. E. and Windrem, R., *Critical Mass: The Dangerous Race for Superpower Weapons in a Fragmented World* (Simon and Schuster: New York, 1994), pp. 200–1, 473–74.

[36] 'Irakische Superbombe von MBB?' [Iraqi superbomb from MBB?], *Frankfurter Rundschau*, 24 Sep. 1990, p. 1; Barrie, D., 'Fuel–air warhead for Iraqi Scuds', *Flight International*, 10 Oct. 1990, p. 5; and Starr, B., 'Probe urged into FAEs for Iraq', *Jane's Defence Weekly*, 20 Oct. 1990, p. 739. A good summary of the affair can be found in Krosney, H., *Deadly Business: Legal Deals Outlaw Weapons: The Arming of Iran and Iraq, 1975 to the Present* (Four Walls Eight Windows: New York, 1993), pp. 169–78.

China unveiled its own FAE project less than one year after the MBB project with Iraq was revealed. It is telling about the nature of the technology that this weapon is a bomb for manned aircraft, very similar to the US Navy's CBU-55 introduced 20 years earlier, presumably with similar capabilities and drawbacks.[37]

The capabilities of fuel–air explosives are sufficiently worrisome to justify stringent export controls. They have found a special role on the modern battlefield and undoubtedly will spread among the world's arsenals, but they have yet to mature into the horror weapon envisaged by some. They cannot be dismissed as a missile armament, but they remain a remote possibility. Rather than providing a reliable alternative to weapons of mass destruction, the experience with fuel–air explosives leads to the conclusion that, for the foreseeable future, serious ballistic missile programmes will continue to stress chemical, biological or nuclear armaments.

IV. Chemical and biological weapons

Although the proliferation of ballistic missiles and chemical and biological weapons (CBW) can be traced back to the 1950s, recognition of the relationship between them developed very gradually. Early studies of missile proliferation assumed that the only choices for missile armaments were conventional or nuclear weapons. The spread of chemical and biological weapons was a minor aspect of proliferation worries, and links to the spread of missiles were all but ignored.[38]

It took a series of surprising revelations to make the potential synergism apparent. The first and most important event shaping this new awareness was Iraq's use of chemical weapons against Iran, first confirmed by the United Nations in early 1984. Previously, Western observers had confused their own abhorrence of chemical weapons with a universal moral assumption. Iraq's use alerted the West that chemical weapons had not lost all their appeal, especially to countries lacking nuclear weapons.[39] Second came intelligence disclosures in the mid-1980s revealing that the Soviet Union had embraced new military doctrines emphasizing chemical weapon options. To some Soviet planners, chemical weapons were especially intriguing, promising greater destructive potential than conventional explosives but without the tremendous risks of nuclear esca-

---

[37] Weighing 250 kg, the Chinese weapon is 10% larger than the US CBU-55 but uses a similar configuration with 3 bomblets. Its blunt shape suggests that delivery must be at speeds of less than 200 km/h. In a press release, the Chinese export company Norinco emphasized the anti-personnel capability of the weapon. Silverberg, D., 'China firm takes wraps off new fuel air bomb', *Defense News*, 24 June 1991, p. 46; and 'China eyes fuel air bomb market', *Defense Week*, 24 June 1991, p. 6.

[38] See, e.g., Eisenstein, M., 'Third world missiles and nuclear proliferation', *Washington Quarterly*, summer 1982, pp. 112–15; and Steinberg, G. M., 'Two missiles in every garage', *Bulletin of the Atomic Scientists*, Oct. 1983, pp. 43–48.

[39] It was these events of the Iran–Iraq War that led this author—who can claim no special prescience—to write that 'CBW has not been legitimized by these events, yet it may be an increasingly viable option between conventional and nuclear weapons'. Karp, A., 'Ballistic missiles in the Third World', *International Security*, vol. 9, no. 3 (winter 1984/85), p. 169.

lation.[40] Third, it was discovered that many countries investing in long-range rocketry also had aggressive chemical weapon programmes, including Iran, North Korea, Libya and Syria. By the time of the 1988 War of the Cities, the possibility that chemical or biological weapons could potentially give regional missiles new capabilities was an accepted fact.[41]

The problem of chemical and biological weapon proliferation has grown into an independent field of study with a literature so extensive that it seems to mock the more modest efforts to understand missile proliferation. This section examines only those aspects of the problem directly relevant to ballistic missile armament. The overlap between the two phenomena is dominated by three questions: How effective are chemical or biological weapons when delivered by ballistic missiles? What are the technical problems of using chemical or biological weapons and missiles together? Will emerging powers be able to solve these problems by themselves?

The answers to these questions are more hypothetical than for other missile armaments. Judgements on conventional high explosives can be based on considerable experience, including thousands of actual missile attacks. Even with fuel–air explosives, more is known about the performance of the weapons, although serious technical questions remain unresolved. As for nuclear weapons, huge test programmes by the superpowers leave little room for doubt concerning their effectiveness or feasibility. When it comes to chemical and biological weapons, there is a lot of very unfortunate experience but little of direct relevance to likely attacks with ballistic missiles. CBW technology itself is old and open, but the technology of missile delivery is frustratingly enigmatic.

As a general rule, chemical and biological missile armaments do not overcome the basic doubts about the effectiveness of missiles armed only with conventional explosives. Although they can be more deadly, there is every reason to believe that they are even less reliable. The effectiveness of CBW armaments for missiles depends on too many particular conditions and circumstances to be predicted. While proliferators may have sound strategic reasons for investing in CBW warheads, they cannot afford to rely on them. Their advantages are few and the disadvantages many. CBW warheads share all the worst characteristics of other armaments: the limited destructiveness of high explosives, the unpredictability of fuel–air explosives and the ethical impediments of nuclear weapons.

---

[40] Krause, J. and Mallory, C. K., *Chemical Weapons in Soviet Military Doctrine: Military and Historical Experience, 1915–1991* (Westview Press: Boulder, Colo., 1992), pp. 168–72.

[41] Among the first to debate the implications were Bingaman, J., 'New threat; poison-tipped missiles', *New York Times*, 29 Mar. 1989, p. 23; Carus, W. S., *Chemical Weapons in the Middle East*, Research Memorandum no. 9 (Washington Institute for Near East Policy: Washington, DC, Dec. 1988), p. 10; and Jacchia, E., 'The spector of missiles with chemical payload', *Los Angeles Times*, 6 Nov. 1988.

How effective are they?

The potential for destruction with chemical or biological weapons is great but depends on too many factors to be stated in any but the vaguest terms. In reviewing likely and extreme possibilities, Steven Fetter argues that a single Scud missile loaded with nerve agent and fired under ideal conditions could be very deadly indeed. 'If used against an unprotected city with a population density of 35 per hectare (for example, Tel Aviv or Riyadh), 200 to 3,000 people would be killed and a somewhat greater number seriously injured, depending on weather conditions'. He concludes that 'they may be 50 times more deadly (than equal amounts of high explosives) if civil defence is ineffective *or* weather conditions are favourable, and 500 times more deadly than conventional warheads when used against unprepared populations under favourable conditions'.[42]

Deadly they may be, but it is an exaggeration to call chemical weapons 'the poor man's atomic bomb'.[43] In so far as the phrase has any meaning, the parallel is not military but psychological, measured in terms not of destruction but of political pressure. Chemically armed ballistic missiles may help to deter an adversary, especially one who is highly sensitive to civilian casualties. Iraqi President Saddam Hussein apparently had this in mind when he threatened to use chemically armed missiles against Israel in April 1990, declaring that 'by God, we will make the fire eat up half of Israel if it tries to do anything against Iraq . . . We do not need an atomic bomb. He who threatens us with an atomic bomb will be annihilated by the binary chemical'.[44] Indeed, as the ultimate Allied response to Iraq's invasion of Kuwait drew near, there was great public concern in Israel. The Scud attacks which began on the night of 17 January 1991 were of greatest effect because of the fear that the missiles would be chemically armed. As it became apparent that this was not the case, and as Patriot missile defences appeared to take effect, these fears eased. Saddam Hussein's strategy apparently was not to deter Israel but to force it into the war. Had the missiles carried chemical warheads, it is likely that he would have succeeded.[45]

Against purely military targets, it is difficult to challenge the conclusion of Thomas McNaugher that 'chemical weapons used tactically fall somewhere between high explosives and battlefield nuclear weapons, but closer to conventional ordnance. Indeed, CW is not very effective at all against troops equipped

[42] Fetter (note 7), pp. 22, 23.

[43] This phrase is often used by regional spokesmen to justify their country's right to chemical weapons. Ironically, it was originated by then US Assistant Secretary of Defense Richard Perle in 1984, when he was trying to draw Western attention to the problem.

[44] Cowell, A., 'Iraq chief, boasting poison gas, warns of disaster if Israelis strike', *New York Times*, 3 Apr. 1990, p. A1. As Lawrence Freedman and Efraim Karsh point out, Hussein's real intentions remain very obscure. This speech contained both threats of uninhibited bellicosity and surprisingly conciliatory reassurances. See their analysis in *The Gulf Conflict, 1990–1991: Diplomacy and War in the New World Order* (Princeton University Press: Princeton, N.J., 1993), pp. 32–33.

[45] Navias, M., *Saddam's Scud War and Ballistic Missile Proliferation*, London Defence Study no. 6 (Brassey's and the Centre for Defence Studies, King's College: London, July 1991).

with protective gear and trained in its use'.[46] In World War I, the first exposure of an unprotected unit could produce casualty rates as high as 30 per cent. This rapidly declined to an average of about 3 per cent as troops gained experience and protective gear, and even that casualty rate was achieved only when artillery bombardments mixed CW shells with high explosive shells which tore away protective gear. More recent experience tends to confirm this low level of destruction. According to the Iranian Government, over 99 per cent of its soldiers injured by Iraqi chemical weapons survived the experience.[47]

A range of options

Not all chemical warfare agents are equally suitable for missile delivery. Their maximum effectiveness varies, determined largely by differences in each agent's lethality and volatility. As shown in table 6.3, the most deadly agents also tend to be the most persistent; once dispersed over a target they remain for as long as several months. Some, such as VX, are also very sticky, making decontamination difficult. These agents—especially VX and mustard—are best suited for use with long-range ballistic missiles, intended to knock out distant targets and keep them out of action for as long as possible. Other agents, such as hydrogen cyanide, are far less deadly and considerably more evanescent; they have their worst effects immediately and then dissipate rapidly. This makes them more suitable for use with artillery rockets and other short-range systems firing close to the battlefield on targets which may soon fall into friendly hands.

Contemporary studies of the military effectiveness of chemical weapons have concentrated not on the goal of killing but on incapacitating an enemy. Rather than trying to destroy an enemy outright with enormous quantities of chemical weapons—probably an impossible task—smaller quantities of chemical munitions may be sufficient to reduce his ability to resist. Limited chemical attacks may make it impossible for troops to fight effectively by forcing them to wear protective clothing for extended periods, inhibiting their mobility and efficiency, or by covering such facilities as air bases or communications centres and forcing them to cease operating until they can be decontaminated.[48] Highly lethal and persistent agents, such as VX, are best suited to this task.

Despite their potential, the established powers never invested heavily in chemical warheads for their missiles. There are a few examples. The United States stockpiled Sarin-filled cluster warheads for its short-range Honest John missiles, although these were withdrawn in 1973. The Soviet Union had chemical warheads for its FROG and Scud-B missiles, bulk-fillable with VX, which Russia is obliged to destroy under the 1990 US–Soviet Agreement on Destruc-

---

[46] McNaugher, T. L., 'Ballistic missiles and chemical weapons: the legacy of the Iran–Iraq War', *International Security*, vol. 15, no. 2 (autumn 1990), p. 30.

[47] Carus (note 41), p. 7.

[48] Cordesman, A. H., *Weapons of Mass Destruction in the Middle East* (Brassey's: London, 1991), pp. 55–59; and Krause and Mallory (note 40).

Table 6.3. Chemical weapon characteristics

Type	Agent	Lethal dose[a]	Duration of lethality[b]	Regional countries likely to possess them
Nerve agents	VX	36	3–21 days	None identified
	Sarin	100	1/4–4 hours	Iraq,[c] N. Korea, Syria
	Tabun	400	1–4 days	Iraq,[c] N. Korea, Syria
Blister agent	Mustard	1 500	2–7 days	Egypt, Iran, Iraq,[c] Libya, N. Korea, Syria
Blood agents	Hydrogen cyanide	5 000	Few minutes	Iraq,[c] Libya, N. Korea
	Cyanogen chloride	11 000	Few minutes	None identified

[a] Lethal dosage by inhalation (LCT_{50} standard) in milligrams per minute per cubic metre.

[b] Duration of lethality varies greatly depending on atmospheric conditions. The durations given here assume ideal conditions: sunny weather with light breezes and temperature of 15°C (approximately 60°F).

[c] Most of Iraq's chemical stockpiles were destroyed under the supervision of UNSCOM in 1992–94.

Sources: Burck, G. M. and Floweree, C. C., *International Handbook on Chemical Weapons Proliferation* (Greenwood: New York, 1991); Carus, W. S., *Chemical Weapons in the Middle East* (Washington Institute for Near East Policy: Washington, DC, 1988); and Cordesman, A. H., *Weapons of Mass Destruction in the Middle East* (Brassey's: London, 1991).

tion and Non-Production of Chemical Weapons and on Measures to Facilitate the Multilateral Convention on Banning Chemical Weapons and the 1993 Chemical Weapons Convention. There are unconfirmed reports that the USSR developed chemical options for longer-range missiles such as the SS-12 and SS-23. The US Army also considered chemical warheads for its Lance and Pershing missiles, although these plans were never put into effect.[49]

According to an influential study by the US Defense Intelligence Agency, the contamination pattern from a single Scud-B loaded with 500 kg of VX could stretch over an area 3.7 km (2.3 miles) in length by 0.4 km (one-quarter mile) in width, with the strength to cause 50 per cent casualties among personnel caught within that area (see figure 6.2).[50] Whether or not such casualties are inflicted is a secondary matter; a few strikes could succeed just by making a major facility temporarily unusable. Even if actual casualties were closer to 10–20 per cent—a more realistic estimate—the tactical effects could be substantial. Once contaminated with a persistent agent, a military facility cannot operate at anything more than a fraction of its peak efficiency. Some facilities, like supply dumps or bases, might have to cease most operations while awaiting decontamination. Closing a few essential installations at a key moment could influence the outcome of a battle or even of a war.

[49] Perry Robinson, J. P., 'Chemical weapons proliferation: the problem in perspective', ed. T. Findlay, *Chemical Weapons and Missile Proliferation* (Lynne Rienner: Boulder, Colo., 1991), p. 29.

[50] *Soviet Chemical Weapons Threat* (US Defense Intelligence Agency: Washington, DC, 1985), pp. 5, 8.

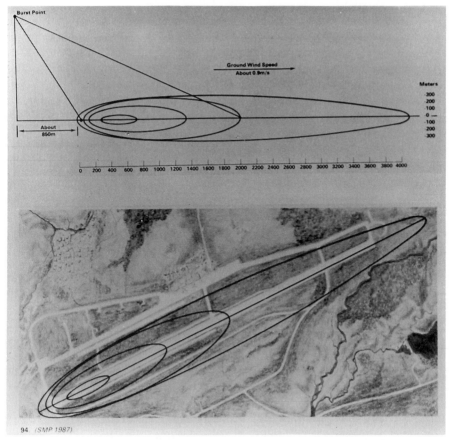

Figure 6.2. Possible target contamination of a chemical weapon-armed Scud-B missile (Photograph: US Department of Defense)

Despite their tactical advantages, synthesis of the most toxic chemical weapons is far from easy. The agents that are the easiest to manufacture also tend to be the least toxic and shortest lived. The ideal chemical weapon for ballistic missile delivery, VX—which is highly toxic, long-lived and difficult to clean—is also by far the most difficult of the orthodox chemical agents to make. Even the most advanced and dedicated proliferators have apparently been unable to manage the process. United Nations investigations never found evidence of its presence in Iraq, and it appears that North Korea still lacks it.[51] Instead, a proliferator is likely to rely on easier-to-produce but less toxic and more short-lived agents such as Sarin or mustard. When used to arm ballistic missiles, such an improvisation would greatly reduce the potential destructiveness of their forces. The estimates of destruction given above—all based on the

[51] Bermudez, J. S., Jr, 'North Korea's chemical and biological warfare arsenal', *Jane's Intelligence Review*, May 1993, p. 228.

assumption of missiles armed with VX—would have to be revised sharply downwards if less sophisticated agents were used instead.

Possession of highly lethal and persistent chemical agents is not proof that a country is using them to arm its ballistic missiles. Rather, possession creates an option. Whether or not a proliferator intends to act on this option, outside powers must take this possibility seriously in their planning. Iraq remains the only emerging power whose development of chemical missile warheads has been confirmed. Whether or not countries like Iran, North Korea, Libya and Syria are chemically arming their ballistic missiles is extremely difficult to prove, but the possibility cannot be discounted.

Biological weapons can potentially cause much greater destruction than chemical ones. A single missile loaded with only 30 kg of anthrax spores released over a large, unprotected city could cause 20 000–80 000 deaths. This would equal the destructive capacity of a small nuclear weapon the size of that dropped over Hiroshima (12–20 kt). Extensive civil defence measures might reduce the deaths from such an anthrax attack to some 2000.[52] More deadly agents are conceivable. All suffer from serious military disadvantages. Not only are they liable to the same problems of weather and dispersal as chemical weapons, but they are living organisms which must be treated with great care to remain useful. Even if biological agents can be delivered successfully, most of them do not take effect for several days.

The question of whether or not proliferators actually will try to mate their missiles to biological agents is even harder to resolve than the doubts surrounding chemical armaments. According to the US Central Intelligence Agency, 10 countries are working on biological weapons.[53] This has been confirmed only in the cases of Russia and Iraq, where laboratories admitted to working on military applications of anthrax and botulism (botulinum toxin).[54] Iraq insisted that their efforts never progressed beyond purely basic research. There is no evidence that any country has developed biological warheads for ballistic missiles, although Iraq and Syria may have tried.

General barriers to CBW armament

The factors militating against CBW armament of ballistic missiles fall into three general categories. First, and of greatest importance, are those considerations that have led most of the international community to abandon chemical and biological weapons altogether. The ethical abhorrence of these weapons is a major force for most countries. The 1925 Geneva Protocol banning the use of CBW and the 1972 Biological Weapons Convention prohibiting the possession

---

[52] Fetter (note 7), p. 27.

[53] Oehler, G. C., Testimony before the Senate Banking Committee, Washington, DC, 25 May 1994, p. 2.

[54] Engleberg, S., 'Iraq said to study biological arms', *New York Times*, 18 Jan. 1989, p. 7; and Aita, J., 'U.N. team confirms Iraq's biological arms capability', *USIA Wireless File*, 14 Aug. 1991, pp. 1–2.

of biological weapons leave little doubt about the convictions of most of mankind. The prohibitions and stringent verification terms of the Chemical Weapons Convention will make it very difficult for any signatory country to accumulate chemical weapons on the scale required for missile applications. Regional disarmament agreements in South Asia and Latin America leave little doubt that most countries would prefer to have nothing to do with chemical or biological weapons. The greatest risk of CBW armaments is restricted to regions where governments refuse to join such agreements or might treat them with contempt, especially the Middle East.

Second, moral objections to chemical and biological weapons are supported by doubt of its military utility. Among Western military experts, there is a consensus that these weapons are effective only against unprotected civilians. Their meagre tactical benefits on the battlefield, moreover, are easily offset by the huge logistical demands they impose, which tend to reduce the forces available for use with more flexible weapons. These problems are especially severe with biological agents, some of which have a limited storage life.[55]

The efficacy of chemical or biological weapons depends overwhelmingly on the specific circumstances of the attack. More so than for other munitions, chemical and biological weapons require surprise to be effective since minimal preparations by a defender like donning protective gear greatly degrade their deadliness. Even then, their effects are unpredictable.[56] Unlike high explosives or nuclear weapons, their effectiveness varies greatly with changes in the weather and topography of the target area. Rain or high winds can sweep a large bombardment away or even turn it against the attacker. When CBW can be delivered perfectly, their dangers can be minimized with sufficient warning and use of defensive measures such as face masks, protective clothing, decontamination equipment and training.

Compounding the general weaknesses of chemical and biological weapons is a third category of problems that make ballistic missiles an especially poor delivery option. Chemical weapons—but not biological agents—are similar to conventional explosives in that their effectiveness depends largely on the quantities and accuracy with which they are delivered. To achieve the greatest effect, an attacker must get the largest possible amounts as close to the target as possible. Consequently, chemical weapons are most effective when delivered by normal artillery or manned aircraft, which can deliver huge quantities with precision.[57] Among the various missile systems, the shorter the range the better the efficiency with chemical weapons. Because artillery rockets can carry the most payload as a proportion of total launch weight, they are the best and long-

---

[55] On general military considerations, see Perry Robinson, J. P., SIPRI, *Chemical Weapons: Destruction and Conversion* (Taylor & Francis: London, 1980). An author somewhat more impressed with the military potential is Spiers, E. M., *Chemical Warfare* (University of Illinois Press: Urbana, Ill., 1986), pp. 120–74; and Spiers, E. M., *Chemical Weaponry* (Macmillan: London, 1989), pp. 1–68.

[56] Burck, G. M. and Flowerree, C. C., *International Handbook on Chemical Weapons Proliferation* (Greenwood: New York, 1991), chapter 1; and Roberts, B., *Chemical Disarmament and International Security*, Adelphi Paper no. 267 (International Institute for Strategic Studies: London, 1992), appendix I.

[57] Harvey *et al.* (note 7), p. 52.

range ballistic missiles the worst option. By contrast, when targeting biological armaments against cities, ballistic missiles can be fully efficient because of the small quantities of agent required.

The particular riddles of missile delivery

One of the many popular misconceptions regarding ballistic missile proliferation is that adapting missiles for chemical armament is virtually child's play. 'All you have to do', explained one Western intelligence official, 'is unscrew the top, pour in the chemical, make one or two adjustments to stop it slopping around and you have a chemical weapon'.[58] Nothing could be further from the truth. Such an improvisation might fool an impressionable journalist, but even a very desperate commander would hesitate before relying on it. Delivery of chemical or biological weapons by ballistic missiles requires solving several serious and very difficult technical problems, none of which has been fully mastered by weapon engineers anywhere.

Special re-entry vehicles are needed, especially for long-range missiles, and dispersal problems must be overcome. Both chemical and biological agents are sensitive to heat. Unless properly protected they may be rendered inert and harmless by the heat generated by a long-range missile's re-entry. All major chemical warfare agents deteriorate rapidly at temperatures above their boiling point, the highest of which is 298°C for VX. McFate and Graybeal have pointed out that virtually all chemical agents decompose almost instantly when exposed to temperatures over 700°C. Anthrax spores and other biological agents are even more sensitive to heat (see table 6.4).[59] To manage temperature problems, CBW re-entry vehicles must be specially designed. For short-range missiles up to the size of a Scud it is probably sufficient to rely on quite simple insulation. Long-range missiles, however, will require specially designed CBW warheads to keep lethal materials cool.

Assuming that the CBW agent survives re-entry, it must be correctly released and dispensed over the target. If it is released too high, the agent may float away on the wind, causing no harm to the target below. If released too low, the liquid will be driven into the ground, with minimal effect. A liquid agent also must be dispensed as an aerosol cloud, in particles of proper size to ensure deadly effects. The orthodox release and dispersal technique is simply to fill the warhead in bulk and explode it at a predetermined altitude. This is a technically undemanding approach but potentially an ineffective one, too. It fails to take into account variations in winds over the target. More importantly, the bursting charge will destroy some or most of the CBW agent.

---

[58] Quoted by Adams, J., *Trading in Death: The Modern Arms Race*, 2nd edn (Pan: London, 1991), p. 268.

[59] McFate, P. A. and Graybeal, S. N., 'A new proliferation threat from space?', eds W. T. Wander and E. H. Arnett, *The Proliferation of Advanced Weaponry: Technology, Motivations and Responses* (American Association for the Advancement of Science: Washington, DC, 1992), pp. 95–96. Their data refer to agent half-life at various temperatures.

Table 6.4. Chemical and biological weapon deterioration at high temperatures

Agent	Boiling point (°C)	Half-life temperature (°C)
Chemical agents		
Sarin (GB)	158	150°/2.5 hr; 230°/1 min.; 350°/1 sec.; 720°/1 msec.; 980°/100 µsec.
Soman (GD)	228	130°/4 hr
VX	298	150°/36 hr; 295°/1 min; 400°/1 sec.; 760°/1 msec.; 950°/100 µsec.
GF (unstable sarin derivative)	239	150°/2 hr
Tabun (GA)	245	150°/3 hr
Distilled mustard (HD)	228	210°/1 min.; 310°/1 sec.; 620°/ msec.; 800°/100 µsec.
Biological agents		
Anthrax spores[a]	..	35°–40°/20 yr; 80°/138 hr; 90°23 hr; 100°/270 min.; 140°/3 min.; 500°/1 msec.
Anthrax (active bacterium)	..	55°/1 hr, 65°/30 min.; 500°/1 msec.

[a] Anthrax forms pseudo-spores when exposed to temperatures above 32°C.

Source: McFate, P. A. and Graybeal, S. N., 'A new proliferation threat from space?' in eds Wander, W. T. and Arnett, E. H., *The Proliferation of Advanced Weaponry* (American Association for the Advancement of Science: Washington, DC, 1992), pp. 95–96.

Biologically armed missiles appear to be especially susceptible to self-destruction in this way.[60] Carus notes that tests during World War II revealed that the heat and blast of explosive dispersal of biological bombs killed 95 per cent of the microbes, while the surviving droplets were too large to be retained in the lungs.[61] The surviving biological agent must still be taken very seriously, but a proliferator will almost certainly try to develop a better system. Developing a more sophisticated warhead is not an easy task; even the Soviet Union relied on bulk filling and bursting charges to dispense chemical agents from its FROG and Scud warheads.[62]

Effective use of CBW armament in ballistic missiles requires cluster munitions. These divide the load into dozens or hundreds of individual bombs. This ensures proper dispersal but does not solve the problem of agent survival since a bursting charge is still needed. It also introduces an entire new range of problems associated with the design and operation of cluster munitions. Several cluster munitions are already widely available for aircraft bombs. Israel and

[60] Tucker, J. B., 'The future of biological warfare', in Wander and Arnett (note 59), pp. 71–73.
[61] Carus, W. S., *'The Poor Man's Atomic Bomb?': Biological Weapons in the Middle East,* Policy Paper no. 23 (Washington Institute for Near East Policy: Washington, DC, 1991), p. 60.
[62] Krause and Mallory (note 40), pp. 156–58.

South Africa have their own designs, while Chile produces a US design.[63] The latter was illegally transferred to Iraq.[64] Adapting these cluster munitions for ballistic missiles would require substantial modification, yet this is almost certainly within the capabilities of many regional defence industries with some outside assistance.

The Iraqi enigma

The difficulties of arming ballistic missiles with chemical or biological agents may explain one of the greatest enigmas of the Persian Gulf War: Why did Saddam Hussein not use his chemically armed Scud missiles? The possibility that he would was the most daunting risk facing Allied commanders planning Operation Desert Storm. Battlefield evidence and interrogation of prisoners of war after the fighting revealed that the Iraqi Army was equipped and ready for offensive chemical warfare.[65] Had chemically armed Scud missiles fallen on Israel, direct Israeli retaliation would have been all but certain and would probably have shaken the Allied coalition apart. Although about 88 Scud missiles were launched, none carried chemical armament, despite Iraq's enormous investment in deadly chemicals. The first UNSCOM inspections after the war revealed that Iraq had 45 Scud warheads designed for chemical warfare, one-quarter of all the Scud warheads the UN found.[66] Why were they not used?[67]

Many reasons for Saddam Hussein's restraint have been suggested. Many have nothing to do with technology. Among the most compelling is the possibility that he was deterred by fear of retaliation, of massive Allied bombing of Baghdad or even of an Israeli nuclear strike.[68] In their statements, Allied leaders deliberately countered the Iraqi leader's worst threats with fiery threats of their own.[69] Despite its appealing logic, however, there is no direct evidence for successful deterrence. On the contrary, interceptions of radio transmissions reportedly revealed that Saddam ordered chemical attacks during the final hours of the war, attacks which never came, probably because of the collapse of his command structure and supply system.[70]

---

[63] Lennox, D., *Jane's Air-Launched Weapons* (Jane's Information Group: Coulsdon, Surrey, 1988), articles on Chile, Israel and South Africa.

[64] Friedman, A., 'US Government says Chilean exported bomb parts for Iraq', *Financial Times*, 8 Apr. 1992, p. 4.

[65] Roberts (note 57), p. 20.

[66] 'U.N. still waiting for data on Iraqi weapons', *USIA Wireless File*, 6 Apr. 1991, pp. 8–9.

[67] By the summer of 1993 several studies had noted that some US veterans of Operation Desert Storm displayed vague medical symptoms—such as nervous conditions, chronic nausea and hair loss—that might have been caused by exposure to chemical warfare agents. Small samples of chemical agents were also identified near the battlefields. At the time of writing, in late 1994, there is no evidence that post-war maladies were related in any way to chemical weapon exposure. The tiny samples of CW agent were probably released from damaged Iraqi stocks. Schmitt, E., 'Gulf troops' ills bewilder doctors', *New York Times*, 11 Nov. 1993, p. A11.

[68] Terrill, W. A., 'The Gulf War and ballistic missile proliferation', *Comparative Strategy*, vol. 11 (1992), p. 170.

[69] Herby, P., *The Chemical Weapons Convention and Arms Control in the Middle East* (Peace Research Institute, Oslo: Oslo, 1992), pp. 28–31.

[70] Roberts (note 56), p. 20.

It is likely that Saddam's fears of retaliation were reinforced by serious doubts over the viability of his chemically armed Scud missiles. The problems of developing a chemical warhead had prevented Iraq from using chemically armed ballistic missiles during the 1980–88 war with Iran. Against Iran, Iraqi chemical attacks relied entirely on bombs, artillery, small-calibre rockets and spraying from propeller aircraft. There are no credible reports from the Iraq–Iran War of attacks with chemically filled FROG or Scud missiles.[71] As late as the important April 1989 Baghdad military exposition, which revealed a great deal of information about Iraq's missile programmes, there was no evidence of developments in missile warheads appropriate for chemical or biological weapons.[72]

It was not until after the invasion of Kuwait in August 1990 that press reports indicated flight-testing of an Iraqi Scud chemical warhead, and these may have been exaggerated.[73] According to John Gee, Chief of the UNSCOM Working Group responsible for destroying Iraqi CBW capabilities after the Gulf War, 'I don't think they had developed the system sufficiently. They told us they had carried out one static test. But it was a very primitive system and I don't think they had gone very far down the road in testing it'.[74]

The missiles themselves suffered from the faults inherent in the Scud design and lacked the accuracy to ensure that if they were fired at Israeli cities their victims would not be Jordanians or Palestinians. The crude design of the Scud's chemical warhead could not ensure greater effectiveness than proven warheads with conventional explosives. Filled with the quickly dissipating nerve agents that Iraq was able to manufacture (Sarin or Tabun), they could not guarantee high casualty rates even if they were launched and dispensed with complete success.[75] Clearly, several factors led to Saddam's restraint. Technical considerations were at least as relevant as logistic chaos and possible deterrence, but a satisfying explanation still alludes us.

An option that will not go away

Iraq's miserable military performance may have discouraged some governments from seriously pursuing CBW missile armament. Other countries have already selected the option, however, and seem unlikely to abandon it:

---

[71] The most comprehensive study lists the following Iraqi chemical munitions in use in 1987: 250-kg gravity bombs; 122-mm BM-21 artillery rockets; 90-mm air-launched rockets; 30-mm howitzer shells; and 155-mm howitzer shells. See Dunn, P. (ed.), *Chemical Aspects of the Gulf War, 1984–1987: Investigations by the United Nations* (Defence Science and Technology Organization, Materials Research Laboratories: Maribyrnong, Australia, Nov. 1987).

[72] Timmerman, K. R., 'In the crucible of the war: the Iraqi arms industry', *Mednews*, 8 May 1989, pp. 1–8; and Willis, G., 'Open sesame! Baghdad show reveals Iraqi military–industrial capabilities', *International Defense Review*, June 1989, pp. 835–38.

[73] One of the first reports of an Iraq chemical Scud warhead test was in the *Los Angeles Times*, 14 Sep. 1990.

[74] Interview with Gee in *Pacific Research*, Nov. 1991, pp. 3–4.

[75] Roberts (note 56), pp. 20–21.

1. *Syria's* interest in chemical weapons has been proven conclusively, but its missile capabilities are more obscure. There have been several reports since 1987 that it has filled Scud warheads with mustard gas or Sarin. Since Syrian technical capabilities are poorly regarded, these are considered poor improvisations. Anthony Cordesman, who accepts most claims regarding Syrian chemical weapons, maintains that the more advanced 'SS-21s in Syrian hands do not have chemical warheads and that Syria would find it extremely difficult to develop such a capability without Soviet support'.[76]

2. It has also been reported that *Libyan* technicians modified Scud missiles in the late 1980s to carry mustard, Sarin or Tabun.[77]

3. *Iranian* missile and chemical weapon capabilities are less advanced than the countries mentioned above, yet in 1992 the Director of US Central Intelligence, Robert Gates, testified: 'we expect Iran to develop chemical warheads for its Scud missiles within a few years'.[78]

4. The only proliferator outside the Middle East that appears to have developed a CBW warhead for its ballistic missiles is *North Korea*.[79] Although no definitive information has been revealed, one source asserts that 'The DPRK is now known to produce chemical or biological munitions, or both, for large calibre mortars, artillery and artillery rocket systems greater than 122-mm, FROG-5/7A tactical rockets, "Scud" variant ballistic missiles, and air delivered ordnance'.[80]

It is difficult to escape the conclusion that chemical and biological weapons are a serious alternative missile armament, but they cannot be considered a reliable choice. Despite the heated rhetoric, chemical warheads do not compare to nuclear armaments in any but derisory terms. Nor do they escape the fundamental problems of conventional armaments, which are effective with short-range missiles and lose credibility as missile range increases. Biological weapons have much greater destructive potential as an armament for long-range missiles, but difficult technical problems must be resolved before a national commander could rely on them in a contest with a nuclear-armed foe.

In terms of destructive capability other weapon platforms, including artillery and manned aircraft, can carry greater CBW payloads for less cost and deliver them with much better accuracy. Seth Carus is undoubtedly correct when he concludes that 'cruise missiles are particularly well suited to the delivery of chemical and biological weapons'. Not only are they less expensive than long-range ballistic missiles, but they 'can fly slowly over a target at a low altitude, making them better able to disseminate chemical and biological weapons than

---

[76] Cordesman (note 48), pp. 144–46; and Burck and Flowerree (note 56), pp. 208–21.

[77] Cordesman (note 48), pp. 153–55; and Burck and Flowerree (note 56), pp. 276–77.

[78] Gates, R., Testimony before the US House Armed Services Committee, Subcommittee on Defense Policy, 27 Mar. 1992.

[79] Bermudez, J. S., Jr, 'CW: North Korea's growing capabilities', *Jane's Defence Weekly*, 14 Jan. 1989, p. 54.

[80] Bermudez (note 51), p. 227.

ballistic missiles'.[81] Although there is no evidence that an emerging power has tried to develop CBW-armed cruise missiles, the possibility is too alarming to overlook.

The threat of chemically or biologically armed ballistic missiles must be taken seriously, if not for their military capability, at least for their frightening appearance and the psychological stress they place on voters and decision makers. But they are not a poor man's atomic bomb. To the contrary, their development requires large investments and considerable technological skill. As the Chemical Weapons Convention gains adherents and moral force, moreover, countries clinging to the CBW option will find themselves compelled to pay ever greater diplomatic penalties for their fascination.

---

[81] Carus, W. S., *Cruise Missile Proliferation in the 1990s*, Washington Papers no. 159 (Praeger: Westport, Conn., 1992), p. 25.

7. The deadly technology II: nuclear armaments

I. Introduction

In the popular mind, ballistic missiles are inseparably linked with nuclear weapons. If they are not nuclear-armed today, it is normally assumed that they sooner or later will be. Although ballistic missiles were originally designed to carry ordinary high explosives, after the bombing of Hiroshima the two technologies immediately fused, not only in the public mind but also in the views of military planners and weapon designers. Ever since then any other armament for long-range missiles has been seen as a temporary substitute. So the inevitable question raised by a proliferator's acquisition of ballistic missiles is: When will they be nuclear-armed?

The relationship between nuclear weapons and ballistic missiles is partly technical, partly political. The technical link arises from the immense destructiveness of nuclear weapons—a force that is potentially sufficient to compensate for the expense and inaccuracy of long-range missiles. A hypothetical intermediate-range missile might be able to reach a target 1000 km away, but with a typical CEP of 1–3 km it cannot be expected reliably to hit any but the largest targets. No country can afford enough such missiles to inflict significant damage with conventional warheads. Even chemical warheads are unlikely to achieve the level of destruction needed to justify the expense of such a weapon. Biological weapons might be more effective, but only a nuclear warhead can provide reasonable certainty of actually destroying a target such as a city or a military concentration from long range.

The political link between ballistic missiles and nuclear weapons arises from the basic motive for weapon proliferation, which invariably reflects a state's quest for power. The tremendous importance of political power makes it impossible for an ambitious government to rely on a single tool of peacetime influence or wartime capability. To be fully effective, the instruments of power must be broadly based and diverse.[1] It is no mere coincidence that the countries of greatest concern in one area of weapon proliferation also rank high in other proliferation threats.

The emerging powers with the most advanced ballistic missile programmes also tend to be developing nuclear or chemical weapon options, accumulating large conventional armed forces and cultivating diversified defence industries. The need for many instruments of power does not mean that all must be pursued or that they must be sought with equal vigour. Several emerging powers have shown little interest in particular options. For example, despite their endemic rivalry, neither India nor Pakistan has offensive chemical weapon pro-

---

[1] Knorr, K. E., *The Power of Nations: The Political Economy of International Relations* (Basic Books: New York, 1975), chapter 3.

Table 7.1. Nuclear weapon capabilities of the 18 leading missile proliferators in 1992

Country	A-bomb capability[a]	Year achieved	Max. missile range (km)	Boosted A-bombs	H-bombs
Ukraine[c]	1 656[b]	1992	11 000	Confirmed	Confirmed
Kazakstan[c]	1 410[b]	1992	11 000	Confirmed	Confirmed
Belarus[c]	72	1992	10 500	Confirmed	Feasible
Israel	75–300	(1967)	1 450	Feasible	Feasible with testing
India	75–100	1974	2 500	Feasible	Feasible with testing
Pakistan	5–20	(1986)	300	Feasible	–
S. Africa[c]	7	1981	1 450	Unlikely	–
N. Korea[c]	1–5	(1993)	(1 000)	Feasible	–
Iraq[c]	–	(2000)	900	Unlikely	–
Iran[c]	–	(2000)	600	–	–
Saudi Arabia[c]	–	–	2 500	–	–
Egypt[c]	–	–	(600)	–	–
Syria	–	–	600	–	–
Brazil[c]	–	–	450	–	–
Libya[c]	–	–	300	–	–
Argentina[c]	–	–	140	–	–
S. Korea[c]	–	–	140	–	–
Taiwan[c]	–	–	120	–	–

[a] Confirmed number of nuclear warheads or number of warheads that can be fabricated from existing stocks of fissile material, assuming moderately efficient weapon design with critical mass of 5–7 kg of plutonium-239 or 15–25 kg of uranium-238 per weapon.

[b] Ukraine and Kazakstan have additional nuclear weapons for delivery by manned bombers.

[c] Party to the Non-Proliferation Treaty or a regional non-proliferation agreement.

Sources: Albright, D., *South Africa's Secret Nuclear Weapons* (Institute for Science and International Security: Washington, DC, May 1994); Lockwood, D., 'Nuclear weapon developments', *SIPRI Yearbook 1993: World Armaments and Disarmament* (Oxford University Press: Oxford, 1993); *Military Balance 1992–1993* (International Institute for Strategic Studies: London, 1992); Spector, L. S. and Foran, V. I., *Nuclear Proliferation Status Report* (Carnegie Endowment: Washington, DC, July 1992); Oberdorfer, D., 'CIA chief reiterates North Korean nuclear threat', *International Herald Tribune*, 14 Jan. 1993; and Sciolino, E., 'CIA draft says Iran nears nuclear status', *International Herald Tribune,* 21 Dec. 1992.

grammes. Even in the Middle East, most countries have forgone one prominent option by signing the Non-Proliferation Treaty. A few have signed the Chemical Weapons Convention, including Algeria, Israel and Morocco. These are exceptions, however. States which are insecure or ambitious will not risk relying on a single arm of military force. They will instead strive to maximize their power and insulate themselves from the vagaries of a complicated world by building as many sources of power as possible.

As a rule, emerging powers try to develop long-range rockets and nuclear weapons together (see table 7.1). Israel started constructing its Dimona nuclear reactor in 1958 and launched its first sub-orbital sounding rocket in 1961. India's decision in 1971 to develop a nuclear explosive was followed by its decision in 1973 to develop space launch vehicles. Iraq and North Korea found it easier to acquire ballistic missiles first, in the 1980s, but they were determined to develop nuclear weapon capabilities in the early 1990s. The connection is also shown by those countries which, when they decided to abandon their nuclear weapon programmes, quickly left their long-range rocket programmes in abeyance as well. Examples include South Korea and Taiwan in the 1980s and Argentina and Brazil in the early 1990s. It is safe to assume that, should any of these four countries renew either their rocketry or nuclear programme, the other programme will be revived soon after.

The exceptions to this rule are numerous but mostly involuntary. Countries such as Iran, Libya and Syria would undoubtedly have preferred to develop nuclear weapons and ballistic missiles simultaneously but lacked the domestic resources and international connections to acquire the necessary nuclear technology. Instead they were able to acquire the missiles alone and have had to rely on unsatisfactory substitute armaments. These countries almost certainly would prefer to develop their nuclear capabilities if international controls were relaxed. Pakistan succeeded in mastering nuclear enrichment by the mid-1980s, but found the path to long-range ballistic missiles blocked by its own industrial weakness and adamant US diplomacy. Saudi Arabia, after acquiring Chinese DF-3 missiles in 1988, quickly felt compelled by pressure from the Bush Administration to sign the NPT.

The only example of a government maintaining one weapon option after surrendering the other voluntarily is Egypt, which has been much keener on ballistic missiles than nuclear weapons. Egypt's ballistic missile programme is anomalously non-nuclear. In the late 1950s President Gamal Abdel Nasser went to great lengths to acquire ballistic missiles, as did his successors in the 1970s and 1980s. However, after initial frustrations with nuclear energy in the mid-1960s, Egyptian leaders lost interest and never tried to mobilize comparable resources to acquire nuclear weapons.[2] Despite Egypt's investments in Scud missile production and development of the Condor-2, Leonard S. Spector safely states that: 'Since concluding its peace treaty with Israel in 1979 and ratifying the NPT in 1981, however, Egypt's nuclear intentions have appeared entirely peaceful'.[3] Few if any other countries have been as willing to overlook the nuclear missile connection.

The relationship between missiles and nuclear weapons also seems to work in reverse; when nations lose interest in one, they also tend to cease working on the other. Rather than cling to the Condor-2 in the late 1980s, Egypt was easily pressured by the United States into abandoning a costly ballistic missile project that made little strategic sense. Among the many countries surrendering nuclear weapon capabilities in the early 1990s were several—for example, Argentina,

---

[2] Cohen, A., 'Patterns of nuclear opacity in the Middle East', ed. T. Rauf, *Regional Approaches to Curbing Nuclear Proliferation in the Middle East and South Asia*, Aurora Paper no. 16 (Canadian Centre for Global Security: Ottawa, Dec. 1992), chapter 2.

[3] Spector, L. S., *The Undeclared Bomb* (Ballinger: Cambridge, Mass., 1988), p. 162.

Brazil and South Africa—with major rocketry programmes.[4] At first they all indicated a continuing interest in rocket research, if only for civilian space launch. Despite official intentions, however, their rocket programmes withered rapidly. Should the former Soviet republics of Belarus and Kazakhstan abandon their inherited nuclear weapons, it is very unlikely that they will retain their ballistic missiles.[5] Without a nuclear weapon option to make them credible, military rocket projects are unlikely to survive as anything more than a shadow of their previous form.

The NPT and the ethical sentiments it codifies are the most important barriers to the nuclear arming of ballistic missiles. Any measure that strengthens the nuclear non-proliferation regime directly reduces the likelihood that nuclear-armed missiles will be successfully developed by would-be proliferator states. Other elements of that regime, especially regional nuclear weapon-free zones and the Nuclear Suppliers Group, which restricts the export of relevant technology, also have the side-effect of inhibiting the spread of nuclear missile capabilities.

The nuclear non-proliferation regime is not the only barrier to nuclear missile armament. In those cases where the regime fails and a proliferator acquires the basic technology of nuclear weapon production, several other hurdles must still be overcome before nuclear missiles can be deployed with its armed forces. These include other general impediments to nuclear proliferation, such as ethical, political and strategic considerations that led some proliferators to cultivate nuclear capabilities—to create the ability to go nuclear or even to assemble key bomb components—without crossing the final threshold by building actual weapons.[6]

Of more immediate relevance here are the technical problems of adapting nuclear weapons for missile delivery. Although the two technologies are highly complementary, they do not fit together automatically. It is not enough to build a few bombs. After building its first nuclear weapon and long-range ballistic missile, a proliferating country must still overcome serious engineering problems before the two can be integrated into a single weapon system. Three problems deserve special attention: reducing weapon size, boosting weapon yield and nuclear testing.

II. The importance of size

The physical dimensions of a nuclear device are the most critical considerations in adapting it for delivery. Any country's first-generation nuclear weapons will probably be too large for missile delivery. Extensive redesign will be essential

---

[4] Spector, L. S., 'Repentant nuclear proliferants', *Foreign Policy*, no. 88 (fall 1992), pp. 21–37.

[5] Ukraine is a special case because it also has factories for constructing long-range rockets. It seems likely that, even after giving up their nuclear weapons, Ukrainian leaders will try to find business opportunities in the space launch field.

[6] Wohlstetter, A. *et al.*, *Moving Toward Life in a Nuclear Armed Crowd?* (Pan Heuristics: Marina del Ray, Calif., 1976); and Wohlstetter, A. *et al.*, *Swords from Plowshares: The Military Potential of Civilian Nuclear Energy* (University of Chicago Press: Chicago, 1979).

to adapt them to missile payload limits and re-entry vehicle dimensions. The first nuclear weapon, the Fat Man bomb tested at Alamogordo, New Mexico, on 16 July 1945 and dropped on Nagasaki on 9 August 1945, weighed 4900 kg (about 2250 kg for the explosive mechanism alone), making it far too large to be carried by a V-2 rocket with a payload capacity of 750 kg. Even the Little Boy bomb dropped on Hiroshima on 6 August 1945 was only slightly smaller at 4045 kg.[7] Not until 1959, with the first flight of an Atlas-D, did the United States have a missile capable of carrying a warhead that large. To this day no country has flown an IRBM capable of lifting a weapon the size of the Fat Man or Little Boy.[8]

A proliferator's first nuclear weapon is likely to be considerably smaller than the first US designs. The first nuclear weapons owed much of their bulk to very conservative design assumptions; uncertain of whether the concept would work or generate sufficient yield, the Manhattan Project added large and unnecessary margins to all elements of the first bombs. During the next five years these designs were refined through a series of steps culminating in the Mk-V bomb, released to the US Air Force in 1952. This was an implosion bomb based on the same concepts as Fat Man but weighing less than one-third as much, with a total weight of about 1450 kg.[9] A bomb of this weight includes a plutonium core weighing 5–8 kg and an even larger quantity of uranium-238 tamper. This was an impressive technical accomplishment, but the bomb was still too large for short- or intermediate-range missiles designed to carry a complete warhead weighing no more than 1000 kg.

Assessments of the process of nuclear proliferation routinely rest on the premise that a proliferator's first nuclear weapon will weigh about 1000 kg, close to the threshold for missile delivery.[10] Implicit in this premise is the assumption that a would-be proliferator can act with greater certitude and proceed directly to a finer design than could the bomb's inventors at the Los Alamos Laboratory. This undoubtedly is the case, but it would be excessive to assume that a country can skip several stages of development to begin with a design which US physicists developed only after considerable experience.

The evidence regarding other countries' first efforts to build nuclear weapons is incomplete, but the emerging impression is that newcomers can now safely skip the most conservative stage in bomb design. Dispensing with weapons like the Fat Man, they can move directly to second-generation weapons similar to

---

[7] On Fat Man weight, see Cochran, T. B. *et al.*, *Nuclear Weapons Databook, Vol. 1: U.S. Nuclear Forces and Capabilities* (Ballinger: Cambridge, Mass., 1984), p. 32; and Mark, J. C., 'The purpose of nuclear test explosions', eds J. Goldblat and D. Cox, SIPRI and the Canadian Institute for International Peace and Security (CIIPS): *Nuclear Weapon Tests: Prohibition or Limitation* (Oxford University Press: Oxford, 1988), p. 33.

[8] The IRBM with the largest throw-weight is probably China's DF-3, which can carry a warhead weighing 2150 kg (half the size of Fat Man) a distance of 2800 km. Lewis, J. W. and Hua Di, 'China's ballistic missile programs: technologies, strategies, goals', *International Security*, vol. 17, no. 2 (autumn 1992), p. 10.

[9] Cochran (note 7), pp. 7–9.

[10] A similar point is made by Van Cleave, W., 'Nuclear technologies and weapons', eds R. M. Lawrence and J. Larus, *Nuclear Proliferation, Phase II* (University of Kansas Press: Lawrence, Kans., 1974), pp. 50–55.

the US Mk-V. Assuming that this rule holds, an emerging power's first nuclear device is likely to weigh less than 2200 kg but more than 1300 kg. A clear example is France, whose first nuclear weapon, the AN-11, tested in February 1960, was a bomb intended for aircraft delivery, weighing 1500 kg.[11] South Africa's nuclear weapons were of a similar class.[12]

Even though their first-generation nuclear weapons will probably be smaller than Fat Man, they will still tend to be too bulky to be loaded into a rocket. Only Saudi Arabia's Chinese-supplied DF-3s are designed to carry warheads heavier than 1000 kg, and Saudi Arabia's ratification of the NPT probably makes its nuclear potential moot. A few other countries have missiles capable of lifting a warhead weighing in the neighbourhood of 1000 kg. Examples include unmodified versions of the Scud-B (985 kg), the 150-km range version of India's Prithvi and its long-range stable-mate the Agni (both capable of lifting approximately 1000 kg), and possibly Israel's Jericho-2 as well. Most other regional long-range ballistic missiles are designed for a throw-weight of no more than 500 kg—including not only the weight of the warhead but also its fusing and the re-entry vehicle.[13] Few nuclear proliferators, it can be concluded, will be able to deliver their first nuclear weapons by missile. The only exceptions can be countries that already have enormous rockets ready when they first go nuclear. Japan is the only country in this position today, with its H-2 launch vehicle, and India could be in a similar situation if it successfully develops its PSLV space launcher, although both rockets would require substantial modification to be used in this role.

Most emerging nuclear powers will require several iterations of the design process to perfect a nuclear weapon small enough for missile delivery. The process of reducing weapon size may be analogous to the experience in the 1940s and 1950s of the United States, the only country for which details of its nuclear weapon developments are available for careful comparison. The rate of refinement is shown in figure 7.1. Although other countries will undoubtedly develop their nuclear weapons on different, probably much slower time scales, the physics of nuclear explosions will force them to progress through comparable stages. Note that the United States needed six successful implosion designs before reaching dimensions suitable for missile delivery—the 450-kg Mk-12 bomb introduced after a crash programme in 1954. Modified as the

[11] Norris, R. S. *et al.*, *Nuclear Weapons Databook, Vol. V: British, French and Chinese Nuclear Weapons* (Westview: Boulder, Colo., 1994), pp. 184, 185.

[12] Early reports following South African disclosure of its nuclear weapon programme claimed that the weapons were advanced and small, weighing 1000 kg according to one report, reiterated in Albright, D., *South Africa's Nuclear Weapons* (Institute for Science and International Security: Washington, DC, May 1994), p. 12. Other investigations revealed that the devices were less advanced and so large that they could be delivered only by the largest South African aircraft, then British-supplied Buccaneers. This would place their total weight at 1800 kg. Simpson, J., Howlett, D. and Ginifer, J., 'Inside South Africa's atomic laager', *Financial Times*, 20 May 1993, p. 4.

[13] 'Missile and space launch capabilities', *Nonproliferation Review*, vol. 1, no. 2 (winter 1994), pp. 96–98.

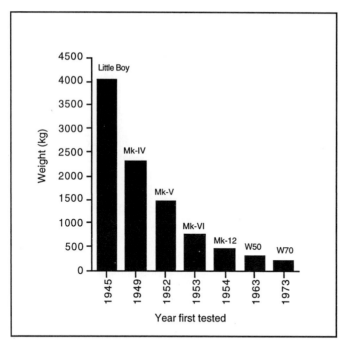

Figure 7.1. Weights of the smallest US nuclear weapons, 1945–73[a]

Applications: In respective order, Little Boy, Mk-IV, Mk-V, Mk-VI and Mk-12, aircraft bombs; W50, Pershing-1/1a missiles; and W70, the Lance missile.

[a] This figure does not include nuclear artillery, demolition mines or other weapons with yields of under 10 kt.

[b] Aircraft bomb weights include bomb casings. It is not clear whether all missile warhead weights include the weight of re-entry vehicles.

Source: Cochran, T. B. *et al.*, *Nuclear Weapons Databook, Vol. I: US Nuclear Forces* (Ballinger: New York, 1984).

slightly larger W7 and subsequent W31, this weapon armed the first US Army nuclear missiles, the Honest John and Corporal, deployed in the mid-1950s.[14]

Reducing nuclear weapons to these dimensions was made possible by numerous improvements in such areas as the efficiency of high-explosive lenses, initiators and tamper design. Of greatest importance was the fractional critical mass or 'fractional crit', a method which made it possible to build a nuclear explosive of smaller size and using less fissile material. Based on concepts identified in 1944, this was ready for testing by the United States in Operation Ranger of 1951. The fractional crit achieved nuclear fission with a core smaller than the theoretically necessary critical mass. This is compressed, by implosion, to a higher density, resulting in a nuclear explosion.[15] Using this approach, the

---

[14] Cochran (note 7), pp. 3, 10–11, 282.

[15] Bethe, H. A., 'Comments on the history of the H-bomb', *Los Alamos Science*, autumn 1982, pp. 44–45; and Cochran, T. B. and Norris, R. S., 'Development of fusion weapons', *The New Encyclopedia Britannica*, 15th edn (Encyclopedia Britannica: Chicago, 1990), vol. 29, p. 580.

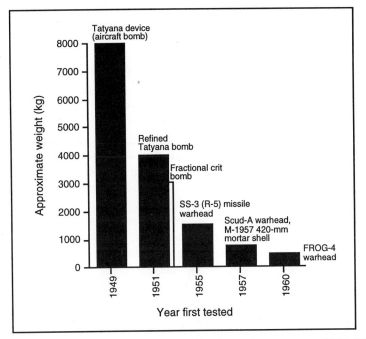

Figure 7.2. Weights of the smallest Soviet nuclear weapons, 1949–60

Sources: Cochran, T. B. *et al.*, *Nuclear Weapons Databook, Vol. IV: US Nuclear Weapons* (Ballinger: New York, 1989); and Zaloga, S. J., *Target America: The Soviet Union and the Strategic Arms Race, 1945–1964* (Presidio: Novato, Calif., 1993).

critical mass of a plutonium device could be reduced from an orthodox 5–8 kg to as little as 1–3 kg, with proportionate reductions in other components such as chemical explosives, tamper and casing. The fractional crit also facilitates production of more bombs by reducing the amount of fissile material required for each one. The approach is not without disadvantages; of special relevance here, destructive yield is reduced, falling from 20 to 70 kt in a normal plutonium weapon, down to 1–8 kt in a fractional crit device.[16]

Although details of Soviet nuclear weapon development are scarcer, it appears that Soviet bomb designers went through a similar process, gradually improving the suitability of their weapons for missile delivery (see figure 7.2). At first, greater difficulty was encountered in merely fabricating a functioning device, which required several attempts. After the first successful detonation of an oversized experimental device in 1949—a copy of the Fat Man device—the major challenge was refining the design to conserve plutonium and facilitate long-range delivery by aircraft. Weight reduction was less of a priority, at first,

[16] Holden, R. F., 'New measures show N. Korea may have 5 nuclear bombs', *USIA Wireless File*, 22 Aug. 1994; and Fialka, J. J., 'IAEA says its plutonium threshold for making nuclear bombs is too high', *Wall Street Journal*, 23 Aug. 1994, p. A4.

than raising explosive yield.[17] Not until the early 1950s did weight reduction receive equal priority as work on the first major ballistic missile, the Soviet SS-3 Shyster, neared completion. The result was a warhead, available in 1955, weighing about 1500 kg. For the Scud-A missile and the M-1957 420-mm mortar, which were first displayed in 1957, an even smaller nuclear warhead was needed. This was the first Soviet nuclear weapon weighing less than 1000 kg and was ready for service by 1960. Also in that year the FROG-4 and FROG-5 missiles went into service, with a warhead weighing 450 kg, although nuclear versions may not have been available until 1962.[18]

The Soviet pattern of development shows that it is not enough to have the essential equipment or basic knowledge of weapon design to produce compact warheads. A huge investment and the advantage of espionage data (discussed below) were only enough to make the Soviet bomb programme competitive with that of the United States: it was still considerably slower at every step. The Soviet example also shows the importance of priorities; nuclear newcomers must decide whether to emphasize small size or large yield. By any standard of measurement, the Soviet pattern was remarkably inefficient; but even if it does not offer guidance to modern proliferators, its warnings must not be over-looked. The difficult and iterative nature of the process that US and Soviet bomb designers encountered seems inherent in the technology. Here is a pattern almost certain to be seen again as regional powers try to adapt nuclear weapons for missile delivery.

For nuclear newcomers, the most immediate implication of 50 years of nuclear history and knowledge is that they can skip the first stage in the development of fission weapons. Instead of building crude 5000-kg bombs, their first nuclear weapons are likely be engineered to much finer tolerances and weigh 1300–2200 kg. Despite this advantage, the other developments required to reduce the weight of their weapons to the levels needed for missile delivery cannot be skipped. Further weight reductions will require such innovations as the composite core or other methods such as the fractional crit. After first developing a functional nuclear device, addressing these problems will require at least 5–10 more years.

The basic characteristics of a country's nuclear weapon programme will also affect its ability to develop weapons that are suitable for missile delivery. The kind of fissile material it has available—plutonium or uranium—may be of great importance for weight reduction. The smallest nuclear devices tend to be plutonium weapons, based on a critical mass of plutonium-239. This is recovered by reprocessing material exposed in a nuclear reactor. While an orthodox uranium bomb usually requires a critical mass of 15–25 kg of 93 per cent pure uranium-235, plutonium designs require a critical mass of no more

[17] Evangelista, M., *Innovation and the Arms Race* (Cornell University Press: Ithaca, N.Y., 1988), chapter 5.

[18] Zaloga, S. J., *Target America: The Soviet Union and the Strategic Arms Race, 1945–1964* (Presidio: Novato, Calif., 1993), pp. 89–90, 94, 133, 252; and Cochran, T. B. *et al.*, *Nuclear Weapons Databook, Vol. IV: Soviet Nuclear Weapons* (Ballinger: New York, 1989), pp. 190–200.

than 5–8 kg of 93 per cent pure plutonium-239 if designed with an efficient tamper or neutron reflector. The size of the core sets parameters for other components. A smaller core requires a smaller tamper, less conventional explosive and smaller casing.[19]

Not all proliferators have access to plutonium. Consequently, those countries which acquire fissile material through plutonium reprocessing facilities—such as India, Israel and North Korea—are in a better position to develop missile-sized warheads than those relying on uranium enrichment techniques—such as Pakistan today, or Argentina, Brazil, Taiwan and South Africa prior to signing the NPT. Some countries may be able to stretch limited supplies of plutonium by designing composite cores containing a mix of both fissile materials, but those without access to plutonium will face greater obstacles to developing nuclear-armed missiles.

The importance of plutonium adds further significance to the discovery in the summer of 1994 that weapon-grade plutonium was being shipped out of the former Soviet Union. In the most serious case, smugglers were apprehended in Munich with 300 g of Russian plutonium-239. The material would be useful to any country or terrorist trying to assemble a nuclear bomb.[20] If it fell into the hands of a country that already had a serious nuclear programme in place, such material would be especially useful, particularly a country trying to fabricate warheads for missiles. A country such as Pakistan, for example, relies on uranium and it currently probably cannot perfect nuclear warheads suitable to arm its missiles. With foreign plutonium, it probably could.

Uranium weapons have one advantage that is potentially important for missile applications: they alone are suitable for gun-type bomb designs such as the Little Boy. Based on the principle of shooting one part of a critical mass of uranium through a tube and into another to create fission, gun assemblies are long and thin compared to the bulbous shape of implosion weapons.[21] The Los Alamos physicists were sufficiently confident of the performance of Little Boy not to have tested the weapon before it was dropped on Hiroshima. Although they are less efficient, with yields typically below 15 kt, the shape of gun devices is especially suitable for use in nuclear artillery shells. The first nuclear artillery of the 1950s relied on gun assemblies.[22] The gun device could appeal to an emerging missile proliferator for the same reason.

III. The importance of yield

For many proliferators, the symbolic and deterrent effects of any nuclear missile they can acquire will be sufficient, so long as the weapon is reasonably

[19] Cochran (note 7), pp. 23–24.

[20] 'Fund 13: Alarmstufe rot' [Find 13: condition red], *Der Spiegel*, no. 29 (1994), pp. 18–22; and Whitney, C. R., 'Fear of nuclear mafia widens in Germany', *International Herald Tribune*, 17 Aug. 1994, p. 1.

[21] Plutonium is not suitable in a gun design, since it tends to begin fissioning before a critical mass has been achieved, leading to a premature detonation with a small yield.

[22] Cochran (note 7), p. 26.

reliable and has sufficient range. With political, peacetime goals of influence and deterrence in mind, they do not require the certainty of destruction assured by more powerful types of nuclear weapon: the mere possession of nuclear missiles will serve their requirements.

For others, the mere possession of nuclear warheads is no panacea for the shortcomings of their missiles. A few countries may have more sophisticated targeting plans, calling for greater and more certain ability to destroy an adversary's cities or strategic sites. Whether this is because they find themselves in more delicate strategic environments, or is due to independent military demands, they may feel compelled to develop larger and more destructive missile warheads.

Just as was the case for Britain, France and the superpowers, the simple possession of a few nuclear weapons may not be enough for some emerging powers. Nuclear explosives are the most effective way to compensate for the inaccuracy of long-range missiles, but there are limits to the effectiveness of low-yield nuclear weapons. At short ranges there can be no doubting the lethality of any, even the clumsiest, nuclear-armed missile. As missile range increases, however, the effects of inaccuracy tend to outstrip the destructive radius of their nuclear armament. At longer ranges, the limitations of missile accuracy become more serious, making accurate delivery of a low-yield (up to 20 kt) nuclear device problematic.

This is illustrated by the problems of using Scud missile versions as nuclear delivery vehicles (the data in this section are derived from appendix 2). At its normal maximum range of just under 300 km, a Soviet Scud-B missile is a very deadly weapon, even when armed with a relatively small, 20-kt nuclear warhead. It is virtually certain to hit close enough to a city centre or an unprotected military base to inflict a blast of 4 psi, sufficient to destroy most buildings. The loss of life could be enormous. In similar nuclear attacks in South Asia, deaths from a single strike could be as high as 234 000 in Karachi or 163 000 in Bombay.[23]

Against a hardened military target such as a modern air base or communications centre, the probability of destruction with a normal 20-kt Scud warhead is also reasonably high, even after basic protection steps have been taken. With vulnerable facilities built of steel-reinforced concrete or underground, almost any essential military base can be hardened against overpressures of up to 10 psi.[24] Although this may seem low to observers trained in the standards of superpower strategy—where destruction of missile silos typically requires overpressures of 1000 psi or higher—the 10 psi standard of blast resistance is more typical of protection for other key military installations. This became the norm for air base hardening in NATO countries and on the Korean peninsula by the 1970s. In the Middle East the effects of Israel's extraordinary success in

[23] Khalilzad, Z., *Regional Rivalries and Nuclear Responses*, vol. 1 (Pan Heuristics: Marina del Ray, Calif., 1978).

[24] The 10 psi standard is described in Glasstone, S. and Dolan, P. J., *The Effects of Nuclear Weapons*, 3rd edn (US Department of Defense and Department of Energy: Washington, DC, 1977), pp. 214–30.

1967 led many Arab armed forces to build to similar standards in the 1980s. South Asian armed forces are still building to this level of protection for key installations, but countries in other regions have not made serious attempts to do so.[25] Against such facilities, the probability of destruction with a 20-kt Scud-B warhead is about 65 per cent. An attacker would have to fire at least two missiles to be reasonably sure of destruction, a ratio most attackers would find acceptable.[26]

At longer ranges the limitations of combining Scud missile technology with low-yield nuclear weapons become evident. As range increases, large numbers of nuclear-armed Scud types have to be fired to ensure destruction of a target. A typical Scud version, such as the Iraqi al Hussein or North Korean Scud-C, has a CEP of about 2 km at its maximum range of 600 km. If fired to its maximum range with an early-generation nuclear weapon yielding 20 kt, it has about a 60 per cent chance of destroying the centre of an unprotected target such as a city or military cantonment, requiring the use of at least two, preferably three, missiles per target. Against a military target protected against blast effects up to 10 psi, at least five such Scud missiles would be necessary.

At the maximum ranges of Scud technology, nuclear weapons cease to compensate efficiently for the missile's low accuracy. Using a missile such as the Iraqi al Abbas or North Korean NoDong-1 with a CEP of about 3 km at a range of 900 km and armed with a 20-kt nuclear weapon, the chance of destroying the centre of even an unprotected target is less than 27 per cent. Destruction of a city centre or an unsheltered military target under these conditions would require at least five missiles, despite their nuclear armament.[27] Destroying a military target protected to 10 psi—an 8 per cent probability—probably would require at least 12 of the same kind of missile, several more if their mechanical reliability is not high. The use of so many missiles on a single target might be judged acceptable, but the expenditure of so many nuclear warheads probably would not.

The most efficient solution to the weakness of a nuclear-armed Scud type is improving accuracy. A more accurate missile similar to the Condor-2 or Jericho-2 is considerably more effective with the same 20-kt warhead that seems potentially inadequate on a Scud missile. If accuracy cannot be improved significantly, small increases in nuclear yield will not compensate. To offset serious inaccuracy, large increases in destructive capability are necessary. Nuclear destructiveness can be enhanced through three techniques: incremental improvements, boosting and thermonuclear weapons.

The incremental improvement of nuclear weapon designs is a valuable approach for reducing weight and size or improving safety and reliability. Better designs, especially improvements in key bomb components such as the

---

[25] Brown, N., *The Future of Airpower* (Croom Helm: London, 1986), chapter 4.

[26] With a 65% probability of kill, 2 missiles must be fired to compensate for inaccuracy. A third missile would be desirable to compensate for mechanical unreliability.

[27] This assumes that destruction is caused only by blast and associated fire. At longer ranges with less accurate weapons, radiation and fallout could be more deadly over a period of months or years.

initiator and tamper, which often involve the use of beryllium, can double and sometimes triple the yield. However, the physics of pure fission still limit the maximum yield to about 50–70 kt.

Boosted fission weapons

More can be accomplished through boosting. First tested by the United States in 1951, boosting works by incorporating the hydrogen isotopes deuterium and tritium (D-T) into the core of an implosion weapon, enabling the neutrons released through the initial fission reaction to propagate additional reactions, releasing greater energy. The technique is well within the capabilities of most emerging nuclear powers, offering some of the capabilities but few of the complexities of a genuine hydrogen weapon. The boosted fission technique is used in most strategic nuclear weapons deployed by the United States since the mid-1960s. After the initial fascination with hugely powerful thermonuclear weapons dissipated in the mid-1960s, US strategic forces evolved almost entirely around boosted fission devices. These can produce yields of up to 400–500 kt, although weapons with yields of 100–200 kt appear to be more reliable and common.[28]

For most regional powers the improved destructive capabilities of boosted fission weapons will be sufficient to assure the military utility of their long-range ballistic missiles. With a 100-kt weapon, a relatively inaccurate Scud version can destroy any but the hardest targets at the full extent of its range. Against a hardened military target of the kind described above (10 psi), a 900-km range Scud version carrying a 100-kt warhead would have a 25 per cent chance of effectiveness, requiring an attack with a total of four or five missiles to be reasonably certain of destruction. While this is far from efficient, such an attack will probably be within the means of an emerging nuclear weapon state with a total arsenal of 100 or more nuclear weapons and only a handful of the highest-priority targets.

With a more accurate Condor-2 or Jericho-2 type missile, the improvement in capability with a boosted nuclear warhead is even more dramatic. The combination of higher accuracy and yield makes a single missile of this class virtually certain of destroying a soft target like a city, even at ranges as great as 2500 km. The probability of hitting and destroying a hardened military target is nearly 100 per cent up to a range of 1500 km, falling to about 35 per cent at a range of 2500 km.

Boosted fission warheads are the most efficient improvements in missile destructiveness likely to be sought by emerging powers; their acquisition is of extreme importance, necessitating the close attention and concern of the international community. Nevertheless, progress in this direction will be difficult for outside observers to detect and even more difficult to stop. Only illegal attempts to purchase deuterium or tritium from foreign suppliers are likely to be

---

[28] Bethe (note 15), p. 46; and Cochran and Norris (note 15), p. 580.

exposed. In the only confirmed examples, in 1984 a German company supplied India with 95 kg of beryllium, a material used to enhance normal fission reactions, and Pakistan received a tritium extraction plant from another German company.[29]

Export controls offer only weak leverage since a determined proliferator can produce both hydrogen isotopes domestically and need not rely on the caprices of foreign supply. Deuterium can be produced by the fertilizer industry, in much the same way that Iraq and Syria relied on pesticide plants to make chemical weapons. Tritium production is much more demanding but it can be produced in a heavy-water reactor; the key is possession of a reactor of sufficient size (usually at least 5-MW capacity) and free from international safeguards.[30] Israel is suspected of having deployed boosted weapons by 1982, probably using tritium generated in its Dimona reactor with no indication of foreign help, although this has not been confirmed. India can probably produce tritium in the same way. Similar facilities in Algeria and North Korea were placed under international safeguards in 1991–92.[31]

In light of the weakness of export controls against boosting, the most important international restraints left are injunctions against nuclear testing. Testing appears to be necessary to determine the reliability and yield of a boosted weapon design. The role of test restraints is discussed below.

Thermonuclear weapons

The single most alarming technology, with the greatest potential for maximizing the effects of ballistic missiles, is thermonuclear weapons—the hydrogen bomb. Although no regional power has such a weapon today, as they invest in ballistic missiles it is virtually certain that they will try to develop an H-bomb option for their long-range missiles.

By employing fusion reactions to generate yields of 1 Mt or more, thermonuclear weapons turn any ballistic missile into a weapon of unquestionable magnitude. The successful development of the H-bomb in 1952 was one of the crucial factors that led the United States to initiate a crash programme in 1954 for the its first long-range missiles, the Jupiter and Thor IRBMs and the Atlas ICBM. Although rapid progress was being made in missile guidance, the US Air Force and Defense Department agreed that the destructive power of fission weapons was too small to justify development of long-range ballistic missiles up to that time. Only the H-bomb was sufficiently destructive to compensate for their inaccuracy and make long-range missiles militarily effective.[32]

[29] Albright, D. and Zamora, T., 'India and Pakistan's nuclear weapons: all the pieces in place', *Bulletin of the Atomic Scientists*, June 1989, pp. 21–25.

[30] Kramish, A., 'The bombs of Balnibarbi', ed. R. W. Jones, *Small Nuclear Forces and U.S. Security Policy* (Lexington Books: Lexington, Mass., 1984), pp. 22–23, 30–31.

[31] Spector, L. S. and Foran, V. I., *Nuclear Proliferation Status Report, July 1992* (Carnegie Endowment: Washington, DC, 1992).

[32] Beard, E., *Developing the ICBM* (Columbia University Press: New York, 1976). Beard argues that other factors, especially bureaucratic resistance from the Air Force and Department of Defense, also contributed to US officials' initial lack of interest in long-range ballistic missiles.

Considerable information on the theory of nuclear fusion has been released over the years, including the general schematics of the first H-bombs, giving potential proliferators a head start.[33] Even for latecomers, however, development of a fusion weapon is an enormous undertaking. A typical H-bomb is triggered by a *primary* fission reaction which initiates a *secondary* reaction, producing fusion. The first fusion explosion, the Mike test of 1 November 1952, used a device the size of a village primary school building and weighing roughly 60 tonnes. The huge size was largely due to the use of liquid deuterium (which required large cryogenic refrigeration equipment) as a fuel for the secondary reaction. To reduce the size of the weapons to manageable proportions designers pursued a series of refinements not unlike those previously involved in tailoring fission devices, requiring several years to perfect a weapon suitable for delivery by any but the very largest rockets (see figure 7.3).

It is inevitable that emerging nuclear powers will require more time to go through this process of refinement; even with the advantages of hindsight and declassified information, they cannot spend resources on the same scale as the United States did when caught in an extreme arms race with the USSR. Of greater precedence for proliferators is the number of iterations of the design process. As shown in figure 7.3, the USA required five major generations to reduce the size of a thermonuclear weapon down to dimensions comparable to the payload of a likely regional ballistic missile. Newcomers may find shortcuts around one or more stages, but they cannot eliminate the process altogether.

The first step in reducing the weight of fusion devices was the switch to lithium-6 deuteride, a solid or powder fuel that did not need refrigeration. The second step was the reduction of yield. The scale of a fusion reaction is largely proportional to the amount of fuel available for the secondary detonation. In theory there is virtually no limit to the size of a fusion explosion; one need only keep adding fuel and stages, as the Soviet Union demonstrated with its freakish 58-Mt blast on 3 October 1961, the largest-yield nuclear device ever detonated.[34] The limiting factors for fusion weapon performance are the vast bulk of such a weapon and common sense. Much of the weight reduction illustrated in figure 7.3 comes from reducing yield. Yield fell from 10.4 Mt for the Mike device to 1 Mt for the B43 bomb of the 1960s. Later refinements in ICBM accuracy facilitated even greater reductions in H-bomb yield down to 0.33 Mt (330 kt) for the W78 missile warhead of the US ICBMs of the 1980s.

Although the process of perfecting thermonuclear weapons must proceed through incremental stages, the process is neither direct nor certain. Even the United States had problems at several points. An especially relevant mistake came when attempts were made to reduce bomb weight too rapidly. In 1954 the Los Alamos Laboratory introduced the Mk-14 bomb, weighing 13 500 kg. At

---

[33] The making of the first H-bombs is described in Rhodes, R., *The Making of the Atomic Bomb* (Simon and Schuster: New York, 1987), pp. 770–78. On declassification of fusion details, see Broad, W. J., 'The (bomb) secret's out: foreign moves to harness electricity from fusion forces U.S. to open up', *International Herald Tribune*, 29 Sep. 1992, p. 1.

[34] York, H., *The Advisors* (W.H. Freeman: San Francisco, 1976), p. 93.

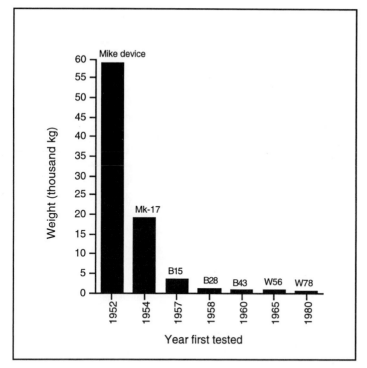

Figure 7.3. Weights of the smallest US hydrogen bombs, 1952–80

Applications: Mike, stationary test device; Mk-17, first aircraft H-bomb; B15, B28, B43, aircraft bombs; W56, for Minuteman-2 ICBM; and W78, for Minuteman-3 ICBM.

Sources: Cochran, T. B. *et al., Nuclear Weapons Databook, Vol. 1: US Nuclear Forces* (Ballinger: New York, 1984); and Cochran, T. B. *et al., Nuclear Weapons Databook, Vol. II: US Nuclear Warhead Production* (Ballinger: New York, 1987).

one-quarter the weight of the Mike device, this was an extraordinary accomplishment. It was also one of the most dangerous and unpredictable nuclear weapons ever and was withdrawn just a few months later in favour of the much heavier (by 50 per cent) but far safer Mk-17 bomb.[35]

Thermonuclear weapons make long-range ballistic missiles complete, and it is no surprise that every declared nuclear weapon power has rushed to develop them. Britain tested its first fission weapon in 1952, followed by a boosted weapon in May 1957 and a thermonuclear device in April 1958, although the exact steps and timing of these events are subject to debate.[36] France tested its first nuclear weapon in 1960 and successfully tested a thermonuclear design in 1968. China progressed very rapidly from its first nuclear weapon in 1964 to

[35] Gibson, J. N., *The History of the US Nuclear Arsenal* (Brompton: Greenwich, Conn., 1989), pp. 86–92.

[36] Paloczi-Horvath, G., 'More bark than bite? Britain's air-delivered nuclear weapons', *Air International*, vol. 47, no. 2 (Aug. 1994), pp. 102–7. See also correspondence by Eric Grove and Paul Jackson in the Sep. and Oct. issues of *Air International*.

test boosted fission devices in 1966 and a genuine fusion explosion in June 1967.[37]

The evidence for more recent thermonuclear proliferation is more ambiguous. Israel reportedly built boosted fission weapons beginning in 1982, and it has been claimed—in greatest detail by the renegade engineer Mordechai Vanunu—that fusion weapons have been designed and experiments conducted with lithium-6.[38] There is no reason to suspect that this work has gone any further, however. According to the congressional testimony of then CIA director William Webster, in 1989 there were 'indicators' that 'India is interested in thermonuclear weapons capability', although he refused to be more specific.[39] In the most certain case, the inspection of Iraq's nuclear programme by the UN Special Commission on Iraq after the 1991 Gulf War found documents showing that a project was under way to produce lithium-6 deuteride, which has no use other than fuelling thermonuclear explosives. Algorithms and computer software to predict thermonuclear dynamics were also found, confirming Iraqi interest.[40]

IV. The test barrier

Among the nuclear weapon designers it is widely accepted that basic, fission nuclear weapons can be fully developed and deployed without full-scale testing. As noted above, the gun device dropped on Hiroshima had not been detonated in tests before. Implosion designs are more complicated and require testing of individual components (especially the conventional explosives), but testing is not essential for the fully assembled weapon. Veteran weapon designers seem convinced that: 'The beginner state can unquestionably manufacture reliable nuclear weapons without conducting test explosion of those weapons'. In more concrete terms, 'It seems clear that a country could, without testing, develop, and probably produce and stockpile with confidence, warheads that would be regarded as sophisticated by, say, 1950 standards'.[41]

Not all authorities are convinced of this. The proliferation expert David Fischer points out that statements asserting the relative ease with which rudimentary nuclear weapons can be built invariably originate with experienced US bomb experts. Regional actors may be unwilling to commit themselves to untested weapons, especially when there is no proof of their reliability other than the assurances of their designers. 'A nuclear establishment of a developing country', he suggests, 'might have more difficulty in persuading its politicians

[37] Norris, R. S., Burrows, A. S. and Fieldhouse, R. W., *Nuclear Weapons Databook, Vol. V: British, French, and Chinese Nuclear Weapons* (Westview: Boulder, Colo., 1994).

[38] Barnaby, F., *The Invisible Bomb* (I.B. Taurus: London, 1989), pp. 38–40.

[39] Ottaway, D. B., 'Signs found India building H-bomb', *Washington Post*, 19 May 1989, p. 30.

[40] Simpson, J., 'The nuclear non-proliferation regime in 1991', eds J. B. Poole and R. Guthrie, *Verification Report 1991* (Vertic: London, 1992), p. 250; and 'Iraq has advanced nuclear weapons program, IAEA says', *USIA Wireless File*, 9 Oct. 1991, pp. 5–6.

[41] Westervelt, D. R., 'The role of laboratory tests', eds Goldblat and Cox (note 7), p. 47; and Van Cleave (note 10), p. 53.

and its military to rely . . . upon an array of untested "rudimentary" weapons'.[42] From this perspective, countries that are not committed to nuclear weapons may find the test issue especially vexing, leading to political disputes that may end the programme.

While testing of initial bomb designs may not be essential, development of more advanced bomb designs makes testing progressively more necessary.[43] Although an emerging power can probably build, without testing, a stockpile of crude nuclear weapons suitable for delivery by manned aircraft, this is not so for a nuclear-armed ballistic missile force. The sophisticated designs required to reduce the size and increase the yield of a missile armament can be only partially developed without actual testing. Once a country has acquired long-range ballistic missiles and its first-generation nuclear weapons, the need to test more advanced weapon designs is probably the greatest hurdle that must be overcome before a strategic missile force can be created.

Departures from basic fission weapon designs introduce large sources of theoretical error and unpredictability in performance. Incremental improvements in a basic implosion weapon create the least uncertainty and might be judged to be adequately reliable without testing, but this is not true of more advanced designs. According to the former Director of the Los Alamos National Laboratory, Donald Kerr, 'Strategic weapons with yields much above 50 kt could not be developed' without testing them at their full yield.[44] Development of a new fractional crit or boosted fission device is especially dependent on testing. Laboratory and computer simulation have essential roles to play in the design process but cannot substitute for test data of more advanced designs: 'The conclusion that has been forced upon US weapon designers by nuclear test experience is that the design of boosted fission devices is an empirical science . . . laboratory experiments have been and continue to be incapable of accurately predicting the results of nuclear tests of boosted devices, because conditions for the boosting reaction are established only after considerable fission energy has been released'.[45]

As a result of the inherent uncertainty of more advanced weapon designs, repeated testing is necessary to establish their yield and assure reliable performance. Britain needed an average of 4–5 tests before finalizing a new nuclear weapon design, the USA some 6 explosions or more, and France as many as 20 detonations.[46] Even a modified design based on a proven weapon can create unexpected problems that only testing can identify. An example was the US Army's W52 warhead developed by the Los Alamos National Laboratory for

[42] Fischer, D., *Stopping the Spread of Nuclear Weapons: The Past and the Prospects* (Routledge: London, 1992), p. 158.

[43] York, H. F., 'The great test-ban debate', eds B. M. Russett and B. G. Blair, *Progress in Arms Control?* (W. H. Freeman: San Francisco, 1979), pp. 20, 23. This point is not disputed by Fischer. See Fischer, D., *Towards 1995: The Prospects for Ending the Proliferation of Nuclear Weapons* (United Nations Institute for Disarmament Research: Geneva, 1993), p. 153.

[44] Kerr, D. M., 'The purpose of nuclear tests explosions', eds Goldblat and Cox (note 7), paper 2, p. 45.

[45] Westervelt, D. R., in Goldblat and Cox (note 7), p. 56.

[46] Goldblat, J. and Cox, D., 'Summary and conclusions', eds Goldblat and Cox (note 7), p. 5; and Fetter, S., *Toward a Comprehensive Test Ban* (Ballinger: Cambridge, Mass., 1988), pp. 172–73.

the Sergeant missile. Although it was based on the proven warhead used in previous missiles such as the Honest John and Corporal,

The nuclear warhead for the Army's Sergeant Missile was designed during the 1958–61 test moratorium, so its design was based on non-nuclear hydrodynamics tests and on computer design calculations. It was fielded in April 1962. Because warhead design was based on a successful warhead tested earlier, there was great confidence that the Sergeant warhead would perform as expected. When the warhead was finally tested, however, it gave only a fraction of its expected yield, a yield so small that it was militarily ineffective.[47]

The problems with the Sergeant warhead were corrected a few months after its shortcomings were revealed. Whether regional powers are equally sensitive to the performance of their advanced warheads is unclear. Some may not care sufficiently to undertake testing, although this seems unlikely in the light of the cost of such warheads and the missiles they are intended to arm. Others may judge that the political repercussions of overt testing outweigh the benefits. If so constrained, they are unlikely to invest in production and deployment of advanced nuclear warheads whose capabilities cannot even roughly be established.

Israel is suspected of having deployed boosted fission devices in the early 1980s, a few years before introducing the Jericho-2 missile which is believed to carry them. What then of Israel's apparent failure to test? One possibility is that Israel tried to test covertly with the aid of South Africa in the late 1970s. In the best known incident in 1979, a flash resembling that of a nuclear explosion was observed in the Indian Ocean, east of South Africa. The most systematic study of the event (commissioned by the Carter Administration) concluded that it was probably a random 'zoo event', an error in the satellite which reported the flash, with no nuclear connection. This did nothing to calm speculation that the event was a secret South African or Israeli nuclear test, possibly of a boosted fission device.[48] Even if such speculation has some substance, a single test would not suffice for deployment of a new and advanced weapon. A more likely possibility is that Israel has deployed a slightly boosted warhead (in the range of 70–100 kt) which has not been tested but can still be expected to generate a normal fission yield (20–50 kt) should the boosting fail.

---

[47] US Department of Defense White Paper on Nuclear Testing, quoted in 'Nuclear testing: why it's still needed', *USIA Wireless File*, 11 June 1992. Although it is not named in the White Paper, the Sergeant's warhead is identified as the W52 with a designed yield of 60 kt, in Cochran (note 7), pp. 8, 11–12. According to another source, the original W52 warhead generated 'only a few kilotons' instead of an anticipated 200 kt, rendering the Sergeant 'essentially useless'. Hansen, C., *US Nuclear Weapons: The Secret History* (Orion Books: New York, 1988), p. 198.

[48] *South Africa's Plan and Capability in the Nuclear Field*, Report of the Secretary-General, UN document A/35/402 (United Nations: New York, 1981); and *South Africa's Nuclear-Tipped Ballistic Missile Capability*, Report of the Secretary-General, UN document A/45/571 (United Nations: New York, 1990).

Illegal assistance and espionage

The only other method of circumventing testing may be to acquire foreign technical assistance or data, cooperatively or through espionage. Israel's nuclear weapon programme benefited from massive French support before 1967, and there is suspicion that French scientists supplied designs and data for advanced weapons.[49] The possibility that a developing country will recruit foreign nuclear weapon experts is not a new danger, but it has become considerably worse following the disintegration of the Soviet nuclear weapon establishment. The possibility that designers from other countries could serve a proliferator also cannot be excluded. Whether the help of nuclear weapon designers alone can be sufficient to justify deployment of a new weapon without testing is doubtful. The experience of Britain indicates that even access to detailed design information and results from another country's test programme may not be sufficient,[50] but clearly such help can greatly accelerate a country's nuclear weapon programme.

Proliferators may also try to acquire designs and test data through espionage, a possibility which deserves much greater attention. Again, there is nothing novel here. The Soviet Union benefited from spying by Klaus Fuchs and other agents at Los Alamos, but still felt compelled to repeat early US test experience.[51] Spy cases from the 1970s and 1980s leave no doubt that proliferators are trying to avail themselves of the same resource, using Western know-how as a cow to be milked for their own nuclear weapon programmes.[52]

Some of the most disturbing examples involved no illegality. Engineers and scientists from known proliferators have been found to be studying in major US nuclear weapon laboratories and European nuclear facilities.[53] In an extraordinary case, Iraqi scientists attended a US Government meeting in 1989 on detonation of conventional explosives, a subject with direct relevance to nuclear weapon design.[54] What they gain is not always clear. In general, espionage usually appears to save a nuclear proliferator time and expense. It is not neces-

[49] Pean, P., *Les deux bombes* [The two bombs] (Fayard: Paris, 1982).

[50] Howlett, D. and Simpson, J., *The NPT and the CTB: An Inextricable Relationship?*, Issue Review no. 1 (Programme for Promoting Nuclear Non-Proliferation, University of Southampton: Southampton, UK, Mar. 1992), p. 5.

[51] Williams, R. C. and Fuchs, K., *Atom Spy* (Harvard University Press: Cambridge, Mass., 1987). How the Soviet Union benefited from its espionage remains the subject of bitter debate. Revelations from former Soviet intelligence officials show that the reports transferred through the Fuchs–Rosenberg and possibly other spy rings saved the Soviet nuclear programme 'several years' in developing fission and fusion weapons. Former Soviet designers now admit that the first Soviet nuclear device was a direct copy of the US Fat Man. Dobbs, M., 'Ex-Soviet spy master tells of stealing A-bomb secret', *International Herald Tribune*, 5 Oct. 1992, p. 1; and Schmemann, S., 'Soviets copied first A-bomb from U.S.', *International Herald Tribune*, 15 Jan. 1993, p. 2.

[52] For a prominent example from the 1970s, see 'Taiwanese program at MIT ended', *Washington Post*, 16 July 1986, p. 5.

[53] Wines, M., 'China reportedly stole nuclear secrets in U.S.', *International Herald Tribune*, 23 Nov. 1990, p. 2.

[54] 'U.S. help for Iraq's bomb', *Newsweek*, 10 Dec. 1990; and *Nuclear Nonproliferation: Failed Efforts to Curtail Iraq's Nuclear Weapons Program*, Hearing, US House Subcommittee on Oversight and Investigations and the Committee on Energy and Commerce, 24 Apr. 1991 (US Government Printing Office: Washington, DC, 1992).

sary for weapon development—there is no evidence of a lack of espionage stopping a country's bomb project, nor is espionage alone sufficient—but it does make nuclear R&D faster.

Although the espionage threat is merely a new permutation of an old problem, law enforcement and counter-intelligence organizations are not accustomed to dealing with a spy threat from the developing world. Until recently they were not equipped to anticipate this threat or organized to react promptly. Many of the cases that have been revealed were discovered largely through luck and were pursued on an *ad hoc* basis. In an attempt to cope with this new form of an old threat, the United States has reoriented parts of its intelligence establishment, creating a Non-Proliferation Center in the Central Intelligence Agency to anticipate foreign threats and a similar group in the Federal Bureau of Investigation to deal with the dangers of espionage domestically.[55] Intelligence and counter-intelligence establishments in other countries have been reoriented in the same way, often with help from their US counterparts.[56] Redirecting organizations schooled in two generations of the cold war will be a tremendous task everywhere, but it is essential to meeting this aspect of the proliferation challenge.

The role of a CTB

A comprehensive test ban (CTB) has been pressed as a prominent symbol of global commitment to nuclear disarmament.[57] Its relevance to missile proliferation, however, is unclear. A CTB would not prevent nuclear arming of ballistic missiles. Technically advanced nuclear proliferators potentially can tailor their early weapon designs—as did Israel—to missile-size proportions without actual testing.

While it cannot prevent the proliferation of nuclear-armed missiles, the value of a CTB should not be ignored either. It is still the most powerful impediment the international community can raise before the proliferation of advanced nuclear warheads for ballistic missiles. It would make refinement of boosted and fractional crit weapons extremely difficult or impossible. Although regional actors would remain free to try to acquire long-range missiles, and nuclear arming would remain feasible, a CTB would create a strong and durable barrier limiting their military effectiveness.

The potential value of a CTB has been demonstrated by Chinese nuclear tests in the 1990s. While the other nuclear powers have observed test bans since

[55] Sims, J., 'The intelligence requirements for non-proliferation policy', eds W. T. Wander and E. H. Arnett, *The Proliferation of Advanced Weaponry* (American Association for the Advancement of Science: Washington, DC, 1992), pp. 271–81.

[56] Burns, T. *et al.,* 'Secret services unite against crime', *Financial Times*, 22 Nov. 1993, p. 3; Erlanger, S., 'Old enemies now allied against crime', *New York Times*, 6 July 1994, p. A3. Rising concern about nuclear smuggling greatly accelerated police collaboration in the summer of 1994; see 'Nuclear fears spur Europol', *Financial Times*, 8 Sep. 1994, p. 2.

[57] For a thorough discussion of the CTB, see Arnett, E., *Implementing the Comprehensive Test Ban: New Aspects of Definition, Organization and Verification,* SIPRI Research Report no. 8 (Oxford University Press: Oxford, 1994).

1992, China conducted a series of tests, including detonations on 5 October 1993, 9 June 1994 and 7 October 1994, culminating in a series of five tests scheduled for 1995.[58] Undertaken in the face of strong international condemnation and at no small cost to its reputation, there can be no doubt that China's leaders believed the tests to be essential to the country's military aspirations. To many observers it appeared that these tests were part of a last-minute rush to perfect smaller warheads suitable for China's tactical ballistic missiles or as MIRVs for its future ICBMs, a rush brought on by the impending completion of a CTB treaty in the Geneva Conference on Disarmament negotiations.[59] These are probably boosted, fractional crit warheads of the kind that need testing most, warheads weighing under 750 kg, the payload of a new generation of Chinese missiles. Had a CTB already been in place, China's programme probably would have been permanently stymied and its ability to field more advanced missiles seriously impeded.

By placing a 40- to 50-kt ceiling on the yield of their nuclear armament, a CTB would directly limit the destructive potential of regional ballistic missiles. The best missiles available to these countries, based on relatively advanced designs such as the Condor-2 or Jericho-2, are unlikely to be sufficiently accurate to be militarily effective at ranges beyond 2000 km when carrying warheads no larger than 50 kt. Hitting targets at greater ranges without larger warheads will require massive bombardments, on a scale almost unimaginable, or tremendous improvements in accuracy, to levels beyond the present capabilities of all missile proliferators and unlikely to be seen for several decades.

V. Conclusions

The connection between ballistic missiles and nuclear weapons may be a virtually natural one, but it is not automatic. The recurrent theme of this chapter is the serious technical problems that must be overcome before a country can deploy nuclear-armed missiles, first in acquiring a basic nuclear weapon capability, then in tailoring a bomb design for missile delivery, and finally in increasing the weapon's destructiveness in order to accomplish specific military objectives. The severity of these problems is enough to explain why only one regional power, Israel, has actually combined the two technologies.

Other countries undoubtedly have programmes to develop nuclear-armed missiles. The limited evidence suggests that India and Pakistan are working in this direction and that Iraq was as well, until stopped by the United Nations.

---

[58] Dawkins, W., 'Japan cuts aid over N-tests', *Financial Times*, 23 May 1995, p. 5.

[59] Lockwood, D., 'Nuclear weapon developments', *SIPRI Yearbook 1994* (Oxford University Press: Oxford, 1994), p. 304; and Walker, T., 'Beijing defies West with N-test', *Financial Times*, 11–12 June 1994, p. 3; Tyler, P. E., 'Chinese test atomic bomb underground', *New York Times*, 8 Oct. 1994, p. 3; and Walker, T., 'China defiant after second nuclear test', *Financial Times*, 8–9 Oct. 1994, p. 3. A more benign interpretation of Chinese testing, avoiding any firm conclusion about its motives, is Dingli Ghen, 'The prospects for a comprehensive test ban treaty: implications of Chinese nuclear testing', eds W. T. Wander, E. H. Arnett and P. Bracken, *The Diffusion of Advanced Weaponry* (American Association for the Advancement of Science: Washington, DC, 1994), pp. 271–82.

Although less advanced, Iran, North Korea and Libya are recognized to be interested. A few may succeed in the coming decades. Even so, the proliferation of nuclear-armed ballistic missiles will be far slower than the spread of missiles themselves and other—less deadly—armaments. The inherent difficulties of the technology and the need for nuclear testing are sufficient to make the process, at its worst, relatively gradual.

Not all rocketry and nuclear programmes are well-suited to develop nuclear-armed missiles. While experts and the general public alike will continue to assume that the two technologies usually go together, as will many would-be proliferators, the link is not a necessary one. Emerging missile powers will be mostly likely to perfect nuclear armaments for their ballistic missiles under the following circumstances.

1. They are able to acquire rockets with *large payload capacities.* A regional rocket usually must be able to carry a warhead weighing at least 500 kg to be considered a potential nuclear weapon delivery vehicle, but a payload capacity of at least 1000 kg is especially desirable to lift early-generation nuclear weapons.

2. The nuclear industry is capable of reprocessing suitable quantities of *weapon-grade plutonium*, or can acquire the material from foreign suppliers, facilitating development of smaller warheads.

3. The nuclear programme has the *skills and resources* to perfect reasonably reliable weapons that are small enough to be adapted for those rockets, preferably with a boosted yield or thermonuclear capability.

4. The nuclear programme has *active foreign support*, in the form of sponsorship by an established nuclear weapon state and direct technical assistance, or by hiring experienced nuclear weapon designers, or by acquiring fissile material or complete nuclear weapons from abroad.

5. *Full-scale testing* of actual nuclear devices is undertaken to establish the performance and reliability of improved designs.

The more of these criteria which can be fulfilled, the greater the possibility that nuclear-armed ballistic missiles will emerge. Given the inherent uncertainties of both rocketry and nuclear programmes, however, the outcome of the process is far from pre-ordained. Even 50 years after the introduction of the modern rocket and nuclear weapons, there is nothing routine about combining the two.

The only short cut is acquisition of complete nuclear missiles or nuclear warheads suitable for available missiles. Libyan efforts to buy nuclear weapons off-the-shelf, while futile so far, leave no doubt about the seriousness of this possibility. There are only two examples of actual transfers, however, and they seem unique. The United States, as part of a long-standing policy, has supplied a variety of Polaris missiles and nuclear warheads to Britain and is currently supplying Trident D-5 SLBMs but not the warheads. The collapse of the Soviet Union in 1991 led to the transfer of control over its ICBMs in several former republics. This left Belarus with 72 SS-25 Sickle single-warhead ICBMs, Kazakhstan with 104 MIRVed SS-18s and bombers, and the Ukraine with a force of 176 MIRVed SS-24 and SS-19 ICBMs plus bombers. This was hardly intentional, however, and since then these weapons have been transferred, slowly but steadily, back to Russia.[60]

It stretches the imagination to envisage a similar process elsewhere leading to additional transfers of complete nuclear missiles or warheads. Yet one would be foolish to exclude the possibility. Might, for example, a Chinese revolution lead to chaos resembling the 1920s or could anarchy in South Asia lead to the birth of previously unimagined states or unknown groups complete with nuclear missiles? The risks of such transfers are real enough to require continuous attention, but they remain the least likely way in which nuclear missiles will spread.

[60] The Military Balance 1993–1994 (International Institute for Strategic Studies and Brassey's: London, 1993), pp. 71, 86, 133. It is expected that all of these systems will be eliminated through implementation of the START I Treaty. A thorough accounting of these weapons appears in Spector, L. S., McDonough, M. G. and Medeiros, E. S., Tracking Nuclear Proliferation (Carnegie Endowment for International Peace: Washington, DC, 1995), chapter 5.

8. Conclusion: strategies of proliferation and control

I. Introduction

As the title of this book suggests, the spread of ballistic missiles is the result of a profound and complicated union of politics and technics. Although much of the technology is old and familiar and the politics little different from that surrounding any large and complicated project, this union between the two is new and disturbing. It is only a modest exaggeration to say that missile proliferation represents a completely novel threat to international security—the first of many that will undoubtedly test the skills of statesmen and commanders for many years to come.

There is no obvious precedent to guide the efforts to steer between the post-cold war Scylla of political fluidity and the Charybdis of rapid technical change. Both phenomena are familiar individually; rapid shifts in alliances and alignments between countries were typical characteristics of international relations until the sclerosis of the cold war, and continuous technical change is one of the defining characteristics of the modern era. In the past, however, national decision makers usually had the luxury of facing only one threat or the other—threats usually came from political instability or technical change, rarely from both at the same time.

After 1945 the pace of technical innovation accelerated rapidly, but its destabilizing consequences could be managed largely because the cold war all but eliminated political uncertainty.[1] Forty years of political stability made it much easier to cope with the nuclear arms race and armed confrontation in Europe, for example. Now technical and political change come together. One of the greatest challenges of the new world order is the need to cope with both of these problems together as they interact in ways almost without precedent.

The most important implication of this new situation is greater contingency. The political and technical considerations outlined in this study create general parameters, guidelines, expectations and probabilities but very few certainties. Ballistic missile proliferation is not inevitable, but it is likely; control and reversal of the process are not impossible, but they are not easy either. Exactly what will happen in any of several dozen particular cases depends on specific choices, resources and luck. In situations like this, where the risks of inaction are clear and the results of particular responses are unpredictable, the responsibility of national leaders is greatest.

---

[1] Deutsch, K. W., 'The impact of science and technology on international politics', *Daedalus*, vol. 88 (autumn 1959), pp. 669–85; Waltz, K. N., 'The stability of a bipolar world', *Daedalus*, vol. 93 (summer 1964); and Waltz, K. N., *Theory of International Politics* (Addison-Wesley: New York, 1979), pp. 170–76.

All too often studies of weapon proliferation assume that the world is moving towards a particular vision of the future, bleak or beautiful depending on the disposition of the writer.[2] Whether such strong views have been shaped by years of careful introspection or by just a glance at the latest headlines, such conviction obscures the fundamental reality of proliferation—the rise of uncertainty and the expansion of choice in international security.

Proliferation is not the inevitable result of technical imperatives or political momentum. The further spread of ballistic missiles is certainly feasible and perhaps even likely, but in no sense is it predestined. Weapon proliferation rather is the product of technical opportunities and political efforts. The most serious disputes of the coming years will be dominated by a contest between two rival images of the future—a contest shaped by political structure and physical fact but ultimately determined through the effort or inaction of the parties involved.

II. Mirror images

From the contingency of ballistic missile proliferation emerge two alternative visions of the future. The politics and technics create an invitation to struggle. With little room for compromise, would-be proliferators and would-be controllers must counter each other's efforts as they strive to achieve their own mutually exclusive objectives. One side sees its security in the acquisition of long-range rockets. The other side sees its security undermined by their spread. In this sense proliferation represents another permutation of the same security dilemma that characterizes most contests over international security. The same possibilities that appear so enticing for one side pose serious threats for the other. One side's strengths are the other side's weaknesses and vice versa.[3]

For countries trying to develop or acquire long-range rockets, the essential fact is the feasibility of successfully building or buying them. As shown in chapter 2, the existence of the technology and its continuous ageing make proliferation possible, even if it is not inevitable. Over time technology acquisition becomes easier as yesterday's exotic hardware progressively becomes banalized. As shown in chapter 3, missile proliferation gives countries new political and military capabilities, if not for outright destruction then at least for intimidation and provocation. The result is a permissive situation which makes the spread of ballistic missiles feasible and appealing. The exact motives behind regional rocketry ambitions are too numerous to pin down precisely. Indeed, this study deliberately avoids the difficult question of proliferation motives for just this reason. Suffice it to say that motives will vary greatly from case to

---

[2] Compare, e.g., the gloom of Clancy, T. and Seitz, R., 'Five minutes past midnight and welcome to the age of proliferation', *National Interest*, no. 28 (winter 1991/92) with the relative optimism of Atkeson, E. B., 'The Middle East: a dynamic military net assessment for the 1990s', *Washington Quarterly*, vol. 16, no. 2 (spring 1993).

[3] The classic but highly formal treatment is in Jervis, R., 'Cooperation under the security dilemma', *World Politics,* vol. 30, no. 2 (Jan. 1978). A more accessible review is Buzan, B., *People, States and Fear* (Harvester: Brighton, 1983), chapter 7.

case, ranging from military insecurity to financial profit to national prestige or the infatuation of a powerful individual with an intoxicating tool of statecraft. It is no surprise that many countries seek weapons like ballistic missiles. Indeed, a country must have compelling reasons to resist their appeal.

For governments trying to halt the spread of ballistic missiles, the threat they face results from the same basic possibility, but it is balanced by the inherent difficulties of the process. In just the past few years, the rate of proliferation has already slowed. It is more than just ironic that the Libyan programme that first warned much of the world of the dangers of missile proliferation, the programme mentioned in the introduction to this study, has made scarcely any progress over the years. Had the Libyan effort been better organized or received greater foreign assistance, the outcome could have been very different. As other examples have shown even more dramatically, control over missile proliferation is feasible, as is the reversal of even highly advanced programmes. Proliferation threats cannot be entirely eliminated—in so far as the civilian industry of any moderately advanced nation has the latent ability to create major weapons—but the threat can be stripped of its immediacy and reduced to a remote shadow of what is today.

This is not to say that the regional missile threat can be dismissed. Efforts to escape the dangers of ballistic missiles by defining them as mere psychological weapons, as Allied commanders tried to do during Operation Desert Storm, convinced no one, not even themselves. In many situations ballistic missiles are intrinsically destabilizing, giving their owners new military capabilities even when they carry nothing but conventional high explosives. Of greater importance is the fact that in any but the most absurd configurations they affect perceptions and through these perceptions the willingness of nations to risk war and their attitudes towards its conduct when war breaks out. In this, as in many other respects, would-be controllers are at a permanent disadvantage. They cannot eliminate the possibility of proliferation or deny its implications. The essential risk of proliferation gives the initiative and a fundamental advantage to would-be proliferators; no matter how hard they try to get ahead of the game, controllers cannot lead, they must react.

The difficulties of control are clearest in the soft technology of ballistic missile acquisition, examined in chapter 4. The conceptual, organizational, human and financial aspects of rocketry are by far the most important. Sufficiently good soft technology can usually compensate in the long term for weak mastery of the hard technology of rockets. North Korea's success with Scud technology brilliantly illustrates the ability of good organization to triumph over poor equipment. There is relatively little that outside powers can do to detract from a programme's internal make-up. Here the choices belong almost exclusively to potential proliferators. If they can establish appropriate objectives, implement them through top–down decision making and centralized authority, and pursue their goals incrementally, then their programme will be largely insulated from the machinations of external influence. A few aspects of soft technology are within the reach of outside powers, such as foreign bank credits, the openness of training centres and the movement of expatriate engineers. However, these levers provide relatively little influence over the long term. For advocates of control, monitoring the soft technology of regional rocketry is less useful as a basis for stopping proliferation than as a source of insight about their prospects. Close attention to soft technology is especially useful for evaluating the likelihood that a regional missile programme will be successful.

It is in the hard technology of rocket building, the physical parts and processes explored in chapter 5, that the cat-and-mouse game matures most fully. For neither side is there a single key technology that absolutely must be pursued, either to develop long-range missiles or to halt the process. The hard technology of ballistic missiles provides both sides with several alternatives, encouraging them to try to circumvent each other at every turn. A determined proliferating country can design its rockets around solid fuels, but if necessary a programme can be redesigned around liquid propellants. Even propellants long ago discarded by the US and Soviet military, such as liquid oxygen and aniline, may be adequate for regional applications. The same is true of guidance systems: inertial guidance systems may be ideal, but less advanced alternatives, such as strap-downs and radio guidance, are still suitable. Even in more demanding areas, such as re-entry vehicles and flight-testing, there is still room for alternative methods.

Export controls do have a few natural strengths. Above all, every newcomer to rocketry starts out being heavily reliant on foreign technology, a reliance they never outgrow entirely. Some hard technologies are also intrinsically important and warrant special attention because they could greatly facilitate the development of long-range ballistic missiles: composite solid fuels, storable liquid fuels, internal guidance, ablative re-entry vehicles, and so on. It would be extremely risky, however, to base control efforts on one or two supposedly essential technologies. As this study has repeatedly shown, there is no key to non-proliferation. Export controls are essential, but they are not a panacea. Rather, they must evolve along with the proliferation problem.

Chapters 6 and 7 show that the problems experienced in arming ballistic missiles are much the same as for other hard technologies. Proliferators have numerous alternatives and, if the ideal armament is not possible, other armaments, still adequate for most purposes, can be developed. High-explosive armaments can be used to destroy a target fully only in rare situations, but they may be enough to enable ballistic missiles to achieve their psychological and political goals. The effects of some other armaments, such as fuel–air explosives, have probably been exaggerated, and the effects of chemical and biological armaments are too idiosyncratic to generalize, but this is not to say that they can be dismissed. An ideal nuclear weapon to maximize the destructiveness of a ballistic missile is difficult to develop, but a crude weapon suitable for missile delivery is much less challenging. Export controls appear to be less useful against armament than controls on the migration of engineers and broad measures such as a nuclear test ban.

III. The technical plateau

Whether or not an emerging power's efforts to master rocketry can be controlled depends primarily on the physical size of the rockets it is trying to acquire. Above all, a rocket's range is the critical variable for determining how difficult it will be for a would-be proliferator to master or for outside powers to control. Regardless of which country is being considered, the individual rocket programme or the particular technology in question, in this study missile range emerges time and again as the factor that is most critical for determining the likely outcome.

As a rule, the difficulties of missile proliferation increase directly with the range of the rockets in question. Short-range, small-payload rockets are nearly always easier to acquire from abroad or develop domestically than those able to carry larger payloads to greater distances. As ranges increase, so do the demands on all the technologies involved, be they soft, hard or deadly. It is for this reason that proliferators do not advance inevitably from small rockets to progressively larger ones. Because rockets become so much more difficult to acquire as their range and payload increase, few of the many countries currently interested in rocket technology have any chance of ever developing highly capable systems.

At the shortest ranges, the technologies of rocketry development are too widely dispersed to permit easy control. At the longest ranges, the technologies are too demanding to permit easy proliferation. There is one critical exception to this rule of rapidly increasing complexity: the technological plateau. This can be conceived as a level plane in the middle of the otherwise rapidly sloping curve of technological complexity. It is within this area between the simplest and most demanding rocket technologies that the most serious disputes over missile proliferation will be fought.

Within the plateau, proliferation is feasible and likely but far from inevitable; and control is difficult but far from impossible. The exact position of this plateau is flexible. It has shifted up somewhat over the past decades, gradually rising in range. It will continue to shift in the future with changes in the availability of rocket technology. Currently it embraces those technologies for missiles capable of carrying a useful warhead to a distance of roughly 150–1000 km.

Below the plateau, at the shortest ranges, proliferation is relatively easy and control is extremely difficult. Rockets relying on double-based fuels, requiring no active guidance and effective with high-explosive warheads, are within the means of virtually all countries and many sub-state groups. Almost any country can find a supplier willing to sell 40-km range artillery rockets. Any country with basic chemical and machine-building industries can develop its own rockets. Even the worst organization and management need not be a barrier. Rockets able to reach targets 70–90 km away are already becoming nearly as

Figure 8.1. The first launch of India's Polar Space Launch Vehicle on 20 September 1993

Although the PSLV is intended exclusively to launch civilian remote sensing and research satellites, it also demonstrates that India has the ability to build ballistic missiles of any range. More than any other rocket in development today, it symbolizes the contingency and uncertainty of proliferation. (Photograph: Indian Space Research Organization)

readily available. It is only at a maximum range of 120–150 km that the limits of easy availability are reached.

Control of the shortest-range rockets is not completely impossible. The increasing hesitancy of major suppliers to sell sounding rockets, for example, has probably done much to reduce that side of the rocket trade. Potential suppliers also appear to be less willing to share manufacturing technologies specifically for artillery rockets, but these are only partial examples. Generally, export controls on such systems must be draconian to have any chance of success, applying adamant pressure on unsophisticated dual-use technologies and all potential suppliers. In most cases, too much is at stake with the countries involved to poison diplomatic relations over anything so seemingly inconsequential as an artillery rocket.

At the other extreme are the longest-range rockets, those capable of carrying a 400- to 500-km warhead at least 1000 km. At such ranges the technology is scarce and demanding; control advocates have the natural advantage. Only well-organized programmes have any chance of successful rocket development, and these must find solutions to the innumerable technical problems like propellants, engine cooling, accurate and reliable guidance, staging and integration, re-entry and armament.

Emerging powers can develop such rockets only by establishing an almost entirely new technical infrastructure. The level of political organization required is beyond the competence of many governments. Several individual technologies usually cannot be mastered without large-scale foreign assistance. Potential short cuts like clustering and staging are no less demanding. For most emerging powers, the only hope for procuring missiles capable of delivering a warhead 1000 km or more is to buy them directly from a foreign supplier. Today no government is willing to sell such a rocket. A critical aspect of nonproliferation policy will be to ensure that no willing suppliers appear in the future.

It is between these two extremes where the most serious proliferation contests will be fought. Within the technological plateau neither proliferators nor controllers have a natural advantage. The technology for rockets capable of hurling a warhead 150–1000 km can be mastered by many well-organized regional powers, but only if key elements can be acquired from abroad first. Typical of plateau technology is the Scud missile, the technically humble symbol of missile proliferation. A single-stage, liquid-fuelled system with adequate guidance, it can be modified by a determined regional power to achieve ranges of roughly 900–1000 km without altering its basic structure. Comparable weapons, like China's M-series and India's Prithvi, probably have a similar potential.

For control efforts to deny plateau-type technology, they must be conceived broadly and implemented early on. Compared to short-range rockets, there are numerous more exotic items and processes which are essential to plateau-range missiles. Compared to longer-range rockets, however, there are no inherent barriers or key items. Instead, there are several paths developers can take, substituting new approaches when others become unavailable. Controlling rockets between the extremes requires strict implementation of broad lists of specialized and dual-use technologies. Direct diplomacy will often be necessary, especially with more advanced programmes, when control is possible only if one is willing to put it at the top of the bilateral agenda.

IV. The strategy of control

The spread of ballistic missiles, like all proliferation problems, is an ever-changing phenomenon. The task of controlling proliferation will never be reduced to a few set policies for application in predetermined scenarios—rules like 'in situation B use policy Y'. Any attempt to reduce the problem to a few propositions or formulas misses the interactive nature of proliferation. As with all strategic confrontations, this one is dominated by the efforts of one group of countries to circumvent the efforts of another. This is what Edward Luttwak called the paradoxical logic of strategy, by which successful policies, if repeated too often, inevitably bring failure.[4] In such an interactive environment, no single policy will suffice for long as others can learn to counter it.

The technology of missile proliferation itself facilitates this process of interactive evolution. If denied the technological help it wants by one supplier, a would-be proliferator will search for others; if prevented from acquiring one technology it will substitute another; if unable to complete one design it can try another. Each act of control invites an adaptive response. If the process is allowed to continue, it inevitably undermines the entire basis of control. It was in this way that export controls of nuclear proliferation became effective and then lost all effectiveness in less than a decade. Drafted in the 1970s to stop unregulated sales of reactors, nuclear export guidelines were undermined in the 1980s as proliferators purchased dual-use equipment for uranium enrichment instead. In 1991–92 the international nuclear export controls were rewritten and gained new force, but one can be certain that the process is not over.[5] Nor will the evolution of barriers against missile proliferation ever be complete.

The real job of export controls is not to stop and reverse the spread of long-range rockets all by themselves. Rather, they are crude instruments, sufficient only against the least advanced and the most ambitious proliferators; those with the greatest need for outside assistance. In more typical cases they are a source of influence, aiding domestic forces in their opposition to provocative rocketry programmes. Even when least effective they help to slow proliferation, buying time for political settlements. In the end, only arms control schemes that deal with political forces, such as the regional and general initiatives outlined in chapter 2, can achieve an enduring solution.

Although missile proliferation cannot be stopped by export controls alone, they remain by far the most powerful instrument available for the foreseeable future. Even with their inherent weakness, no other mechanism can be applied with so little effort but such great result. The problem is to identify the specific technical weaknesses of a regional missile programme and target them with the strongest possible controls. In another context, J. F. C. Fuller once wrote that 'weapons, if only the right ones can be discovered, form 99 per cent of victory'.[6] The same is undoubtedly true of export controls on the spread of ballistic missiles.

The essential point is that the numerous paths leading to ballistic missiles cannot all be permanently blocked by a single barrier. Tactics must change with the threat. In some cases the existing system of export controls, stressing specific rocketry and related dual-use technologies, has proven its effectiveness. In other cases it may be more effective to stress controls on less visible exports, such as finance, training and migration of engineers, or counter-

---

[4] Luttwak, E. N., *Strategy: The Logic of War and Peace* (Harvard University Press: Cambridge, Mass., 1987), part I.

[5] Fischer, D. *Towards 1995: The Prospects for Ending the Proliferation of Nuclear Weapons* (United Nations Institute for Disarmament Research: Geneva, 1993), pp. 97–116.

[6] Fuller, J. F. C., *Armament and History* (Eyre and Spottiswoode: London, 1946), p. 31.

intelligence against espionage. In some situations controls on related technologies for missile armament, such as chemical or nuclear weapons, may be of more immediate importance. Over time it may be necessary to use all these tools, and others not yet imagined, against an especially adaptive regional missile programme. Like other non-proliferation contests, this one will go on for a very long time but the lengthy struggle, far from signalling defeat, will be proof of success.

Once countries have mastered long-range rocket technology, their programmes lose their sensitivity to export controls. Instead, non-proliferation policy must adopt strategies stressing regional confidence building and conflict resolution to minimize the dangers of the new capabilities as well as regional arms control and disarmament to roll back the threat. These ideas are not examined here, not because they are unimportant but because they go far beyond the distinct problems of ballistic missile proliferation. In the end, ballistic missiles cease to be a unique phenomenon requiring special responses. They become merely one of many elements of regional security, part of a mass of security problems which must be resolved together.

Appendix 1. The global dispersion of artillery rockets, sounding rockets, ballistic missiles and space launch vehicles, 1994[a]

Country	Artillery rockets Range: 20–40 km	Artillery rockets > 40 km	Sounding rockets	Ballistic missiles < 150 km	Ballistic missiles 150–1000 km	Ballistic missiles > 1000 km	Space launch vehicles
Europe							
Armenia	BM-21 122-mm BM-16 130-mm BM-22 220-mm	BM-30 300-mm					
Austria	M-51 127-mm						
Azerbaijan	BM-21 122-mm						
Belarus	BM-21 122-mm BM-22 220-mm	BM-30 300-mm		SS-21	Scud-B		
Belgium	LAU97 70-mm			Lance			
Bulgaria	BM-21 122-mm M-52 130-mm	FROG-7			Scud-B SS-23		
Croatia	BM-21 122-mm M-77 128-mm						
Cyprus	RT61 120-mm						
Czech Republic	RM-70 122-mm M-51 130-mm	FROG-7		SS-21	Scud-B		
Estonia	Various						
Finland	BM-21 122-mm						

Country	Artillery rockets Range: 20–40 km	Artillery rockets > 40 km	Sounding rockets	Ballistic missiles < 150 km	Ballistic missiles 150–1000 km	Ballistic missiles > 1000 km	Space launch vehicles
France	MLRS 227-mm		Centaure-2 Dauphin Dragon-3 Eridan	Pluton	Hadès	M-4 S-3	Ariane
Georgia	Various						
Germany	MLRS 227-mm LARS 110-mm		Maxus Skylark Texus	Lance			
Greece	LARS 110-mm	Honest John					
Hungary	BM-21 122-mm	FROG-7			Scud-B		
Italy	FIROS-30 MLRS 227-mm		Various	Lance			
Moldova	BM-22 220-mm						
Netherlands	MLRS 227-mm			Lance			
Norway			Nike-Cajun Skylark				
Poland	BM-21 122-mm RM-70 122-mm WP-8 140-mm	FROG-7	Various		Scud-B		
Portugal	LARS 110-mm						
Romania	M-51 130-mm APR-40 122-mm				Scud-B		

Country							
Russia	BM-21 122-mm BM-22 220-mm BM-25 250-mm	FROG-7 BM-30 300-mm	Various	SS-21	Scud-B	SS-11 SS-13 SS-17 SS-18 SS-19 SS-24 SS-25 SS-N-6 SS-N-8 SS-N-17 SS-N-18 SS-N-20 SS-N-23	SL-3/6 (R-7) SL-8 SL-12 Proton SL-14 SL-16 Zenit
Serbia	M-77 128-mm	FROG-7 M-87 262-mm					
Slovakia	M-51 130-mm RM-70	FROG-7		SS-21	Scud-B SS-23		
Spain	Teruel 140-mm						
Sweden			Skylark Maxus Texus				
Turkey	MLRS 227-mm RM-70 122-mm	Honest John					
UK	MLRS 227-mm		Skylark-8 Skylark-10 Skylark-14	Lance		Polaris Trident-2	
Ukraine	BM-21 122-mm BM-22 220-mm	FROG-7 BM-30 300-mm	Various	SS-21	Scud-B	SS-19 SS-25	

Country	Artillery rockets *Range: 20–40 km*	Artillery rockets *> 40 km*	Sounding rockets	Ballistic missiles *< 150 km*	Ballistic missiles *150–1000 km*	Ballistic missiles *> 1000 km*	Space launch vehicles
North America							
Canada			Black Brant				
USA	MLRS 227-mm		Aerobee-1500 Aries Black Brant Conatec series Nike series Terrier series	ATACMS Lance		Minuteman-2 Minuteman-3 MX Peacekeeper Trident-1 Trident-2	Amroc Atlas Delta Pegasus Space Shuttle Titan
Latin America							
Argentina	DGFM 127-mm		Castor Orion-2 Rigel				
Brazil	Astros SS-30 Astros SS-40	Astros SS-60	Sonda-1 Sonda-2 Sonda-3 Sonda-4				
Chile	Rayo 160-mm						
Cuba	BM-21 122-mm M-51 130-mm	FROG-4/7					
Grenada	BM-21 122-mm						
Nicaragua	BM-21 122-mm						
Peru	BM-21 122-mm						
Venezuela	LAR 160-mm						

Middle East

Country						
Algeria	BM-21 122-mm BM-14 140-mm BM-24 240-mm	FROG-7				
Bahrain	MLRS 227-mm					
Egypt	BM-21 122-mm M-51 130-mm	FROG-7 Sakr-80 325-mm		Scud-B Scud-C?		
Iran	BM-21 122-mm BM-11 230-mm Oghab 230-mm Shahin 355-mm	Iran-130		Scud-B Scud-C		
Iraq	Astros SS-30 BM-21 122-mm	Astros SS-60 FROG-7 Laith M-87 262-mm		Scud-B		
Israel	BM-21 122-mm LAR 160-mm	MAR 290-mm MAR 350-mm	Lance	Jericho-1	Jericho-2	Shavit
Kuwait	MLRS 227-mm					
Lebanon	BM-21 122-mm					
Libya	Astros SS-30? BM-21 122-mm RM-70 122-mm	FROG-7 Astros SS-60?		Scud-B Scud-C?		
Morocco	BM-21 122-mm					
Qatar	Astros SS-30					
Saudi Arabia	Astros SS-30 MLRS 227-mm	Astros SS-60			DF-3	

Country	Range: Artillery rockets 20–40 km	Artillery rockets > 40 km	Sounding rockets	Ballistic missiles < 150 km	Ballistic missiles 150–1000 km	Ballistic missiles > 1000 km	Space launch vehicles
Sudan	BM-21 122-mm						
Syria	BM-22 220-mm BM-21 122-mm	FROG-7		SS-21	M-11? Scud-B Scud-C		
United Arab Emirates	FIROS 122-mm						
Yemen	BM-24 250-mm BM-14 140-mm BM-13 132-mm BM-21 122-mm	FROG-7		SS-21	Scud-B		
Sub-Saharan Africa							
Angola	BM-21 122-mm BM-14 140-mm						
Chad	BM-21 122-mm						
Congo	BM-21 122-mm BM-14 140-mm						
Ethiopia	BM-21 122-mm						
Gabon	Teruel 140-mm						
Liberia	APR-40 122-mm						
Mali	BM-21 122-mm						
Mozambique	BM-21 122-mm						
Namibia	BM-21 122-mm						
Somalia	BM-21 122-mm						

South Africa	Valkiri 127-mm						Jericho-2
Tanzania	BM-21 122-mm					
Zaire	BM-21 122-mm					
Zambia	BM-21 122-mm					
Central and South Asia						
Afghanistan	BM-21 122-mm BM-14 140-mm BM-22 220-mm	FROG-7			Scud-B?		
Bangladesh	Type-63 122-mm?					
Burma	Type-63 122-mm?					
India	BM-21 122-mm		Centaure M-100 Rohini-200 Rohini-560		Prithvi	Agni	ASLV PSLV
Kazakhstan	Various			SS-21	Scud-B	SS-18
Kyrgyzstan	Various					
Pakistan	BM-21 122-mm		Dauphin Eridan Shahpar	Hatf-1	Hatf-2 M-11?	
Tajikistan	Various			SS-21	Scud-B	
Turkmenistan	Various					
Uzbekistan	Various			SS-21		

Country	Artillery rockets Range: 20–40 km	Artillery rockets > 40 km	Sounding rockets	Ballistic missiles < 150 km	Ballistic missiles 150–1000 km	Ballistic missiles > 1000 km	Space launch vehicles
East Asia							
Cambodia	BM-21 122-mm BM-14 140-mm BM-13 132-mm						
China	Type-82 130-mm Type-63 130-mm Type-81 122-mm	WM-1 320-mm Type-83 284-mm	Various		M-9 M-11	DF-3 DF-4 DF-5 J-1	CZ-1 CZ-2 CZ-3 CZ-4
Japan	Type 75 130-mm		Kappa series Lamba series S-520				M-3 N-1/2 H-1 H-2
Indonesia	LAU 97 70-mm		Lapan-150 Lapan-250				
Korea, North	BM-21 122-mm M-1989 240-mm Type-63 130-mm	FROG-7			Scud-B Scud-C	NoDong-1	
Korea, South	Kooryong 130-mm	Honest John		Nike-Hercules			
Mongolia	BM-21 122-mm						
Taiwan	Kung Feng 126-mm			Green Bee			
Viet Nam	BM-21 122-mm BM-14 140-mm Type-63 130-mm						

Pacific
Australia

Aero high
HAD
HAT

a The table in this appendix includes only systems in active service or formal reserve status. Many countries have additional systems in long-term storage where their status and readiness cannot be readily assessed. Nor does it include foreign-owned systems on a country's territory, such as Russian Army weapons stationed in ex-Soviet republics.

Sources: Foss, C. F. (ed.), *Jane's Armour and Artillery 1992–93* (Jane's: Coulsdon, Surrey,1992); *The Military Balance 1993–1994* (International Institute for Strategic Studies and Brassey's: London, 1993); European Space Agency, *10th ESA Symposium on European Rocket and Balloon Programmes and Related Research*, ESA SP-317 (ESA: Paris, 1991); Sietzen, F., *World Guide to Commercial Launch Vehicles* (Pasha Publications: Arlington, Va., 1991); Taylor, J. W. R., *Jane's All the World's Aircraft 1972–73* (Sampson, Low, Marston: London, 1972); Wilson, A. (ed.), *Interavia Space Flight Directory 1989–90* (Interavia: Geneva, 1989); and Wilson, A. (ed.), *Jane's Space Directory 1993–94* (Jane's Information Group: Coulsdon, 1993).

Appendix 2. The destructive effects of nuclear-armed ballistic missiles

Determining the probability that a nuclear-armed ballistic missile will destroy a target depends on the specific characteristics of the target, the missile and the nuclear weapon itself. In general, the lower the blast pressure required to destroy a target, the more accurate the missile; and the more powerful its nuclear warhead, the more likely it is that the weapon will accomplish its mission. In an ideal situation, an attacker targets a soft target like a wooden city or a troop encampment with a highly accurate missile and a very powerful warhead. In reality, the attacker may have little choice over his targets or his weapons.

In this brief review of the problem, two possible targets are used to ease comparison. One is a hardened military facility such as a specially built air base, radar site or communications centre, with key structures built underground or constructed of steel-reinforced concrete, making it secure against blast overpressure less than 10 psi (pounds per square inch). The second example is an unhardened business or residential area such as a city or military cantonment, vulnerable to destruction by blasts of no more than 4 psi.

The proximity of a nuclear detonation required to inflict such levels of destruction depends on the total yield of the weapon. It is assumed here that any nuclear weapon would be detonated at its optimum burst height for greatest destruction through blast to ground targets. Other destructive effects which can increase the total effect of a nuclear detonation, such as radiation, fallout and fires, are ignored here not because they are irrelevant but because of their unreliability and difficulty of assessment. Other disruptive factors which can reduce the destruction, such as topography and ambient temperature, are left out for the same reason.

The maximum distance at which a nuclear explosion will generate destructive overpressures can be calculated on the basis of $R = R_1(Y)^{1/3}$, where the radius of destruction, R_1, extends to the cube root of the weapon's yield (Y). Two equations routinely used to state this relationship are given below.

(1) $P = y^{1/3} (A/R + B/R^{3/2})$,

    where
       P = Overpressure in psi
       y = Yield in kilotons
       R = Radius of overpressure in kilometres
       A = 2.98
       B = 4.61

(2) $P = \dfrac{16.4Y}{R^3}$

Neither equation describes the full range of nuclear weapon effects. The first is strongest for low yields (kiloton range) and overpressures (under 5 psi); the second at high yields (megaton range) and overpressures above 30 psi. Using scaling to account for divergences, this leads to the following maximum distances of lethal blast effects (see table 1).

Table 1. Maximum distances of lethal blast effects of weapons with certain yields

Weapon yield (kt)	Maximum distance (km)	
	10_{psi}	4_{psi}
12	1.0	1.8
20	1.2	2.2
50	1.6	2.9
100	2.2	3.7
400	3.2	5.8
1 000	4.5	8.0

Knowing the maximum distance of lethal blast as well as the accuracy of a particular missile (expressed in CEP or circular error probable, the radius of a circle within which half of all missiles aimed will hit), the probability that a single nuclear-armed missile will destroy its target through blast effects can be determined as follows (see tables 2 and 3).

Table 2. Probability of inflicting lethal blast effects: the Scud-B missile and versions

Missile range (km)	CEP (km)	Nuclear weapon yield and P_k			
		100-kt (4_{psi})	100-kt (10_{psi})	20-kt (4_{psi})	20-kt (10_{psi})
300	1.0	6.85	2.20	2.40	0.72
600	2.0	1.71	0.55	0.60	0.18
900	3.0	0.76	0.25	0.27	0.08

Table 3. Probability of inflicting lethal blast effects, the Condor-2 or Jericho-2 missile, or an equivalent

Missile range (km)	CEP (km)	Nuclear weapon yield and P_k			
		100-kt (4_{psi})	100-kt (10_{psi})	20-kt (4_{psi})	20-kt (10_{psi})
1 000	1.0	6.85	2.20	2.40	0.72
1 500	1.5	3.00	0.98	1.00	0.32
2 000	2.0	1.71	0.55	0.60	0.18
2 500	2.5	1.00	0.35	0.39	0.12

$P_k = 1 - .5 [(R/CEP)^2]$.
P_k = Probability of kill.
R = Radius of maximum damage for the nuclear weapon, in kilometres.

CEP = Circular error probable, in kilometres (estimated in the tables).

Sources: Glasstone, S. and Dolan, P. J., *The Effects of Nuclear Weapons*, 3rd edn (US Department of Defense and US Department of Energy: Washington, DC, 1977), pp. 108–23; the source of equation 1 is: Zimmerman, P. D., 'Rail garrison MX', in Hobson, A. *et al.* (eds), *The Future of Land-Based Strategic Missiles* (American Institute of Physics: New York, 1989), p. 219; the source of equation 2 is: Tsipis, K., *Arsenal: Understanding Weapons in the Nuclear Age* (Simon and Schuster: New York, 1983), p. 57, Appendix H; and Morel, B. and Postal, T. A., *A Technical Assessment of Potential Threats to NATO from Non-Nuclear Soviet Tactical Ballistic Missiles* (Center for International Security and Arms Control, Stanford University: Stanford, 1987).

Index

WIDENER UNIVERSITY
WOLFGRAM
LIBRARY
CHESTER, PA.